SHADOWRUN:
CRIMSON

KEVIN R. CZARNECKI

SHADOWRUN: CRIMSON
Cover art by Ian Llanas
Design by Matt Heerdt

Published by Catalyst Game Labs,
an imprint of InMediaRes Productions, LLC
PMB 202 • 303 91st Ave NE • E502 • Lake Stevens, WA 98258

DEDICATION

Thanks to Jason Hardy for taking a first-time writer on, Patrick Goodman for bringing me in and letting me add to the Sixth World's vampire lore, and John Helfers for making this novel happen, and happen well. A writer is only as good as their editor, and I couldn't have asked for better.

For Kelsey, who got me writing in the first place.

For P.N. Elrod, who wrote the stories that helped me find my voice.

For Tina Jens and Mort Castle, who taught me how to use it.

And for everyone else who has Porphyria and has been called a vampire for it. This book is for you. Let's have some fun with it.

PROLOGUE

ABSENT FRIENDS • SEATTLE, 2064

10

The view from the ninth floor of Hotel Andra wasn't terribly impressive unless you faced away from the window, third eye open, staring back into the rooms. There, dozens of dancers swirled across the floor, doing everything from the Charleston to the Foxtrot to the swells of swing and jazz. Up in the air, back and forth, skirt tassels, spat shoes, slicked-back hair, and laughter. The clink of martini glasses came from the kitchen, and somewhere the crash of broken glass sounded sharp and clear, followed by a yelp and shocked laughter. It was enough to distract me from a pair of dancers so absorbed in their Lindy Hop that I didn't see them until the lady's foot was flying at my face. I flinched as it made contact, then passed through my head, leaving a cold, dissonant ripple in my aura.

Unlike that of the New Century Square Hotel, the Andra's management couldn't figure how to turn their paranormal occupants into a profitable attraction. These were long-standing hauntings, deep-rooted, like a stain, almost impossible to drive out. Unable to knock the place down, they were stuck with a historically preserved and protected madhouse of a hotel. The next best thing was to have a live-in mage who could somehow channel the sometimes mischievous ghosts and act as caretaker.

This is where I lived.

The view was still nice enough on a rainy spring evening, as most Pacific Northwest evenings are wont to be, and a whole floor to myself wasn't bad, either. My geomantic alignments kept the jazz to a quiet level, their power fueling my wards in a circuit of self- sufficient adaptation, and I tapped my toes and sipped my bagged drink. I wished it was warmer, or fresher, but it was guilt-free at least. My PocSec sat inches from my drumming fingers.

The call wasn't late. Su Cheng was never, ever late. It vibrated once, and was in my hand.

His voice was as calm and cryptic as ever, a single syllable. "*Come.*"

<h2 style="text-align:center">9</h2>

Twenty minutes later, I braked my old Yamaha Rapier to a stop in Chinatown. Thermals of steam rose off faux-paper lanterns as the rain pelted onto them, complementing the crimson and gold façade of the Taoist temple the Yellow Lotus Triad called home. The thrum of power was low and quiet in the astral, as calm and potent as a rushing river.

A pair of Yellow Lotus, an ork and a human, watched me from across the street, adjusting SMG-shaped displacements in their fashionable HK knockoff jackets. I was expected, of course, but they had to make their show of strength, keep up face. At least my elven ears weren't out of place among them, the meta-friendly Triad. Giving the door guards a discreet nod, I headed up the steps and past a pair of holy statues of the Dragon and Tiger, their eyes seeming to follow me as I passed into the main hall.

Seated facing me, flanked by great pillars, the ancient Incense Master meditated before the three great forms of Yu Qing, Shang Qing, and Tai Qing. His eyes opened, burning yellow. He never revealed this aspect of his nature to any but those who shared it. I stood before him and bowed low.

"Greetings, great master."

He rose, silent and smooth in crimson and black robes, his yellowed teeth baring in a smile under his drooping Fu Manchu. "You do not try to speak to me in Cantonese any more?" His soft voice belied immense power.

"I try not to speak any language I don't fully grasp. Not after last time."

"I'm quite sure Li Kwan has forgotten it entirely." He chuckled, beckoning at me with a single, long talon as he walked into an antechamber upholstered in burning reds and golds. He sat at a low, carved table, its glossy lacquer making the dark wood gleam.

I sat on a silk pillow across from him as he poured a deep crimson mixture into a pair of small, delicately painted porcelain cups. Someday he would have to tell me what alchemical process he used to prevent it from coagulating. "I have a task for you that should settle our mutual debts to one another."

I accepted my cup with a slight bow of thanks. "I'm surprised you would call upon a *gweilo* for any task of import."

"Hmph. Culture means less among our kind. You should know that. And aren't you and I 'ghost-people' already?"

I nodded, drinking with him. The coppery taste was mitigated by hints of some sort of herbs. We set our cups down, and formalities completed, he drove straight to the point.

"The Kenren-Kai Yakuza have recently engaged in a string of assassinations against other organizations, contracting a specialist to remove those among their rivals that control industries they covet. The assassin is not one of their number, but is quite well-paid for his work."

I nodded. "The Kenren-Kai stand to gain a lot from expanding into rival syndicates. It might even look good to the other Seattle Gumi."

"Quite. But we cannot strike directly against them, and their hired dog is particularly well-suited against more mundane efforts to stop him."

"A mage?"

"More than that. One of us. And one who shares your tradition, but with a decidedly darker bent."

"There aren't many darker paths than Black Magic."

"Except for those few who practice it like you do, perhaps." Su Cheng's smile was almost mocking; he didn't have a high opinion of my morality. "But he stands to stereotype, and has learned sacrificial practices."

"A blood mage, then?"

"Yes. He simultaneously makes an impression, publicly and in the astral, by leaving the results of his work for all to see, and pollutes the site with fear and hatred. His defilements interfere with the feng shui, ruinously disruptive. Hardly good business, but very effective psychologically."

"And you want me to kill him?"

He grinned. "It is my understanding that the Draco Foundation bounty for live blood mages is still a generous sum."

"Why not test some of your disciples, send them after the killer?"

"Because we must marshal our strength. And because we cannot risk association with the deed. It is better we are thought weak by those who would strike at us, and it is better to avoid making a show of force just for the sake of pride. And because this man is a shadowy reflection of you. He is the Hun to your P'o. You are perfect to overcome him. And because you are in my debt, as I am in yours."

He inclined his head to me, his point made. I sighed. I hadn't run the shadows for a year, had largely remade myself into a fixer and consultant. Hunting down a threat like this, I might be a little rusty now.

But a debt is a debt, and it doesn't pay to cross the largest triad in Seattle.

8

Hunting an assassin requires thinking like one. Just the same for a blood mage. Both often have sizable bounties on their heads, and that means the ones who are successful, or just survive long enough, develop a healthy sense of paranoia. They learn to keep their ears open, find out when someone is looking for them as soon as possible, the better to eliminate the threat.

I was spared the risks of working my contacts by the information the Yellow Lotus had found on their tormentor. All that Su Cheng had intimated was there, and more. Vasili Ivchenko, most personal details unknown, and only a sketch gathered from descriptions by one of a very few witnesses. Conjecture, mostly, but it was believed he might have been an operative for Yamatetsu, a Vory triggerman, or any of a dozen other origins.

Current intel stated that he was almost certainly employed by Chimera, the elite cabal of assassins, though no one could confirm if he was currently still among their number. What was certain was that he was called upon not for clean kills, but those meant to make a statement. Scorched earth of a magical nature, burning the life force of his victims to damage astral space itself to leave his mark.

What caught my attention so quickly was not his nature or his crimes (I'd hunted many kinds of monsters over the years), but the traditions he used to do so. Astral forensic analysis of the scenes of his strikes showed the emotions of his ritual sacrifices, aside from the terror of his victims, to be hedonistic ecstasy and terrible focus. The blood was used to paint blasphemous runes, pentagrams, Baphomet goat heads and inverted religious stylings, none of which held any real power beyond the psychological reaction to them. They were the textbook trappings of Black Magic, but with an important caveat: they incorporated technical designs drawn from all kinds of traditions. Hexagrammatic circles, mathematical lemniscate, esoterica from a dozen paradigms, and all of them harnessed purely for psychodrama, which usually confused the authorities. They didn't know that the exercise was only for focus and theatrics, creating the mindset necessary to feel powerful, and exert that inflated ego upon magic, itself.

Dark Magic, my old master would have called it. It was a kind of hybrid tradition, Chaos Magic and Black Magic, which eschewed Chaos' need for scientific methodology and the Machiavellian motives of Black, and instead demanded that magic obey the mage's pure will. Force of personality shaped spells, bent mana, and lent power to the mage's very id, one feeding the other. It was the pure, crude, and immediate pursuit of godhead. A path to absolute command of magic by way of one's own dark, solitary nature.

I knew this, because to my regret, it is the same rare style of magic I was educated in.

7

It took two days to get everything in place, the tracing rituals, bound spirits, and research on his background and tactics, even with Su Cheng's considerable documents and tissue samples recovered from previous assassination sites.

The night of the operation, I pressed the hidden catch on a pair of bookshelves containing my collections of magical hard texts, opening them to my small armory of gear. Past the collections of knickknacks and curious souvenirs I'd picked up during more than a decade of fighting supernatural threats and carrying out contracts for high-paying corporate intrigue were the black long coat, custom Ares Redline chambered to look like a Predator I, an array of sensor packages small enough to fit on a button or in a pocket, and the most expensive piece of equipment I owned: my vibro-katana weapon focus, etched in runes and with a fine

Damascene veining of exotic steels sharpened to a mono-edge. Enchanting something so technologically advanced had required a lot of time and money, but I had yet to find a blade that cut harder or deeper.

From behind me, a voice of water and bells echoed into existence. "Why are you doing this? Do we need the money?"

My eyes didn't leave the sword. I knew my ally as well as I knew myself; a feminine, elven form of water. She was my voice of reason, the calm in my moments of storm.

"We have plenty of money."

"Then what? Settling things with Su Cheng?"

My fingers traced along the treated black leather and steel scabbard, baffled against sensors, the link between us radiating a sense of familiarity, almost like déjà vu. "My style of magic is just rare enough that there are very few of our kind that would know of it. There's a chance this assassin learned it from...the same one I once learned it from."

"Then this is about tracking down your origins? Revenge?"

I smiled. "I don't think revenge would mean anything after all this time."

"Then what?"

"Ivchenko's dossier reads like a demon's resume. And Su Cheng pegged it. This guy... he's everything I'm afraid to be."

"Afraid to try to be?"

"Afraid to let myself be."

I pulled the blade from its sheath. To my astral sight, it glowed with power even as its edge hummed to life, vibrating faster than even I could see. "The world is better off without something like me out there."

"Something like you?"

I turned to her.

"What I could become."

6

The circle was cast in grave dust and oak ash, the ruined products of the mortality that sustained me and the fruits of nature that abhorred me. I could feel in it the echoes of sunlight and pulsing, living wood, both of which would cause me nothing but pain and death. All of it was dust in my hands, and that was proof of my power over them, bone and grain rendered into carbon that formed connective lines. Death to carve a channel. Life to form a link.

My practiced eye took in the shape of the circle, quickly and quietly measuring its dimensions. An imbalanced circle, or one with broken lines, would do me no good. Likely it would ruin the spell. Not because the circle itself was important, but because a perfect circle represented a sound mind, steady nerves. Sure action. Confidence.

At each of the cardinal points I placed the Enochian symbols for Air, Earth, Fire and Water. Widdershins formed into a *Choku Rei* swirl, overlaid with a geometrically reinforced pentagram. Without breaking my concentration, I mused over the misnomer that a pentagram, or even a dark mage should automatically be considered "evil." The pentagram did not point downward to summon demons, but mageward, to focus the harvest to the harvester. To be a Dark Magician was not to be evil, nor even to cast oneself into the darkness, but the see the world—good and bad, dark and light, life and death—for what it is, and accept it, taking it all into oneself and thereby becoming stronger.

The circle was complete and time was running short. At the distant point of the circle, I deposited Ivchenko's blood sample upon the point for Earth to stabilize it. On either side of me were Fire and Air, elements of motion and change, leading to where I stood at Water, ironically the element I philosophically favored, and its accompanying render of data into fluid wisdom.

I watched as the blood seemed to soak into the ash, watched as the echo of Ivchenko's True Name whispered life into the bone dust and oak ash, forming small, red lines that leached quickly across the circle. Waiting for the exact moment, I sliced a finger on my right hand and let a drop of blood hit the symbol for Water just as the lines reached it, one side vibrating with an internal breeze, the other burning like a fuse.

Met with my sanguine offering, a single red drop formed, hovering above the Water symbol, the merged essence of him and me, forming a connection I could use to track him. I grasped it with my left hand, clenching my fist tightly to smear the fluid all over. I could feel the resistance of the forces I called upon, and felt the ecstatic shudder of exerting my own will over them. Quieting, their rebellion became a cowed support, and I held my bloodied hand over the circle and pressed it down into the center of the ash. My palm stopped at the marble table, but my soul pressed through into the astral, and soon I was following the bright red trail of the assassin's blood, passing through time and possibility, and into his plans to know where he would be tonight.

5

Ten in the evening, and the distant rumble of thunder made for a dramatic setting. Except Seattle didn't have thunderstorms. More likely a volcanic gust of fresh ash into the choked sky.

It would probably be raining acid within an hour, and I pulled my hood up out of the collar of my long coat. I had a commanding view of Ivchenko's target from a taller roof across the street, a sleepy motel in Everett that housed a Yellow Lotus brothel, one of the few criminal enterprises they maintained in the up-and-coming neighborhood.

The front doors and lobby were in sight, and a pair of masked watcher spirits kept sight of the back alley entrance. Ivchenko would have masking of his own, but with his astral signature specifically known to me, I had the upper hand. If I had a team, I'd have picked a drone rigger to help patrol the area, posted a sniper where I was, and waited in the motel myself. I worried for the people inside, criminals or not, and my one reassuring thought was that Ivchenko did not favor bombs. He would go in personally and unleash hell with his magic.

And that was when I would stop him.

The watcher spirits proved useless as I spotted a small, hunched man with skin like an old potato slowly approach the hotel. My eyes narrowed as I focused on his aura, masked and fluxed so potently that there was almost no chance to see who or what they really were. Powerful, though, there was no mistaking that. There was a chance this was simply an old mage looking for a good time, but I couldn't stay out here if that really was Ivchenko.

As soon as he passed the threshold, I took my katana by the scabbard and leaped from the roof. A whispered word of power, and I floated down to land, shoe meeting pavement with a gentle *tap*.

The lobby was clear of any obvious security besides a lone surveillance cam. There had to be more hidden throughout the building, considering its hidden enterprise. Piss-yellow carpets and old cream walls trimmed in forest green, dirty black-and-white tile for the lobby floor.

No sign of the old man. I whispered a command for one of the watchers to cover the front door in case I was playing the wrong hunch and headed to the second floor, where an large ork "attendant" sat near a caution-taped off hallway.

"Under construction," he grunted, looking up from his hard copy trog-fetish magazine.

I leaned close. "I brought an umbrella."

He nodded at the code phrase and flipped a switch near the taped wall, causing the web of yellow and black to swing back into the hallway like a gate.

I smirked at the trick. "I need to talk to your boss."

The ork eyed me warily. "What for?"

"Su Cheng sent me."

The ork looked like he knew how to keep his cool, but he flinched slightly at the name, pointing down the hall to a door marked *Manager*. I nodded my thanks as he returned to his magazine without another word.

The door opened without any resistance to a pitch-black room. The light from the hall and my thermographic vision picked out two figures inside, one warm and dying, the other hunched over him, teeth at his throat, heat spreading from the mouth out to the rest of his cool body. The illusion of the old man melted away from the figure on top, revealing the sallow features and dark hair of Ivchenko, his concentration lost in the rush of draining the brothel master. I threw my hand out in a quick stun spell, only to see the bolt unravel as a blood spirit materialized beside its master.

His face caked in blood, the dark mage rose, licking it from the tips of his elongated canines with an indulgent expression. He flicked his wrist at me almost casually, throwing a manabolt spell that came apart as my own ally appeared beside me in a shimmering splash to counter it. She glared at the blood spirit as it gnashed its long, toothy beak and gave an inhuman, fluted growl.

Ivchenko cleared his throat, a wet gurgle of stolen blood, murmuring in a thick Russian accent. "Another Triad dog? Not one of their Wu Jen, though..." He was almost speaking to himself.

I didn't have words for him. He went on without prompting, inhaling through his nose deeply, tasting the air and astral.

"Mmmm...brother, perhaps. Perhaps we are all brothers, yes? Perhaps you have come to kill your *brat, drugh*?"

"You could just surrender and come with me."

"Hmmm. I could. But I like what I am doing now. I like the path I am walking."

"Where could it possibly lead?"

"It does not matter, *brat*. The journey is all that matters."

I smirked. "That's ironically Taoist of you."

"Our tradition embraces all philosophies. All the world. Makes it ours, *da*?"

I pressed my thumb against the guard of my katana, pushing it free of its scabbard for a quick unsheathing. He dropped the corpse of the Triad pimp and drew two long, wicked blades from their forearm sheaths. The grips were wrapped in pale human leather, the metal blades etched in obsidian.

We spoke as one, intoning the ethos of our tradition. *"Until someone stronger takes it away."*

For him, he was speaking pure, elemental truth. To me, there were only the sorry memories of learning magic in such a selfish form, power driven by ego and nothing more. Power through the self-deceptive illusion of power. But for us both, it meant there could be no other outcome but this.

Masking dropped, astral eyes opened, we appraised one another. The grasping darkness and swirled crimson of our auras revealed our natures and traditions, but his was drenched in blood and souls, awash in stolen *anima*. The blood spirit hunched beside him in the astral, anchored to him in spiritual chains that slowly fed it some of the essence he had pulled from his victim. He had somehow made a familiar out of it, and they sustained one another in their mutual thirst. He looked more like it now than he did me. I was ashamed at how relieved that made me feel.

With a telekinetic boost, he kicked the desk toward me, data cards and counterfeit credsticks flying as I jumped up to stand on it. He followed it in a blur, his blades flashing, and I could see the tell-tale patterns of weaponized athame foci in the astral.

His pet blood spirit flooded him with excess essence, and he channeled it into his quickness, slashing over and over with inhuman vigor while I backpedaled off the desk and into the hall. The bouncer had long since run, and I pulled my sword in a fast *iaijutsu* draw to parry where I could. My own reflexes began matching his speed as my ally wove an enhancing spell, and the world slowed so that his attacks became manageable once again. I backed to the stairwell, going up another floor into disused hallways and splintered, half-painted plasboard, hanging plastic tarps, and empty sealant cans.

His blood spirit familiar seeped into existence, bleeding from the astral into the physical, a bloated, beaked tick of crimson and gristle filling the space behind him. Ivchenko's bloody, fanged smile widened as the horrific spirit flowed around him to rush at me. I winced right before the wave of sanguine horror broke against a crystal blue wall, my own spirit appearing before me. Their features were alien, yet their hate for one another was obvious. The blood familiar's scream whistled like steam combined with a lion's roar even as my ally held fast, her aquatic features solemn and set.

Ivchenko dashed to his left, through the thin plasboard and into an adjoining room. I followed through a gap in the construction material covered in grimy, transparent plastic, the hallway behind us beginning to vibrate with the familiars' conflict. From the corner of my eye I spotted Ivchenko speeding toward me, athame held in a reverse-grip. I ducked to counter, only for my blade to pass harmlessly through him. I had just enough time to realize it was an illusion before I felt the slash of his athame. My coat and underarmor did little against the edge of an enchanted blade, and the physical pain was nothing compared to the agony of the knife pulling some of my life force away. Clutching the wound, I heard a *thump* on the ground and glanced down to see a grenade at my feet. I twitched my hand, sending it flying away with telekinetic force. A heartbeat later, the detonation shattered most of the bare bones of the renovation and threw me onto my back. The already-weakened roof collapsed, burying me and allowing the tainted rain to fall in.

"Do you not like what you are, *brat*?"

I pushed against the rubble, heaving it off and rising to my feet, leaning on my sword.

The knife slash wasn't closing, naturally. I pressed my free hand against it, whispering small blasphemies in Latin, quietly and self-consciously extolling my supremacy over magic and flesh. The depths of my heart still swelled at the daring to spit in the face of the divine, and I felt the spell knit the wound shut. Only the gash in my coat and suit to show for it—and the small emptiness that had been torn away from my soul.

Across the expanse of rubble stood Ivchenko, his broad, fanged grin splitting his face like a demon in the Seattle neon and

rain. He shook his head and laughed, stinging chemicals flying off his greasy black hair.

"You fear what you are?"

I clenched my fingers on the katana handle and flicked the thumb switch. The hum of its serrated teeth scattered water in all directions, and began steaming.

Ivchenko spread his arms, knives in hands, taking in the scene, almost as though to embrace me. "We are not unalike."

I grunted. "Funny. That's how Su Cheng convinced me to come after you."

His wide smile melted. His arms dropped, and he began striding at me, boots crunching on the crumbled debris. I matched his steps, and we began chanting.

Forty steps apart.

Stunbolt. Counterspelled. Thirty steps apart.

Manabolt. Counterspelled. Twenty steps.

Blindness. Counterspelled. Ten.

Powerbolt. Counterspelled.

My katana flashed out in *Ono-ha Itto-ryu* form, slashing down from the high left to low right.

He caught the blade between his own pair, but the buzzing metal spat them back apart, the edge slicing with technological power and magical precision through his armor and biting into his chest. He pulled back, mitigating the damage. The cut was shallow, his vest and shirt stained with a quick splash of blood.

A riposte, Wildcat style, aimed at my right shoulder. My sword arm. I turned, avoiding the strike, blooming the fingers of my left hand upward with the whispered hiss of a powerful word. Electricity arced from them, searing his face as he howled. I could see the astral call to his familiar, see the power he had fed it funneling back into him to restore his strength as he called upon its healing arts. With every drop of stolen soul he channeled into himself, the spirit grew darker, weaker, thinner.

He spat his Latin, and I met him word for word. The wounds sealed only by the smallest of fractions, and he roared his frustration. I had spoiled his one chance at magical rejuvenation.

Ivchekno thrust his palm out, reaching with a telekinetic grip. Before I could react, I felt a hammer blow on my kidneys, and looked down to see a shard of broken wreckage that had speared through my gut.

I coughed up blood, gripping the sharp edge. Ivchenko

caught his breath, smiling and wiping an arm across his mouth before sheathing his blades and putting a hand on my shoulder.

"*Da...Da.* It's okay. You fought well. You became much."

He slid his hand into my hair, yanking my head back and exposing my neck. Baring his fangs, he whispered in my ear, "Until someone stronger took it away."

I closed my eyes.

Let the world fade away...

The blood-soaked debris impaling my chest clattered to the ground as I melted into mist, right out of Ivchenko's hands. I rematerialized behind him, fingers outstretched to cast a potent stunbolt. His familiar, already weakened and held captive by my ally spirit, could not help him. The spell slammed into his back, knocking him almost senseless to the ground. I rolled him over face up, and his unfocused eyes fought to see me.

"That...wood..." he slurred.

I wove another bolt in my fingers. "Plasboard doesn't have any wood in it."

I held the spell's blue glow in my hand. It seemed eager to leap into him and rob him of consciousness.

"I know what I am, Ivchenko."

The bolt leaped quickly, and his head thumped to the ground, out cold. I relaxed my hand, ran it across the hole in my stomach, rapidly regenerating. My fangs had extended in response to the pain. I winced until the flesh finished knitting, leaving me whole again.

"I just don't enjoy it like you do."

4

The Draco Foundation's Seattle headquarters was quiet at this time of night, but the two armed guards had their SMGs at the ready when I walked in dragging a known assassin behind me by the boot. They kept their guns trained on me and Ivchenko as I dropped him unceremoniously on the fine marble floor, smiling at the receptionist who, to her credit, did not seemed fazed in the slightest.

"Is there still a bounty on practicing blood mages?"

She pushed up her Novatech I-L glasses and smiled politely. "Yes sir, pending results of metamagical analysis by our experts to verify the telltale astral signatures of blood magic use. You'll have to fill out some forms while we make sure you haven't dragged an innocent man in. Do you have a valid SIN?"

I pulled out a credstick with this month's fake SIN of choice, Malcolm Weaver, on it.

Two hours later, I was presented with another credstick, this one loaded with a substantial amount of credit. I thanked the Draco representative, deposited the cred into an anonymizer account for laundering, and sent Malcolm Weaver into a homeless man's beggar cup with a couple hundred nuyen loaded on it. Anyone who went looking for Malcolm and his payday wouldn't find me at the end of their trail.

3

A beautiful young woman walked into the Temple of the Yellow Lotus until a wave of my hand dropped the illusion, and I stood there instead. It didn't matter to Su Cheng, of course; he could pierce even my masking effortlessly. I did it for the benefit of the watchers from the other powers of the underworld. With this kind of shakeup, all eyes would be on each other, and showing up here now wouldn't do me any favors.

He rose from his position, the chamber empty as before. His smile was serene, smug. "Our accounts are settled."

I nodded. "And mine are considerably healthier."

He considered me a moment, contemplative. "Did you find what you sought?"

"My maker could be dead and gone for a long time now, if that's what you mean. I don't think he has answers I couldn't find for myself."

"What would you ask?"

"Why he did it."

He nodded. "The oldest question."

"It wouldn't matter, though. Not really. Besides, it wasn't him. I couldn't have asked, anyway."

"Then what do you seek now?"

I sighed, my eyes wandering over the statues. "How should I know? Try to build a normal life? Right now I should probably get out of town until the mob shakeup calms down a bit. Travel, maybe. Find some measure of peace."

"I think you may find that peace is a luxury our kind are rarely afforded."

2

Seattle spun above, below and around outside, a lazy, panoramic orbit in the 2 a.m. acid downpour. It might have been unreasonable of me to expect my niece to join me at the Eye of the Needle at that hour, but I tried to make up for it with the view. The private room's opaque black glass door opened silently in the reflection in the window, and I turned with a smile to the only family I had in the world.

Gizelle was the spitting image of her mother, my sister long passed from VITAS for forty years, with long red curls, pale skin and deep blue eyes. Only the touches of elven expression marred the similarity. Her clothes were crisp and professional, though she looked at least a little tired by this hour. As one of the premier experts in parapsychology in the Sixth World, she was endlessly in demand as a "spirit lawyer," handling important conjurations and bindings, overseeing spirit pacts, and brokering the delicate, byzantine, and alien rules of negotiation with free and ancient beings. She made excellent money, took very good care of herself, and as a freelancer, was protected by some of the most powerful spirits I had ever seen bound to service. What's more, they always seemed entirely glad to be doing it. Someone who could do that was a valuable extraction target. Whoever tried would pay dearly.

She sat across from me by the window, a waiter in tow with something green and smelling vaguely of fruit in a martini glass. She knew my nature, and knew not to wait for me to order with her. As soon as the waiter was gone, I smiled.

"No coffee, then?"

She laughed, the drink inches from her lips. "Oh, spirits, no. I've been up for eighteen hours cross-examining an Oath of Youth for some Wuxing exec and his ancestor. As soon as we finish, I'm off to bed, and well-earned, too."

I grimaced ruefully. "I'm sorry to have called you up so late."

She smiled and squeezed my cold fingers across the table. "Don't you worry about it. I'm always happy to see you. And you can't help your hours any more than I can mine."

"Fair enough."

The door opened again, the waiter bringing a fine crystal bowl of fresh fruit. Gizelle was perpetually on a diet. I couldn't imagine why. Moments like this, as she speared chunks of melon and strawberry with fine silver, I missed the entire process of eating and drinking. I'd have given a lot to toast her with a cocktail of my own. It was just one more detachment from the people around me.

"So, Rick, not that I don't like seeing you, but this is very short notice, and the Eye of the Needle is very nice surroundings. Is something going on?"

I folded my hands. "I did some business tonight that might see me in trouble shortly. I need to get out of town for a little while, lay low."

She arched a brow. "What do you mean, trouble?"

"There was a favor that needed repaying."

Gizelle sighed, setting down her fork and steepling her fingers. "Uncle Richard. Let me be entirely clear: I know exactly what you do for a living. You know this. I don't mind it. I don't speak against it. I don't even ask you to keep me out of it. What I do ask is that you be smart. So if you need to get out of town, why in Ghost's name are you not on a plane right now?"

I smiled. "I called in some favors. Right now, there are several records of my departure from the metroplex by different means. When I leave this room, I'll look like someone else, check into a coffin doss, and be out of town tomorrow night by black cab to someplace nice and quiet for a few months."

"So, why are you here now?"

"Because you're my only family, and I don't want you to worry."

She smirked. "You're an idiot, and I love you, too. Can I trust you to stay out of trouble?"

"I plan to be a tourist and catch up on my reading. I'm long overdue for a vacation."

She curled one finger in a beckoning motion, and my ally manifested in a swirl of metaplanar water. "Can I rely upon you to look after my trouble-finding uncle until he returns?"

My ally bowed her head with the deepest respect. "You can rely upon me, mistress."

"You have got to show me how you do that." To this day, Gizelle is the only person I have ever seen who could co-opt a mage's own ally into her service.

She grinned at me. "You've got forever to figure it out."

"Gizelle, if there is one thing I can tell you, it is that the passage of time doesn't always make us smarter. In fact, in my experience, it takes away much more than it gives."

1

Stuck was a great place to get away from attention in Seattle. A little city within a city due to some legal loopholes, the metroplex police held no jurisdiction there, and old man Stuck, the mayor and millionaire ruler of this corner of the sprawl, had connections to the Mob. This suited me fine, since it was the Yakuza who would be gunning for me, and they'd want to steer clear of a place like this. A smuggler haven in the city, I could probably get anything I wanted here, most importantly a ride out of town.

I checked into Stuck's Sleephouse on 88th, a no-frills coffin motel amid the bustling predawn streets and lay back on the mattress, considering where I wanted to go. There were a lot of places I'd always wanted to see, and plenty of old friends to visit all over the world. When my work had taken me to new countries, I was generally too busy to have any time as a tourist. Vampirism only added to the difficulties of seeing the sights, even in an age when most businesses stay open all night.

I was debating enrolling in another college somewhere when the PocSec rang. Activating the anti-trace programs, I picked up.

CHAPTER 1

AWAKENING AND ACCLIMATION

The first thing I became aware of was the blood coursing down my throat.

I was down to the nub; empty, drenched, shaking from the cold and the overwhelming, sanity-rending need that consumed me. I could feel it pouring into me, just enough to whet my appetite. What I really needed wasn't in it. This was dead blood, barely good enough for base nourishment. I needed what was behind it. I needed souls...

I heard the clatter of running feet as I groggily rose. My hands trembled, and my still-dry mouth ached. The blood did little to restore me, but it was enough that my vision returned, enough to sense what was near. I couldn't think about it, only react to need, as a drowning man blindly rips toward the surface of water for air...but then, that's an analogy I understand all too well.

The life before me was too much to resist, and I brought my mouth down on its throat without any pretense of grace. The screams were high-pitched and alien; I didn't know if they were mine or came from whatever was writhing beneath me. Maybe both.

The liquid that flowed into me wasn't human. Not even meta-human. It was clumpy, gooey, acrid. It was revolting, to be honest. But at the moment, I was a starved, crazed beast.

My tunnel vision receded, the dark room bright to my elven eyes. Other senses could make out the fading heat of the corpse before me. I started feeling guilty over going so long without feeding, for letting myself lose control and hurt someone...until I saw my victim.

It was vaguely recognizable as once having been human, but its mutations were too numerous to mistake its nature. The arms and legs were twisted, its flesh half-formed into chitinous growths all over the body. A flesh-form bug spirit. Its head was the worst, reshaped into a half-ant monstrosity, mandibles emerging from a mouth torn open, one eye multifaceted while the other seemed to have simply withered. Hideous. I could see the burn marks on its flanks where it had been shocked to bring it down but keep it alive.

I ran the back of my hand across my mouth to wipe the ichor away, only to find a substantial growth of matted, ginger beard on my face. I reached back to find long strands of hair, ragged and clumped with filth, falling far past my shoulders. Normally I kept it trimmed short, in an unassuming style. *What had happened to me?*

I rose from my crouch and looked around. A concrete room, a single, cold bulb swinging from the ceiling. What little illumination there was came from a metal door, the light through the crack underneath betraying someone's presence. The makeshift cot I had risen from was threadbare but reasonably clean, despite stains prolific enough to cover its entirety. The bug was chained, bolted hooks securing it to the wall and floor.

The whole set-up was competent, but unprofessional. *Where the frag am I?*

A knock sounded from the other side of the door, three soft taps. I tried to respond, but my mouth was sticky, my throat rawer than I could ever remember it being before...

...*Gasping, stirring, metal in my back...*

Okay, maybe once before.

I walked to the door and knocked back. It opened gently. Guns cocked as pale, half-blind eyes stared up at me from the trio of ghouls in the doorway. None I immediately recognized, but I've been on good terms with them most of the time. Birds of a feather and all that.

I stepped back, hands up to show I had come to my senses and meant no harm. There was no telling how smart the female leader was, or the two males that followed her, keeping a shotgun and Uzi trained on me the whole time. Krieger strain had a bad habit of driving many of its victims off the deep, feral end. The guns were actually a good sign.

The girl looked at me while winding a strip of dirty-looking gauze around her arm, which bled a dark, brackish red from two neat points. I smiled in gratitude—now I knew who had given me that first, tantalizing draught.

She surprised me by speaking. "Are you feeling well, Mr. Lang?"

That name also surprised me. It'd been a long time since someone referred to me by my old given surname. After all, I'd been legally dead since 1999.

I coughed, working some precious saliva into my mouth to clear away the gunk. My voice came out like gravel and sawdust, but at least she could understand me. "I feel like I just died and came back to talk about it."

"Not many people can tell that kind of story twice and be honest about it." The familiar voice pulled at my brain, surging a dozen memories from forgotten places.

Steely eyes and razor teeth and a warm smile impossibly in-termingling. The face that came through the door matched all of it perfectly. I was sure Needles' expression must be rare: the ghoul who pitied the vampire.

The chemical showers had become more mainstream beyond the Chicago Containment Zone walls since Needles had ascend-ed to lead the ghouls. He said it was his effort to make more of them civilized, not to mention necessary for keeping outbreaks of Strain-III controlled. I didn't care at that moment, relaxing as the hot water warmed bones that felt like they'd been cold for months. I suppose I was fortunate; they'd been cold for many, many years.

The rest of the warrens hadn't changed since I was last here. A section of the cable car tunnels, almost two centuries old, re-claimed and refurbished. The ceiling stretched up twenty feet at the peak of its arches, old stone browned and ancient wood supports long rotted away or used for fuel, much to my relief. This section covered a quarter of a city block, sealed off long ago and reinforced many times since, the entrance and exit to be found somewhere in the connective ventilation and mainte-nance tunnels, a maze of ducts and passages. The air ducts led to other monitoring stations, unused storage sheds, and the endless reaches of the city's sewage system. But in here, they made the best of scrounged and salvaged materials to create a home.

The ghouls were comfortable in the dark, their white eyes blind, yet seeing into the astral, meaning the only light was the dim glow of heat cells, but it was more than enough for me to see by. They huddled in small groups, wrapped in patched blankets and nursing the cracked chitin of insect spirit-hybrid flesh, quietly sucking it from the exoskeleton like crab from the shell. Others listened to audiobooks played on tiny, dented media players. One or two ran their long-taloned fingertips over ancient Braille print hardcopy, reading to the small, natural-born ghouls. Without exception, the small, hairless children with razor teeth and pale eyes gasped and giggled at the tales, as enraptured by the words as the impressions the storyteller's aura made.

Various rooms had been repurposed to the pack's needs. Sleeping; storage; a kitchen with a vicious array of reclaimed surgical instruments, kitchen knives, and a battery-powered cooler; and a few offices for those who filled specialist roles. I didn't give them much attention as Needles led me to the "cafeteria," a space outside the kitchen where an old, faux-wood table with built-in benches had been recovered from some high school ruin. It was scarred with dozens of claw scratches, right through the enamel coating. A plate of meat was brought for him and a cold, vac-sealed bottle for me. I recognized it as the same kind that attached to a needle cap, used by organ thieves to rapidly harvest blood.

I'd always appreciated the effort he put into it, trying to bring a disadvantaged people up to spec with the rest of the world. Few realized these days how many ghouls were still sapient, especially those who were born into it, as many of this pack were. Given their need for metahuman flesh and their persecution by the rest of the world, who could fault them for forming gangs and roaming the streets at night?

Needles was one of those strange cases. He'd been a guard for a charity relief effort for ghouls when they were attacked by bug spirits. His girlfriend, one of the attending doctors at the refuge, got infected. Unable to cope with the changes, she'd attacked him in a frenzy of pain. He couldn't stop her from rushing the other guards, nor could he protect her when they shot her down. He'd adapted to his own infection much easier, and made it his mission to carry her dream forward, to make sure no other ghoul would suffer as they had in Cabrini. He'd adopted the pack, and had been trying to get them as educated, organized, and re-spected as possible ever since.

I also owed him my life. Twice now, it seemed.

"You remember who you are?"

I shot him a look over the bottle of goopy, cold, hybrid blood that said I could remember how to tell him to frag off. He was all smiles about it, showing off those teeth that were his namesake as he chewed a steak of bug flesh. He was strangely fortunate to live here, where he and his pack could feed without hurting any-one innocent. After all, bug spirits were born out of metahuman flesh, and they were still palatable. Not as tasty, but good enough.

"What the hell happened to me?"

His smile faded a little, and he took another bite of troll wasp tartare before responding. "What's the last thing you remember?"

I tried to dig back...Needles had asked me to come back to Chicago now that I'd hit the big time. I'd invested all of my running money into a small corporation of my own, using it to turn fixer and fence, launder money, and make more. I had a long list of cli-ents still running the shadows, but no matter how good business got, I'd promised myself I'd remember those who had been there to help me get where I was. So I'd responded.

Seemed his pack was trapped between the bug spirits, who'd taken the time to build their ranks, and Knight Errant, who had decided to let the ghouls and bug spirits fight it out until a win-ner was declared. The prize was a final KE sweep to pick off the survivors. Seeing as that was hardly playing fair, I shipped a few crates of AKs and several hundred gallons of insecticides over to my chummer, plus I hired a runner group and made for Bug City myself. If I owed anyone, I owed Needles.

The three weeks of bug hunting were a blur. A new queen was in town, a termite made from the biggest damn troll they could find. We didn't know we'd flushed her hive until they were fly-ing everywhere. It was like the Breakout all over again. Being the leader and an initiate to boot, the queen went for me. A running fight through the old El tunnels all the way to a Wall-Zone bridge saw me facing off one on one with Queenie. Natch, I figured I was dead. An explosion later, and everyone agreed. After that, nothing.

Needles put down his fork and placed his hands on the table. His black claws clacked, and I suddenly felt really nervous. "Tell me what you suppose happened."

I shrugged. "I guess I got knocked unconscious. How long was I out?"

Needles looked pained. His eyes kept flitting to the side, as though he could see something I couldn't.

Come to think of it, I was having a hard time seeing into the astral. Maybe it was because I was so shaky. I felt numb to everything. Why should my magic be any different?

"Red, what year is it?"

Oh, drek...

"It was October, 2064, last time I looked at my watch."

His grimace deepened, uncertain how to proceed. He drew in a deep breath before responding, slowly, carefully.

"It's November 21st, 2076."

The bottom fell out, and I couldn't feel my body. "Happy Thanksgiving, incidentally."

For those who don't know, vampires, or individuals infected with mainstream Human Metahuman Vampiric Virus—usually humans, sometimes other metatypes—are subject to a great many physical quirks. One of the lesser-known ones is that vampires who are cut off from a supply of oxygen do not die, but enter a state of suspended animation. I know this better than most, because the first time I "died," this was the cause.

The short version is that I was born in 1983, before the Awakening. I'd been gifted with small visions, dreams coming true, impressions of people's emotions, all those little manifestations of magic before the Sixth Age that most would have called instincts. I had the good taste to find the occult fascinating, and the bad luck to find a charismatic quack named Karl who claimed he could show me true magic.

After working in his bookstore a while, his coven, led by a tall, blond man who never gave his name, came to show off their powers. When I saw that they intended to sacrifice a young woman to fuel their abilities, I tried, unsuccessfully, to stop them. The wash of blood magic created a small pocket of Awakening in the prepared space of Karl's basement, allowing the coven, led by a vampire, to indulge their skills. Each of them craved the blond man's power and immortality, and drank blood in emulation of him. As their powers faded, he drained me as well, dumping my corpse into the Chicago River. This was in 1999.

I was there for, oh, say, forty-nine years, the transformation holding me in hibernation. The virus activated dormant genes, not unlike a SURGE changeling, Awakening my senses to true magic and revealing my nature as an elf. Usually elves express as Banshees when infected with HMHVV, but I suppose since the virus had already taken its turns, I'm one of the rare exceptions.

By chance, I was picked up by a salvage trawler, and it was Needles who found me in the garbage heaps. From there, I learned about the new world I'd woken up to, and how to make my way in it. As a vampire without a SIN and with a firm grasp of an esoteric tradition of magic, becoming a shadowrunner was almost inevitable.

I've felt a little edgy about large bodies of water since my drowning. So imagine my horror at learning I had just lost another twelve years of my life (Which may or may not be eternal, depending on whom you ask) by the same cause.

Well, now I knew why I was so disoriented. Why my throat had been so raw. Why I had been so starved.

A million questions flooded my brain. The first... "Where is she?"

Needles didn't have to ask. I hadn't had a girlfriend since Gypsi. "Rick!"

She streamed through the wall with her usual liquid grace, blue aquatic form materializing like a chiphead's warped dream of sea nymphs. She might have been a perfect elf, swathed in ancient garments reminiscent of Babylon or Egypt, but for her composition of crystal blue water. She threw her arms around me, leaving only the faintest trace of moisture in their passing. She might have been crying, but who could tell?

Wait a minute...

If anyone could tell, I could tell. She was my ally spirit, my familiar. We shared a connection...

She must have read my thoughts, because she burst into a wailing that might have put a depressed banshee to shame.

I looked at Needles through her translucent face. "Twelve years?"

He shrugged. "We all thought you were dead. When that KE rocket took down the bridge and the queen...it's amazing you weren't blown apart, too. I think she was blown away by the force of the explosion, so she lost you on the way down. But she never stopped looking."

She nuzzled into my collarbone as I took it in. My soul had gone dormant, buried in the muck and astral static, and she was newly born into freedom. No connection to me, no ability to see anything but the contours of skeletons and wreckage for more than a decade, feeling their unmoving shapes to search for a familiar form she was no longer beholden to, with no conception of the passage of all that time.

"She didn't have to," I murmured.

"I know. She was free by then, wasn't she? No, she wanted to look. And with the city the magical mess it is, it's a miracle she found you at all. She found me after she found you. She needed help getting you back up. It cost some cred to get the gear to pull you up, let me tell you."

"What do I owe you?"

His sudden smile was almost hostile. "Don't insult me, Rick. What are friends for?"

I smirked and sniffed, knowing he wouldn't keep track of any debt. But I certainly would. They'd both worked so hard on my behalf, neither one owed me a thing. How was I ever going to pay them back? How could I? I'd lost so much.

I straightened up—I hadn't realized I'd slumped in the first place.

She gazed up at me as I sighed. "Okay. First things first."

I stood in the street, the crumbled ruins of the Sears Tower surrounding me as I weathered the cold wind off the lake. My tattered long coat flared, clouds gathering as the trio behind me watched. Needles and his man were well-armed, in case my exercise in spellwork attracted the wrong sort of attention, bacterially or otherwise. As for her, well, I couldn't get a moment's peace from her if I'd wanted it.

And right now, I certainly didn't.

I was concentrating, fighting off doubt and dread, falling into old patterns I had worked out for myself from the earliest days of learning magic. Pre-Awakening, Crowley-esque, dark mumbo-jumbo in the basement of Karl's new age shop. I even allowed myself the luxury of the old broad hand movements and loud words, chanted in Latin, focusing my will. My hand extended, my eyes fixed upon a broken pile of concrete chunks twenty feet away.

The spell finished, and I waited for the effect to happen. Every fraction of a second that went by made me sweat, hopelessness welling up with tangible force. I could feel it, almost...almost...like fingertips brushing something just out of reach. I could feel something stirring within me, something faint...

The ground rushed up with a suddenness that I usually expect from quicksilver mongooses and wired razorboys. My whole body collapsed, but my hand remained rigid, frozen in place, reaching to the stone. I heard my companions rushing toward me, footsteps crunching on the gravel with frantic intensity. Still, my mind and soul labored.

Their hands reached down to lift me up as I smiled. "Look."

Three faces turned to the place I was clutching at.

A single rock slowly flew through the air toward me, drawn to my fingers until I could grasp it. I gratefully sighed into exhaustion with it in my hand.

I awoke to find a moist hand brushing my brow. I drew into myself and opened my eyes again, finally seeing into the astral, though I nearly shook with the effort. She smiled down at me, sorrowful relief and joy mixing in her liquid features. I smiled back. It was forced. Now that I had eyes to see it again, I knew for certain that she and I no longer carried that connection. It was gone.

"I see you got my message," I said, a tear nearly falling from its pool in my eyes. Her face twisted in a mixture of guilt and laughter.

"I didn't know you'd cast a contingency spell. How'd you keep it from me?"

I smiled more honestly, letting the astral fade from my tired eyes. She was always amazing to behold without it, anyway. No heat signature, yet so alive.

"A man's got to have his secrets," I whispered. "I just felt you deserved a name, in case I..."

"But you didn't," she protested, a look of objection matching her tone perfectly. "You didn't die. Why didn't the spell recognize that?"

"You sound like you'd rather remain tied to me. I thought all spirits longed to become free."

"I was always free, with you," she whispered, looking away. For all the world, she seemed like a girl whose heart had been broken.

"I think I worded the spell poorly. I said, 'If it seems I am to die, gift my ally with her name.' I guess those circumstances qualifed."

She laughed and sniffled, swatting me on the arm. "Well... it is a beautiful name."

"I'm glad you like it, Menerytheria."

Love and pain often look strange enough on a normal, human face.

Now imagine them on an elf made of water.

"My theory is that I was down there so long my connection with magic atrophied."

I sat with Needles again, each of us on either side of a subway tunnel entrance. He was watching me quietly, listening.

"I didn't burn out, thankfully. I can still cast. I just need to work out those magical muscles, as it were. But most of my spells will need to be relearned. Hell, I only remember the ones I designed myself."

"That really slots, man," Needles said.

"Mmmm," I responded, already distracted.

"What's on your mind, chummer?"

I turned to look at him, and he looked worried all over again. "How much has changed?"

"What?"

"It's been twelve years, Needles. Twelve years. The twelve years before I drowned again saw the birth of AIs, the *otaku*, a dragon for president... A lot can happen in twelve years. So what did I miss?"

Needles might have looked uncomfortable again, but I smiled at him. "C'mon, man, this isn't a reproach. I just want to be prepared for what's out there."

He smiled and shook his head. "All right, you asked for it."

It took him two hours to explain the second Crash, the new, wireless Matrix, the rise of technomancers, the fall of Novatech and birth of NeoNET, and a hundred other things. The whole time I couldn't believe what I was hearing. I knew he wouldn't lie to me, but it was still rough. Don't get me wrong, I had more than average experience in adjusting to massive changes. This was hardly the strangest thing to have happened to me. But still, it was amazing how much could happen in so short a time. Every decade brought a whole new world. I had always avoided the idea of an inevitable future of change, and the haunting notion of immortality that promised it.

But it was good news, in some ways. I could be a part of the Matrix using 'trodes and keep up with people now. The shadow community was as alive as ever, and my talents would still be in demand as a result. But I needed to get to a data terminal or hot spot. I needed to check up on my affairs. The apartment. The company. My contacts and family and runner chummers. I was a dozen years dead, as far as anyone knew, so this might be a chance to write off some old enemies and renew old friendships.

I told Needles all this, and he said I definitely wasn't "going into town" looking like I did.

CHAPTER 2

BRAVE NEW WORLD

"Red, this is Pretty."

I agreed, whether it was a street name or not. Sitting at a well-lit mirror with a table filled with cosmetics and every beauty appliance I could imagine, the girl before me held the kind of natural charisma some sim starlets try to get with training and chips. About 1.6 meters tall, she was curvy and pale, with long black hair cascading down a back that invited fingers to trail slowly along it. Her big eyes were a vibrant blue, too deliberate to be real. She turned them on me with a naturally vulnerable look, and suddenly I felt like I really *had* been in cold water for twelve years. She was slipping black gloves off, still wearing a short skirt and black top just this side of immodest.

A second look give way to a double take. There were things about her that stood out as... unnatural, at least to someone with my experience. Her cybereyes. Her natural nails, black yet unpainted. Her hair, too perfect not to be bioware. Her skin, almost a shade of gray instead of pale, and a little too smooth to be natural.

Pretty was a ghoul.

I don't think she could tell if I was staring because of her looks, or because I knew what she was, despite appearances. To tell the truth, I'm not sure I could tell which was the case, either.

She turned to me, almost smiling, with a hint of something feral. She extended a manicured hand to me and shook. "A pleasure. One hears a lot about the famous Red in the warren."

Her voice was ambrosia, throaty and vibrant. She knew her stuff. Even her perfume was perfect to offset the scent a cannibal inevitably exudes. Only my heightened sense of smell, especially for blood, gave me any hint of the taint beneath.

I turned the shake into a bow, lowering my lips to her hand with something resembling grace and kissing it lightly.

"The pleasure is mine."

Needles snickered as Pretty flushed a faint blue, then shook it off with something like a scowl. I wasn't sure where I'd hosed up, but then, some girls were just strange. An unbelievably hot ghoul only had that much more going in that direction.

Needles walked toward her, looking at me. "Pretty here is our girl for going into town. She was a looker before all the mods. I figured it was a worthwhile investment so the rest of the world could see it, too."

Pretty turned from her mirror, taking out black spikes on hooks I assumed were fashionable earrings. She tossed them onto a table, her eyes never leaving my face. They searched over me, for what I wasn't sure. It didn't seem like she found me attractive. I hadn't looked in a mirror yet, so I could only imagine what a mess I was. So what was she looking for?

"Given that she's the only one of us who can go out for supplies and contacts and the like," Needles continued, "I figure she's the one you'll want to talk to before making the trip. Hell, while you're sticking around, you might do a few runs for us yourself, if you're feeling up to it."

Pretty's head snapped to glare at him. Ah, so that was it. I was competition for her role in the pack. Wow. I could already tell she was a ghoul by birth. At her age, I'd have seen her before twelve years ago. I wondered which one she was. She'd have been really young when I last was here, no more than nine or ten...

"Well, I'll let you get to it." And with that, Needles took his leave, leaving me with the glowering young ghoul.

She looked me up and down. "We've got some work to do, don't we?"

A haircut and shave later, and I was feeling a world better. My red locks hung down near my chin, styled with some kind of nano-gel that maintained it in spikes, my new goatee trimmed short. I thought I looked rakish, and loved it. It seemed my hair had de-cided to keep growing while I was sleeping. Another inexplicable mystery of infection. It was good to be rid of my Rip van Winkle, and I said so. Pretty didn't get it at all. She supplied me with a

synth-leather jacket and black tee, and some old, torn-up jeans.
She plopped a commlink and glasses in my hand.

"Unless you use a skinlink out here, it's awful coverage for AR.
Mostly when we use them in the zones, it's a small PAN discon-
nected from the main systems. When you get past the wall, onto
the Corridor and the subsprawls...well, be ready."

I could imagine what she was talking about, but I knew I was
going to be in for a shock.

She pulled some thigh-high boots on and threw me a with-
ering look. I just smiled through it, unsure how to approach her,
feeling like an idiot. How do you handle something so fragile
when you don't understand what it's like to be a part of a pack
mentality?

"Okay, Red, let's get going."

It took us thirty minutes to move through the side passages and
air ducts in the warrens to an exit point. Pretty pushed a cloth
ahead to keep dust off our clothes, but the path seemed well-
traveled enough that it was mostly clean and clear. Her handbag
was loaded with lint removers, perfumes, and colognes to mask
the stench of sewer travel. There'd be pay showers on the other
side, anyway. She was silent almost the whole trip, and it never
seemed more deliberate than when I tried to engage her in conversation.

"Have we met before?"

"So...were you born a ghoul?"

"Tell me about yourself?"

"Do you do this often?"

Silence answered every question.

Finally we came to a metal door that led into an operations
room. The dust told me it had been abandoned long ago.

"The Star and City Hall both think this door is welded and the
room sealed. Thank our resident decker for that."

We went up one last ladder into a shack, and from there, into
the dusk. We both hesitated for a brief moment before stepping
out. Vampires, despite the sims, rarely burst into flames in the sun,
but we burn fast. Hell, UV-A hurts. Even with allergen resistance
magics, you couldn't take all the discomfort out exposure. Not
a lot of vampires hanging around the blacklights at nightclubs.

Ghouls are the same, to a lesser degree. In the dusk, it was more of a psychological reaction, painful but undamaging.

There was no direct sunlight. We were fine.

A few steps out the door, and she turned and started walking away.

"Wait!" I called, stopping her in her heeled tracks. She didn't turn to look. "Are you just leaving me out here?"

Her voice betrayed exasperation. "We'll meet here just before sunrise. You're a big boy. You'll find your way around." And with that she clicked her way into the bustling Corridor of un-walled Chicago.

Since the Sears Tower bombing, the bug breakout, Cermak Blast, Bug City, and Operation: Extermination, Chicago has been irreversibly changed from its old glory. The core of the city's downtown had become a rubble-strewn wasteland ruled over by Zone Lord gang kingpins. It was the picture of post-apocalyptic decay. The distant subsprawls, once the suburbs where I had grown up, had become the new centers for order. In between was the Corridor, an eclectic collective of communes mashed together in a state of freedom and hardship. In the post-sunset gloom, the clouds didn't glow with the neon of a thousand late-nights like they did in other metroplexes. Here the stars were visible, and the markets still chattered with life, lit by gas and battery, snug in the repossessed ruins of better times. The squeal of pigs from a repurposed storefront competed with the tunes of a jukebox in an open-air bar across the street, mason jars of home-stilled moonshine poured in exchange for whatever someone could barter. If I wanted Matrix access, I'd have to make my way to a subsprawl.

I hitched a ride on a rickshaw with patched leather bucket seats from a luxury sports car and mismatched bicycle wheels and was on my way north, back to where the sky washed out and the lights never dimmed. The Northside was a Corridor that merged the freedom and ruin of Chicago's gypsy lifestyle with the remnants of working tech to better do business with the corporate outliers and wageslave day-trippers, and my commlink pinged as it entered an area with wireless Matrix access.

There's an old phrase: "The more things change, the more they stay the same." Even in 2076, it still held true...

...once you were past the Augmented Reality. The streets of the Saturday night were surprisingly quiet, despite plenty of glitterati sashaying to and fro, laughing at jokes unheard or jamming to music I couldn't hear. It was unreal, how quiet it could be. Conversations were muted, the scrape of shoe soles louder than I could ever recall before. I remembered how to work the commlink, slid on the shades, hit the switch for my second-hand Renraku Sensei—

—and the world exploded.

Everywhere, people talking, listening, music, voices, ads, over twenty commercials vying for my attention while a half-dozen profiles popped up with various queries. I remembered how to activate the spam filter for the homemade programming, and things became more manageable, like the volume button for a stereo that's been left on too loud when you first switch it on.

The world was awash in color and sound. Shops rarely used real neon signs anymore, just picked up an AR tag. Clubs and restaurants beckoned; even a triple-X joint joined the chorus of sound with moans that set my long-deprived brain afire. I imagined, with a simlink, I might have felt a moment of simulated ecstasy or the illusion of a caress, just enough of a taste to whet my appetite and lure me inside. Shops of all kinds, blinking on and off with full audio. I was hard pressed to imagine what a more expensive commlink, complete with bells, whistles, and a kitchen sink, might show me.

Another small window opened up, a news bulletin. The stereotypical newscaster held sheaves of paper as though she was actually reading from them. The FastFacts logo flashed across the screen before she started speaking.

"FastFacts News, I'm Bella Luchessi. Tonight's top story: Lone Star Security has announced six new missing persons, all suspected of being the latest victims of the rash of kidnappings plaguing the city. This brings the total of reported disappearances in the past three months to 28, with inside sources revealing that Lone Star has no leads as to the identity of the kidnappers, nor the motivations behind them. No ransom demands have been made as of yet, and no apparent connection between the victims has been found. More on this story as it develops."

A small link popped up with information on the identities of the kidnap victims, as well as contact information to report any leads.

Then the profiles started bleeping for my attention. A half-dozen little e-mail chat requests, each with a picture and link to a bio next to them. I saw the link to my own bio, which Needles had made up for me, and started laughing.

Rick Carmine, age N/A, income...

It went on and on, describing me as a freelance stock trader with an obscene income, as well as a picture of me right after Pretty had finished my haircut, touched up enough to keep me from being recognized. It actually looked really good. I started wondering if any of the people who were trying to chat me up had gotten a look at my ratty clothes.

An hour's wanderings brought me back down from the initial fun of AR. Nice, but still just a tool. I doubted it would change my life all that much, when it got right down to things. At least you couldn't pick my pocket for my credstick any more.

I finally pulled up next to a public data term. The Sensei was good for local interpretation of the Matrix, but for real searches in Chicago, I needed something more grounded.

I went back to my old sites, which, though updated, were still fundamentally the same, and entered my account info and passwords.

Password Denied

I frowned, frustrated. I punched them in again.

Password Denied

I sighed and tried some other sites. The results were always the same. Over and over, the red letters taunted me. My old identity, Kevin Tripp, was *gone*.

I started a Matrix search for my old holding company, Vryce Ltd. Only one smaller database had any info on them. I brought up the results.

Vryce Ltd. Est. 2061, closed 2065. CEO Kevin Tripp.

A private holding firm with at least one warehouse for engaging in import/export ventures, Vryce Ltd. took a major hit when its founder and CEO vanished in the winter of 2064. When the second Crash occurred, its sites were unprotected, and it was erased wholesale. The property was reclaimed in 2066 and resold.

Every runner who survives more than a year or two starts to think about retirement. They think of an out. A perfect escape plan to spend their hard-earned criminal cash. Most go the Caribbean island route, with umbrella drinks and sandy beaches and real food and tanned company. Absolutely every one of those elements was anathema to me. Well, not the tanned company. But deep water, alcohol, and sunlight were no good for me.

Other runners try to set up their skills in legitimate enterprise, becoming security consultants, or Mr. Johnsons, or just opening up a bar. For me, it was to learn and learn some more. Saturday Jones, escape artist to the stars of shadows, had procured an actual PCC SIN for me, along with an apartment in L.A., an account that would slowly accrue interest, and everything I would need to live comfortably, self-sufficiently, ready to be a student at any university I liked with a complete, thorough background against checks. A seemingly-perfect retirement plan that even used my real name.

A way to step out of the shadows and into the world.

All gone...

I felt kind of empty inside. It might have been more of a shock to learn that all my money, all the things I had worked so hard for years to have...all of it was gone. But I'd been expecting this in some way. It wasn't quite like starting all over. I had experience, even if I was physically out of practice. I knew how the biz was conducted. I still had my magic, weakened though it might be. And I could always fall back on the knowledge that I was nigh-immortal. Nothing puts a setback in a positive light like knowing you've got forever to make it up.

Still...3.5 million nuyen...all my savings...all my gear...

I wondered if any of my old emergency caches were still around. My prized vibro-katana weapon focus was at the bottom of the Chicago River, no doubt rusted away even with its magical sturdiness, but plenty of other goodies were scattered here and there. Hell, maybe one of my old chummers might have some of them, and some other swag, as well...

Drek! I had a lot of people to call! A lot of old friends to find. I started punching in the first number when I realized...this is a new chance. A chance to start over.

Who knew who might be watching? I was pretty sure any enemies I used to have thought I was dead and gone. Why throw that away if I didn't get any other perks of coming back from the dead? Still, there was one person who I would never hide from. I finished punching in the number and waited as it rang and rang, deactivating the camera for my face so they would get audio only. The line picked up, clicked for about half a minute with rerouting and antitapping, and finally a heavily warped voice came through on the other side.

"Speak."

I smiled. It's amazing how much you can recognize, when you know what to look for. I twisted my own voice in my throat, something I'd always been good at, and tried to keep my voice straight from holding back the giggles. It was like a prank call from my childhood.

"If you want to remember old friends, take a look in Chicago for a crimson name." And I hung up. I was sure she would figure out the riddle.

It wasn't my first time in this town, in any of its incarnations. I'd practically grown up in Woodfield Mall before the Awakening, before anything. I learned to run the shadows here before the breakout. In 2057, Ares bombarded the Containment Zone with Strain-III Beta Bacteria, a bioweapon that targeted astral forms such as the bugs and ghouls, devastating the insect spirits and ghouls alike. Then-President Haeffner had officially taken down the walls of the Containment Zone in Chicago in 2058, while the government offered up reconstruction contracts and projects to lure new businesses back into the Shattergraves. What they hadn't counted on were the non-Awakened warlords and gangers that would keep UCAS peacekeeping forces busy for a long time. Contracts started to dry up, with no one willing to risk their lives to work there, and magic-users avoided the city due to the Strain-III clouds still floating about, despite ongoing Ares cleanup projects. Smaller businesses started to crop up along the periphery, and enough people were trying to making a living there that walling off the larger area once again was impractical.

The new outbreak of bug hives only complicated things further. For whatever reason, some bugs just didn't want to leave, new ones had come to take up residence, and a few captured insect shamans revealed that the area was especially appealing to them. At the same time, the surviving ghoul population had either found ways to acclimate to the new environment or left for safer parts, and a few new packs had risen up to replace the old. So new walls went up around the highest concentrations of gang, ghoul, and bug territories, slowly contracting to eliminate the "infestation." So yes, Chicago's Containment Zone had been dropped, at least on paper. In reality, it had simply shrunk.

I waited for Pretty across the street from the sewer entrance, pulling up a hood and shuffling around like a beggar for about an hour, almost hoping some poor slot would roll up and try to mug me. "Vamping," we used to call it—vigilantism and hunting rolled into one. I'd started out that way, cleaning up the streets, feeding, and collecting a small arsenal of weapons. The things street scum carried, these days. Knives, pistols, chains, pipes, even the occasional SMG. It was discouraging. I never drained them all the way, only enough to put the fear of beggars into them. I always enjoyed the thought that maybe one of those kids might think about slicing up some poor lady on a street corner for some quick cred, then realize that she might be one of those monsters.

Alas, no one came along to harass me. Maybe Lone Star was too efficient for my liking...

I heard Pretty before I saw her, high heels clicking down the street. Her bio-hair picked up the shine from the streetlights that weren't smashed, and her artificial eyes flitted back and forth. It was hard to tell if she was predator or prey. Looks like she and I played the same game, just used different cards.

She tensed as I approached, unrecognizing. I let my hunger overtake me for a moment and my eyes shone red. I smiled with fangs out, not caring if I scared her. She was being a real slitch to me, and being friendly hadn't scored me any points thus far. Maybe she was one of those backward girls who enjoyed the company of the abusive.

She relaxed, completely impassive. I wondered if that was her natural state, or did pretending for the sake of the warren just exhaust her of her daily allotment of natural emotion?

Pretty opened the door.

Ten minutes passed in silence. She'd changed out of her nice boots to some waders she'd left by the vents. We walked on either side of a stream of filth on the concrete bridgeways under the ancient brown stones, silent as quarreling siblings. She seemed to be pointedly ignoring me whenever possible. Made me wonder just how much of an issue my presence in the pack was to her.

I leaped over the gap and stood before her. She didn't register any surprise, but I felt it in her stance. I was awfully close, a possible miscalculation on my part, but the hell with it. She'd back off if she was uncomfortable, wouldn't she?

"What is your problem with me?"

Her eyes slowly rose up to meet my stare, and suddenly the closeness felt like too much. She was just a kid. Physically we were the same age, but goddammit, I'm ninety-two! Well, almost sixty of those years were spent asleep, but so what? That still made me her elder. It was just too hard to read her. I'd never spent much time around coherent female ghouls, let alone ones who knew what it was like to be found attractive. She was somewhere between feral animal and sophisticated woman. It was an almost intoxicating blend, except for the utter confusion it engendered. And I hate being confused.

Even now, it was a paradox. Her posture, the position of her feet, the inclination of her head, ready to lift up into a kiss. Everything... except those eyes. Not just the cybernetic alien-ness of them, but something cold. It was within her soul and withheld from the surface, something I might never penetrate. I wondered if anyone else saw it. I wondered if anyone else had a problem with it.

I turned and continued walking, with her behind me. I wasn't feeling like I had much to lose, and I might have welcomed a fight, so I didn't care who heard me. I started to rant.

"You know, it's not like I asked to be in this position. I had it all. Money, toys, magic, fun, and friends. I was on my way up—up and out of the shadows. Legit, free to live a life, not just fight and scrape for one. I paid my dues. Now I have to start all over. And it ain't easy, you know? Next to no one remembers me, the world kept turning, and I lost years in a long eyeblink. I know you have no idea what that's like. I know it's unfair to bitch about what I've lost when you've never had something like it in the first place, but damn it all, you might just try being a little friendly!"

I spun around on that last word, the echoes reverberating long and hard down the tunnels, dripping water our accompaniment as we breathed the filthy air and stared at each other.

Her expression was something far too simple to be faked: she was shy. She looked like a child who was terrified of meeting a new stranger. But as I watched, this slowly hardened into a belligerent sneer, her chin lifting, scarlet lip curling, eyes narrowing from that guileless width into something menacing. It was unnerving.

I wasn't even sure if this girl knew herself what she was like deep down. What must it be like, to be born a ghoul, a monster, and then become a human? To live among monsters you call family, yet be forever apart from them? To share their tendencies, but live a double life with those who shun them? How old was she? How long had she been doing this?

Spirits, it was sick what this world did to us all.

"You look awfully thin," Needles remarked as I stripped off my shirt to hop back in the shower. I looked at a broken mirror propped against the wall. He was right. My ribs showed plainly, my stomach caved in. My arms were like twigs, my legs not much better. My skin was almost ash gray, but that could be blamed on a steady diet of bugs and no human blood to give me a healthy blush.

"What'd you expect after a decade-long nap?" I replied.

He smiled. "I seem to remember you in a similar condition the last time you got hauled up."

...*Too weak to move, too weak to breathe, but gotta breathe, gotta...*

"Yeah, I remember."

"Well, then don't worry about it. You looked fine after a while. Just gotta get some exercise, that's all."

I smiled ruefully. "You think you could spare some weights?"

His grin turned feral. "Actually, I was thinking something a bit more...aggressive."

CHAPTER 3

HUNTING

I clutched the AK-97 carbine in my sweating hands. I imagined it was one of the same ones I had shipped to Needles years back. One of the reasons I'd sent them was their durability. Even today, its antique ancestor, the 47 model, was still around, though you'd never see one outside a private collector's case or third-world warlord's army.

I listened, ears perked to pick up the sound of an approaching flesh-form's steps. I could feel it near. Hours of meditation had returned some of my mystical power. I still couldn't astrally project for some reason, but at least I could now see the ebb and flow of magical energy, such as it was in Chicago.

I'd gone bug-hunting many times in my life. It was thrilling. I had a distinct advantage, being what I am and all, but those fraggers were still scary. Each one was born from a human, their soul used as a host for the incubating creature within. That, or consumed in bringing the beast over from the dark, alien metaplane they originally came from, a place I dared not contemplate. No one sane knew for sure. But one way or another, once you were locked in one of their cocoons and it got into you, it was all over.

The Universal Brotherhood had taught us how to hate them back in the '50s, as sure as they preached their ethos of love. The cult used to bring willing, if unknowing, recruits to be used as hosts. That was the most terrifying thing of all—if you went into that cocoon willingly, it might result in your body remaining intact and unchanged, along with all your memories, allowing the bug in your shell to use you to take over your life. The ones who were less willing, well...the merge didn't go nearly as smoothly, and the body became a twisted hybrid. Like the one I'd fed on when I woke up. Like the ones we usually brought home to the warren for supper.

I checked the magazine one more time. Each green-striped bullet was hollow; chemical rounds, filled to the brim with concentrated insecticide. It was one of life's little ironies that the bugs had a severe allergic reaction to the stuff. It made the bullets a little less accurate, but they stung that much more.

Crumbled ruins surrounded me, a grim testament to the terror Alamos 20K somehow felt justified to inflict on the lunchtime crowds of downtown Chicago's Loop. Their bomb had brought the Sears Tower down, killing thousands from the explosion itself and the domino effect of collateral damage. Today it was a picked-over scar, the few standing walls of the depressing landscape usually pockmarked with bullet holes, long-dried blood, human or otherwise, and the ocean of other detritus that accumulates in a forsaken land. No one lived here but us monsters, and the few warlords, gangs, and scavengers crazy enough to take on all the nightmares the world had to offer. In a place like this, I took an odd comfort in being one of the monsters.

It was in the middle of that thought that something far worse than me reared its head.

The buzzing was the first indication, a dull throb that inspired dread. I crouched against the half-wall behind me, AK aimed at the massive, half-formed wasps closing in with death and assimilation on their minds. They may have preferred a perfect human duplicate, but a flesh-twisted monstrosity has its uses, too.

They came in a phalanx of five, swarming overhead and dodging around an errant cloud of Strain-III with a sound that reminded me bombers in old war movies. I could *feel* them more than I heard or even saw them. Alien chitters and impulses linking their minds together, I might have been tapping in on the sanity of a complete psychotic. *Kill. Eat. Expand the Hive.*

I felt a little sick.

I waited, the gray dust and debris blending me into the ruins well enough to buy some time. Luck was on my side as they split up, each heading in a different direction. One landed amidst the husk of an old warehouse. I couldn't see it, so I moved in quickly, staying quiet and picking my footing very carefully. I wished

I could have Menerytheria with me, but she would stand out to them like a flare on a dark night. No, I was safest on my own—at least until they found me.

I edged around a corner, seeing the grotesque thing turning over some rubble. Its wings hung limp. The slightest fall of a rock from the broken ceiling above caused them to flutter for a breath-stealing second, its head twitching to search about with perfectly inhuman movements. My safety was off. I might not get another chance to catch it alone. The others might already be heading back...

Raising the rifle to my shoulder slow and silent, I lined it up in my sights, careful not to make a sound—

Somehow, it sensed me.

I barely registered it moving before it slammed into me. My reflexes, along with my muscles, weren't what they used to be, and the monster pinned me before I could evade it. Its wings twitching, three arms held me down as the fourth tried to claw me. Its extended abdomen, complete with stinger, stabbed repeatedly into the ground, seeking my flailing legs as I dodged for all I was worth. Finally, though, the stinger made contact with my right thigh. I groaned as it punched like a dagger blade into me. I felt my flesh swell as it pumped me with toxins. It hurt like hell, and made me mad.

My rage swelled, drawing out some of the stolen power of my soul to instantly make me stronger. Ignoring its grip on my arms, I lifted it up and threw it off me, one of its wings snapping as it broke the flesh-form's fall. I growled at it, snarling in a way to make any horror-sim aficionado proud, and pounced on the thing. My fists slammed into it over and over, until they punched through its mottled, bulbous carapace. There was no skill in what I was doing; only the fueled rage of a vampire.

As it writhed beneath me, a scream somewhere between human and...something else issued from its mandible-twisted maw as I lowered my mouth to one of its arms. Inside the elbow was a patch of flesh almost completely untouched, pink and soft and vaguely feminine. I could make out part of a tattoo of a brilliant green butterfly with arcane patterns for wings.

I hated this thing. I hated what had been stolen from the person who had gotten that tattoo, what she had been turned into. I gave vent to that hatred with one final punch to knock it out, and then filled up the empty space inside me with its thick, rich blood, drawing out almost all of the spirit within, and feeling more whole than I had since waking up.

I dragged the corpse back to the warren quickly, before my increased strength wore off. It made me heady, enough to completely distract me from the hole in my leg closing up. Another benefit of my condition. Too bad I was filled with venom from the sting. That'd be coming back later, and all too uncomfortably. I was immune, of course. The vampiric virus rejected all competition, be it sickness or poison, but it had to come out somehow, just like bullets and blades.

The body was taken by some of the more primitive ghouls of the warren. Needles had once told me they were far less feral if kept busy with work or play. Some, he said, were even beginning to show rudimentary signs of socialization beyond the primitive animal level. Of course, he said it with much more grounded words and, I think, no small hopeful bias.

It was taken to a chamber filled with knives and saws, next to tables, probably scavenged from old butcher shops, with drains set in them to catch the drippings. Liquid cannibalism was the only way for me, but ghouls had the option of steak or broth. I grabbed a few vac-sealed bottles before going back to my corner of the warren.

I was starting to come down from my high, and the exhaustion of a fight taken to such visceral levels would be hitting me soon. Shaking, I lowered myself to a cot beside a sleeping ghoul woman. She lay half-naked, a gray-skinned infant sleeping in her arms. I shut my eyes and embraced hopefully-dreamless sleep.

I was drowning, sinking like a stone into the black water. Vampires don't float. But there was no limit to the depth. Could a vampire be crushed to death? Eventually.

Regeneration has its limits, surely. The pressure would crush my head, pulverize the delicate, unmendable brain tissues, and that would be it. Nothing more. Just darkness and the endless nothing of a monster's afterlife. That's all there was for a vampire. My soul had already been consumed, the virus puppeting me like an insect spirit, seeking nothing more than to consume, to spread, to thrive. All my abilities were for its benefit, not mine. I was not gifted. I was dead. I was nothing but a host. And I was drowning...

I awoke, gasping for breath. Sweat soaked my clothing, my brow dripped with it, and a sickly-yellow stain of ejected poison discolored my pant leg.

I looked up, and my eyes locked with Pretty's. She was only a meter or two away, her makeup off and her hair messy. Her cybereyes were switched to resemble the natural pearly whites of a ghoul. She fixed me with a stare that communicated nothing, like looking into the eyes of an animal, and then stalked off. My gaze followed her, and I felt a damp pull on my face back the other direction.

"I don't like her."

I nearly jumped out of my cot. Menerytheria had been next to me all along, probably curled up against me as I slept, much like the mother and child next to us. Maybe the moisture hadn't been sweat, after all. She looked angry and innocent all at once. She never failed to amaze.

"I don't like how she looks at you."

I ran a hand across my face, trying to wake up the majority of my brain. I missed coffee so badly sometimes. "What are you talking about?"

"She wants you."

My eyes bulged with an incredulous look. "Maybe for dinner."

"Are you blind?! She desires you! For mating!"

I couldn't believe what I was hearing. Just how did Menerytheria think of me? Some ally spirits viewed their masters as friends, partners, unknowing minions, even as parents. I'd always thought she regarded me as an employer, maybe as a friend. Just how off target had I been?

Seconds ticked as I tried to make sense of her emotions. Her face seemed fit to burst with tears when she flew away from me. I didn't get a chance to speak a word before she was through a wall and out of reach.

Cabrini Green hadn't seen better days since before I was born, its buildings bearing scars over scars that spoke of violence and crime as a way of life for more than a century. The landmark additions, declaring it a monument and museum, looked well cared for, making it an anomaly for the Zone. It was like everything else that had played an important part in my past: nostalgic and changed at the same time.

The guards nodded at me after I passed through the airlock, entering a lobby threshold I hadn't crossed since the '50s. Broken tile floors were swept clean, the squalor preserved in memory of the struggles Needles and his ilk had endured with Tamir Grey. Holograms showed footage of familiar faces, moments of violence and tenderness. I paused at one, a familiar face with an uncharacteristic smile. Nicholas and Sara Macavoy before their infection. Needles, in happier times, with a shock of dark hair and the grin of someone in love. Someone who would leave a lucrative job as a DocWagon HTR specialist for a beautiful young doctor with a caring heart. A girl who would risk her life for victims of HMHVV, and would lose her mind and her life when the infection took her, too.

The portraits led to the gravesite of Tamir. His hologram was projected in front of the headstone, stoic and inspiring as he had been in life. The stone itself was a monument, gray marble of a bald ghoul reaching up to the sky. Reaching, just as he always had.

"Been a long time, old friend."

One of the visitors, a ghouled elven woman, walked over as I said it. "Excuse me, but...are you a vampire?"

I smiled. "I'm afraid so."

"Did you...did you know Tamir Grey?"

I shoved my hands in my pockets, my eyes far away.

"I was there the day he gave a copy of his journal to a group of shadowrunners."

"Ghosts... That's...if you don't mind, what was he like?"

I looked up at the outstretched arm of the monument. "He was a leader. A man who never saw any of us as monsters. No more than any other metahuman, anyway. I didn't know him for very long, but he was both strong and meek. Modest but passionate. For him, leadership wasn't a matter of power, but responsibility. He lived life in service to all people." I turned to face her. "He lived up to his legend and then some."

She was dumbfounded. Probably a pilgrim who had come to this place, a mecca for ghouls and the birthplace of Infected rights.

To the right, the hard copy of his famous journal was on display in a glass case, preserved from the elements and lit overhead. An interactive holoscan of it could be flipped through. The neat handwriting didn't focus on the medical research, but the daily observations of ghouls and those few other Infected who made this place a refuge. Every page extolled their humanity in the face of adversity, the hardships within and without. Grey had the perspective of someone who had gone through the change, knew the hunger, and never forgot what it was to be metahuman. Along with everything he had accomplished, his inspiring words were his enduring gift and legacy.

He was my friend. I missed him.

I fished my Meta-link out of my pocket, turned on the image link in my contacts, and blinked a picture of the ghoulish pilgrim, hands clasped before her as she gazed at the journal. To her eyes, the letters were almost invisible. But the vestigial wisps of his intent clung still, the afterimage in the astral that was a greater insight into him than any words I could offer.

To my camera, the greater tale of souls and echoes was lost, yet the story was still told, somehow, just by her stance.

I was no Tamir Grey, but I'd strayed a long way from the example he set so many years ago. The least I could do now was tell my story.

The high-rise was long since toppled, a victim of the Alamos bombing that never got repaired before the rest of the city followed it into ruin. Only one corner of a wall was left. About twelve floors up, it was one of the larger structures left behind.

The floor bore evidence of its previous uses: old wrappers of instant soy-mixes, a long-dried blood smear, shell casings from what I judged to be sniper rounds. Good to know some things never change.

I sat against that corner, just in the shade against the setting sun. I'd chosen the spot two hours earlier, so the majority of my body was out of the light. I didn't care for fancy cross-legged positions or strange methods for my meditations: it's enough to simply relax. After all, clarity is in the mind, not the body. I hate crutches.

My left hand hung just over the edge of the building, sitting in the dimming sunlight. It had been there since I had started.

It would heal fairly quickly, I was sure, though slower than most things.

Wood, extended sunlight exposure, magic, and brain and spinal damage are the four things hard to heal, going from easiest to hardest. Club me to death in the head and back with a magical spiked wooden cudgel at high noon, and I had problems. Otherwise, I didn't care overmuch what happened to me.

The hand was blistered, the ashen flesh split with burned cracks as dark blood oozed slowly out of the numerous lacerations. My eyes remained closed, my ears deaf to the relative silence of the sky as I let the pain happen. Pain is really just an alarm. Once you get over it (which is easy to do when you know it'll heal quickly), it's not much of a problem. Besides, I wanted the pain. I wanted to be distracted. I wanted it to challenge my concentration. I was behind the times, and I aimed to get back in the game.

The sun set and I pulled my wounded hand back to my lap, opening my eyes to gaze at it.

I could just feel the cells sluggishly moving, wearily mending what was broken. I decided this was the right moment, and started moving my other hand in delicate patterns. I could feel something in me open up, a channel to the astral, my body acting as a gateway from that world to this. There was endless energy, waiting to be tapped, if one could handle the flow.

That was all a mage really was: a transformer. My will shaped the delicate movements and Latin mumblings into something meaningful, twisting that which was without purpose into a healing glow. My hand started fixing that much more quickly. In an instant, it was mostly recovered from the burns, flesh pink and raw but whole. I smiled and relaxed.

And winced. Frag, that hurt!

"I told you, you don't owe me a thing!"

My arms were crossed, my expression angry. Needles had one to match.

"Then let me help out of the goodness of my heart."

"I don't want you here just because you think you owe me something, Red. It ain't about debts. We stick up for one another. That's what friends and comrades do. You'd've done the same for me."

"Yeah. And if I did, I'd think you'd be trying to make it up to me, too."

He displayed exaggerated agreement. "Oh, really?"

"Yeah, I think you would."

He met me stare for stare for a moment, until he started smiling. "Maybe I would, at that."

I let my expression soften, but I held my ground. He finally relented, after giving it some thought.

"All right, all right. To be honest, I'm glad you offered. We can always use the help."

I sighed. "Finally. So, what can I do? I mean, bug hunting only gets you so far, right?"

"Right. Actually, given your face, maybe you wouldn't mind playing dealer for us?"

I knew what he meant, and I'd been half-afraid of it. "You sure you want me stepping on Pretty's toes?"

"Whaddaya mean?"

"I mean she views that as her position in the pack. Maybe if I start picking up her duties, she'll get really pissed. Feel like I'm trying to replace her."

"You're gonna tell me how ghoul packs work, now?"

"No, no, I just mean...she doesn't like me as it is. I *know* you've noticed."

Needles probably had, but he didn't show it. He might have been a little rusty about standard social graces after all these years of isolation, but it still takes mighty charisma to lead a pack of monstrous cannibal humanoids. "I think if she's truly concerned about the pack, she'll welcome the help."

I sighed unhappily. This was not going to go well.

CHAPTER 4

SOIREE

The ghoul before me sat amid piles of cyberdecks and half-constructed commlinks. Bits of microcircuitry hung precariously by wires, dials, keypads, and a dozen other modified knickknacks that looked like an electronic Rube Goldberg machine. Blueprints and user manuals fished out from the garbage were glued to the concrete walls, along with a very old Maria Mercurial poster that must have still been worth something.

The ghoul, the "decker extraordinaire" Pretty had mentioned, was oblivious to my presence, humming along with some tune or another. Old-fashioned headphones covered his ears as his fingers, the sharpened nails filed down, snapped the case off a commlink that looked like it had been hit with a flamethrower, then run over with a truck.

I came around, trying to insinuate myself into his vision. He was as thin as I was, but without my catatonic excuse. A pair of datajacks gleamed dully on his left temple, and his eyes were cyber replacements, adorned with fanged smiley faces. Cute.

His eyes flicked up toward me, unfocused as though looking at the rock poster behind me, when he jumped halfway to the ceiling, yelping with such alarm that I almost feared guards would come running.

"Whoa!" I raised my hands, trying to display confidence and humanity at once, hoping to calm him down. He adapted quicker than I expected, closing his eyes and letting out a shaky sigh, then smiled and actually laughed. He lowered himself back into his chair, tucking his legs underneath him. He was around sixteen, possibly a little younger, and it showed, from his cracking voice to his exaggerated expressions.

"You really glitched me, there, term." He looked up at me as he pulled off his headphones.

"Sorry."

"Nah, nah, its wiz. I just get really...really *involved,* you know?" He emphasized the word with a clutching motion at the half-dissected commlink. His eyes were already darting back between the diagrams on the walls and the pieces on the desk. He didn't look back at me until I leaned back into his line of sight and spoke again.

"I'm, uh, Red, by the way."

He extended a skinny hand to me without taking his other hand from the commlink, or his eyes from the wall. "I'm Slim."

I can see that... "So, ah, Needles told me I should come and find you, something about a person I'm meeting?"

Slim reluctantly turned his eyes to me. "Yes, yes, I've got it all here." He held up an optical chip; old by today's standards, but reliable, plugged it into an older cyberdeck, and held out a 'trode set as he flipped switches. I placed the set on my head and felt my mind slip into the ether of electrons that comprised virtual reality.

A full three-dimensional image of a man appeared in the white room I stood in. Tall, lanky, dressed to the nines in fashions which spoke of old European traditions and tastes. Mortimer of London; custom, conservative, costly. Sandy hair glued into immaculate shape, skin tanned, and fingernails manicured. This guy had money. I wanted to say he was a Johnson, or maybe a classier fixer.

"This is your contact, who we just call Edgar."

Text started flowing before my eyes, including scrollers about his known history, a list of transactions the ghouls had entered into with him, and some pie charts that seemed to serve no discernible purpose.

"He's our primary supplier for gear and stuff. We also fence some of the salvage we find out here through him."

"What kind of salvage?"

"Oh, stuff Star patrols use but we don't really need, artifacts lost during the Breakout, things we claim from local warlords and gangs, spell components from the bugs..."

As he spoke, one of the pie charts enlarged, and I could see a precise breakdown of what had been sold to Edgar, with percentages. Another pie chart showed profit dividends, and there were more beyond that. Two things instantly occurred to me: he had far too much free time on his hands, and most corporations would kill for this kind of natural talent with details and statistics.

"Okay, I get it. He's a big mover and shaker for the pack. He's the one I'm meeting?"

"Oh, no, no, not at all. He's Pretty's contact."

A full dossier on Pretty came up, complete with more charts. I spoke up before he got too far off track.

"Then who am I meeting?"

"Oh! Right, right. She has been working on Mr. Edgar for a couple of weeks now. He doesn't seem to know about her being a ghoul, so she was able to get some names out of him. Since we don't want to ruin our relationship with Edgar by showing how interested Pretty is, it'll be your job to meet with these people and establish contact."

A list popped up displaying aliases, names, commlink numbers, and other data. It streamed past me, showing perhaps a half-dozen names with as much detail on each as could be collected. Despite being unfinished, it was remarkably thorough.

"Do we know what these people do?"

"Most of them. I'm still data mining for the last two."

"Will I be meeting them cold?"

"Huh?"

"Will I be initiating contact with them, or is it all set up?"

"Man...I dunno. I hadn't really thought about it. I've been talking to the first one online. She's the one you'll be meeting with first, I think, since we know the most about her."

"Okay, so tell me about her."

The environment changed into a perfectly still vineyard. A clear blue sky rained painless sunlight onto me, and I found myself nostalgic for a feeling I had all but forgotten. The field seemed to stretch into eternity, the ocean just in view to the west. I'd've placed it as California, if this was lifted from a real location. A large house, in classic Spanish villa style with attached facilities, was a short distance away, and standing by the entrance was a petite woman, probably Japanese, in a conservative business suit. Her stance was relaxed, her eyes dark, her suit expressing a tiny flair of color in the small pin on her lapel, a cluster of red grapes.

"This is Konoko Jones, owner of the *Vino Sanguis* Vineyards in southern CalFree."

The name tugged at my memory, but I couldn't place it. Vine's Blood? Probably just some commercial or something...

"Her vineyard is known for producing not only exceptional wine, but customized vintages for wealthy consumers. The vineyard also hosts several Awakened plants and animals, which they cultivate to produce useful fetish materiel, as well as mixing some into grape vines or directly into the wine itself. Some of their bottles are totally unique for their mixtures and treatments."

I had to whistle. I knew what being a talismonger was like. With land like that, she'd turn a pretty credstick if she could keep the poachers and land grabbers away.

"So, why are we interested in meeting her?" I asked.

"Well, we have a lot of Awakened plants and animals here, too, when they survive the Strain III. Maybe there's something we could sell to her. But Pretty noted that Edgar said she was a good person to talk to when you needed someone to disappear. I don't know exactly what he meant, but I guess Needles thought we could use a contact like that."

Well, who couldn't? I thought.

"So, she's an assassin? Awfully public persona for someone who does wetwork, even if you believe in hiding out in the open."

"It doesn't look like it," he said. "If she is, she cleans up her trail very well."

"Okay. So this means I'm flying out to CalFree?"

Slim laughed. "Sorry, chummer, but we ain't got the cred. No, she's coming to town on a tour to promote this year's vintage and shop around for new plants to add to their gardens. I managed to make an appointment for you to meet with her tomorrow. She's having a wine tasting for the upper crust at an exclusive party at Club Raid. Your name's on the list. Just get some nice threads and make your appearance. Introduce yourself, and mention 'extracting juice without picking the grape.' After that, it's all you."

I had to shake my head and laugh. It was all out of a Z-grade spy flick. But then, that's how some runs went.

I was living a moment out of a romantic comedy from hell.

The elegant elven clerk eyed me with obvious disdain as Pretty talked about what to clothe me in. Most people don't walk into Mortimer of London without their own entourage, let alone in torn jeans and a hoodie. But Pretty looked like a nouveau-riche princess with a shabby boyfriend she wanted to clean up, and if she had the nuyen, who was the clerk to argue?

Her eyes darted all over the store, taking in every garment. I thought I almost saw the glint of something so human as desire, but then it was gone, as fleeting as my realization. I scowled at her, which fit the act perfectly.

It took some effort to act like I didn't enjoy getting fitted for the suit. I used to love this kind of thing, reveling in the trappings of wealth. I opted for something dark, slick in cut but standard in fiber. I only needed to look flash. It didn't need to be made from woven diamond filaments with massaging liners.

That would wait for my fiscal resurrection.

An hour and a half later, I was in a pay shower, enjoying the feeling of warm water and fresh soap. Pretty was right outside, smoking a cigarette and wearing a new mask, seeming to have fully embraced the "tolerant-yet-impatient rich girlfriend" role. It made me wonder just how right Menerytheria had been.

"I don't like the way she looks at you..."

That was a whole other can of worms, right there. "Was it really wise to spend so much on a suit?"

"If you're going to make a few meetings in high-class places, yes," she called back through the booth wall, with just a hint of bitterness.

"I didn't think the warren had so much to spare."

"We're okay, but we have to buy everything carefully. No one can trace what we do out here back to the warren. That always costs extra."

"What about starting dummy corporations, or getting control of one of the city necroplexes?"

"Starting a cover costs even more money we don't have, and it wouldn't mean much in the Zone or the Corridor, anyway. Other ghouls have that territory, and in this town, there's a major competition between the packs."

"Are there many of them?"

"There's Long Pig Farm out by the old golf courses, and a few packs wear 162 colors and tag wherever they can. They just make trouble for the rest of us, but they also keep hunters distracted."

That confused me. "Why don't you all just pack up and make for greener pastures, then?"

The booth door slammed open with sudden ferocity. She stood on the other side, cigarette hanging from her painted lips as she shouted at me. "You think it's that easy? What do you know about having roots? You've never made something in a place you could call your own. You just walked away and started somewhere else! You've never had a home! You left!"

My eyes were wide with surprise, and it took her a moment before hers adopted a similar shocked expression. Even so, she glanced over my form once before slamming the booth shut. The last sight of her face was furious blushing and the dropped mask of her shyness.

I finished my shower in silence.

The general club scene hadn't changed significantly in the past decade, or hundred years, as far as I could tell. On a fundamental level, it was the same as it must have been for its town square pub equivalent in the 1700s, if just a bit more exclusive.

A bouncer stood outside the door with a list of names. Past him, the bar served various forms of delectable toxins, people under their effects moved in and out of rhythm with the music, and everyone did their best to have a good time. The place had been cleaned thoroughly for the event, but it was impossible to get rid of the vague, yeasty stink of spilled beer and dance sweat, sometimes mixed with the sticky sweet of mixed drinks.

On a visual level, however, the clubs were a whole new beast. Same breed, but evolved. Club Raid seemed happy to fly in the face, as it were, of the Chicago fear of bug spirits. Caution tape, bio-hazard signs, plastic sheeting with nano-morphing graphics, slow, throbbing music by a Japanese dwarven DJ, and waiters in various forms of exterminator gear. I was a little dubious of the sex appeal a waitress in a bikini and gas mask had to offer, but some of the *sararimen* really seemed to dig it.

Almost every drink I spotted was wine, served in test tubes, proper goblets, and fluted glasses that must have been worth a fortune in their own right. A long table was lined with bottles, spitting buckets accumulating expensive cargo as sommeliers made their way along the selection, nodding appreciatively and noting hints of this or that to one another while I scanned the crowd for Ms. Jones. I finally spotted her standing by a bank of trideos showing footage of LS security fighting bugs on the walls back in the late '50s.

She was basically the same as she'd been depicted in the Matrix. A little shorter, perhaps. Strangely enough, she seemed a touch younger than I'd expected. I guess that was good business: who wanted to trust their money to a kid? By the time they found out her real age, they were sold by virtue of the quality of her product.

Her gaze turned to me as I approached, casually taking me in. Maybe it was my own apparent youth, but she must have decided I was no threat. She extended a hand and I took it, bowing over it, but not kissing. I decided to slip into a role at the last minute. I felt ill at ease about her, and I didn't want her to have the straight idea about me, not just yet.

With a plainly Irish Tír na nÓg brogue, I started in. "Ms. Jones. You're more radiant in person than I could have imagined."

She smiled, relaxed and in control, and eyed me like a well-fed cat regards a mouse. "Clearly I'm not paying those site-designers enough, Mr...?"

"Donovan, Ms. Jones, Christian P. Donovan, at your service."

She seemed to like the formality of it, and did a little curtsey. I couldn't smell if she had been drinking in this room, and the heat in the club made it hard to catch the details of her thermals. I'd have to play it carefully.

"Have you had the pleasure of tasting my wines, Mr. Donovan?"

My stomach reeled at the thought of alcohol. Vampires can't hold their liquor for more than a moment, and it's never pleasant. I had to bluff.

"I'm afraid not, Ms. Jones. I've got something of an intolerance to spirits."

"Oh?"

"Oh, yes, I never drink...wine."

Her eyes flared for a moment, and I could have slapped myself. I almost bit my tongue for uttering something so cliché, especially for my kind. I had to change the topic quickly.

"All the same, Ms. Jones—"

"Call me Konoko." She smiled mysteriously. I guess she had a thing for guys who weren't interested in her drink.

I smiled. "Konoko. All the same, I do represent a concern interested in your business."

"Oh? Strange that they would send someone who can't handle his wine to deal with me."

"To be sure, to be sure. But I understand the science of wine quite well. In fact, it's the hope of my company that you might collaborate with us for a new extraction technique."

"Oh?"

"Indeed. Without giving too much away, we think we've got a handle on a way to extract the juices from the grapes while they are still on the vine. It provides for much better soil fertilization and production turnaround."

She smiled knowingly, tilting her head back to consider me. After a moment, she nodded at a set of stairs winding up to a private room above the monitors. "Perhaps you'll join me alone, so we might discuss this further?"

I smiled and followed in her wake.

The room was luxurious, set up like a cozy drinking room where any manner of debauchery could take place and yet still seem opulent. Simple, hard lines offset by warm fabrics. None of the insect wasteland theme was to be found. A window facing the dance floor was transparent until Konoko hit a switch, making it as solid as the rest of the walls. She shut the door, which locked with a series of buzzes. I watched as she took a seat in the drinking pit, hitting a series of switches near the center of the table. My ears popped as a white noise generator activated and the lights dimmed.

"Come sit down, Christian."

I sat across from her, stretching my legs out, but keeping my hands free. She just kept smiling at me. The mystery was still there, but it was outshone by something else. A kind of hunger. It was worrying me.

She got up and strode over to the minibar. I could see it was laid out with a number of bottles of wine, each bearing the *Vino Sanguis* label. She pulled one from behind the bar and poured two glasses.

"Oh, Ms. Jones, I really can't—"

"I told you to call me Konoko."

She walked back to sit beside me, holding out a glass for me. "And I'm sure you will enjoy *this* vintage."

She smiled a little too knowingly as I accepted the glass. The rich coppery scent made my fangs extend a little as I realized what she had poured. It was even warm.

"Why all the runaround to contact me?" she asked.

I was still reeling. "Excuse me?"

"Is Ryu watching *that* closely?"

I decided telling the truth was going to get me kicked out very quickly, but claiming yes or no to questions I knew nothing about would get me in deeper than I could bluff. Instead I let my face calm to impassiveness. I contemplated the glass, swirling the contents about and smelling it as she stared at me. No hint of tampering, as far as I could tell. Not even a glimpse into the astral revealed anything but what this was: human blood. I drained the glass in a long, slow pull.

It was the guiltiest pleasure for me. Nothing tasted so good, but there was always the question of where it came from.

I set the glass down, her eyes still on me. I had to say something. I remained confident. Something told me she held me in awe. Probably because of what I was. But it was clear there was nothing disturbing about me to her. After all, she'd poured herself a glass of blood as well. But she was in no way a vampire. I could tell if she was, if only in the astral, unless she was very talented at Masking. But she registered as a plain human. I opted to play the arrogant undead act, maintaining my accent.

"What do you want me to say? I'm not in a position to answer questions like that. They put me in more risk than it's worth." I loved an evasion cloaked in truth. They fool most people, and even a few spells.

"All you had to do was drop the code phrase, and I'd know you were Tamanous. Why all that cloak-and-dagger nonsense trying to get my attention?"

Well, now it was clear this was a case of mistaken identity. If I went any further with this, I would never be able to do business with her. But at least I knew what she had to offer.

"Ms. Jones, please, relax. I'm afraid you've mistaken me for someone else." Her eyes flew wide open, and I could almost hear her thoughts racing.

"We did schedule a meeting," I continued, "though I think there must have been some confusion. I represent a concern interested in your under-the-counter services, but I am not a member of Tamanous, myself."

Now was the gamble. Would she hear me out, or would she decide I was a threat, and try to have me silenced?

"I see... Very well. May I assume you are familiar with my wares?"

I smiled. "If I asked you to give me a rundown of what you offer, you'd assume I was a cop. No, Ms. Jones, I am sadly not very well acquainted with your vintages, though I could hazard a guess."

She still wasn't smiling. She held her own flute of blood, not drinking, but not setting it down, either. "What business do we have then?"

"I represent a cadre of individuals with access to rare spell ingredients. Flora and fauna, as well as an appreciation of such... limited vintages as this." I indicated my glass.

"A coven of vampires, then?" She looked hopeful.

"No, not quite..."

"Ah. Ghouls, then." Her disappointment was obvious.

"Indeed. But well organized and quite industrious."

"And in need of employment, no doubt?"

It's no secret that plenty of ghouls find work with Tamanous. I wondered how Needles felt about the organization. I wasn't even sure how I felt about them. As a person who could use what they were selling, I could appreciate an organization that offered or-ganlegging. On the other hand, there were all kinds of rumors about *where* they got their organs, few of them pleasant. I like to think I don't have to hurt innocents to get my fill. Tamanous made no such promises.

"I would have to discuss that with the party in question. Pri-marily, I am here to open a dialogue, and hopefully create the beginning of a relationship that will prove mutually profitable to both parties."

She considered this for a while, tapping a red fingernail against her glass. After a few moments, she got up and poured another glass. Walking back, she set it before me.

"Am I to assume I would be doing business with a local warren?"

"I'm not at liberty to say. Contact could easily be maintained online, as it has until now."

"I would work out details with them?"

"Yes."

I glanced at the glass on the table. The blood within sat as still as wine, not a hint of coagulation. She grinned as she intuited my curiosity. "A proprietary alchemical blend, and one I am not inclined to share, keeps the blood from coagulating for at least several days after exposure to air. I assure you, it doesn't impact its taste or nutrition."

I could already attest to the latter. Another moment passed before she raised her glass to me. I took up my fresh one, glancing astral to see that she hadn't added wood particles or something equally toxic to me, and drained it as she drained hers. As I set my glass down, her hand covered mine.

"Now that our business is concluded, perhaps you would be willing to meet with me in the future to discuss some other business possibilities?"

I had no idea what she had in mind, but figured there were always possibilities to be had in unlikely places. I smiled, caught up her hand in my own, and squeezed it. "You can contact me via the same channels."

She smiled. It chilled me.

"You gonna meet with her?"

"I don't know. I'm still waiting to see what you do."

Needles reclined in his chair, fingers steepled and sighing noisily.

"I don't know, man, I just don't know. I mean, Tamanous gainfully employs—not to mention feeds—lots of ghouls. But their methods, their reputation...I'm trying to get us some legitimate recognition, here. Having connections to them just makes us a new kind of monster."

I suddenly had a pang of guilt. My ruthless ghoul friend felt edgy about getting into bed with organleggers, but I had no problem doing business with them? My own moral flexibility frightened me. Would I have considered such a deal before I was a vampire? How much had I changed over the years?

"Well, if you want to get some support for that cause, why not start fostering some contacts with the Ghoul Liberation League?"

"All they ever do is ask for money. Most charities are like that. They spend ninety-nine cents out of every UCAS dollar they get paying to stay in existence, while barely any of it goes toward the cause they supposedly exist for."

"Then write some damn memoirs or something! Tell the story, get people sympathetic to your cause."

Needles turned his milky eyes on me. "I wish it was that simple. You remember *The Diaries of Tamir Gray*, back in '57? Before that was Special Order 162 in '53. We got, what, six months of legitimacy in the eyes of the public? Oh, and the Cabrini Refuge, which ended up being a slaughterhouse. Then enough people showed up with bites taken out of them to get it repealed.

"That was six months of citizenship. Six months of real, honest-to-goodness lawful standing in the community. And, if memory serves, it put government-sanctioned ghoul bounties out of business.

"It's not that easy, Rick. It's not like every motion will be the one to make progress. Hell, those memoirs were written from an extremely sympathetic viewpoint. Everything we do has the potential to set us back as much as it might put us ahead, if not more. You think a bunch of guerilla fighters in parts of Chicago that are *supposedly* safe will make for especially romantic protagonists?"

I looked him right in the eye. "Yes."

The long pause was pregnant with thought. I could imagine his: *why should I bother? We need attention paid to things like survival and education and improved living conditions, not releasing PR on an unforgiving public.*

My own ran more like: *why can't he see that every blow struck is in the right direction?*

We didn't talk about it for the rest of the week.

CHAPTER 5

STARS

I could see myself. But I was not me.

I watched the pale figure with red eyes and hair calmly walk up to my sister. Our old family home. In her room. I talked to her about her boyfriend, about school...then ripped her throat out. I drank her eagerly, consuming every last wisp of her soul, beyond what I needed. I hid the body and called to my mother. She was next. With malicious, precise brutality, I slowly worked my way through the house, slaying my two brothers, my other sister, and my stepfather. As their corpses started attracting their first flies, I headed to the last bedroom. There, I stared face to face at myself. My sleeping, unsuspecting form barely shifted as my vampire self came closer. The fangs lowered to my pale neck...

The blast was sudden, rousing me from another nightmare-laced dream into an equally horrid reality.

Bits of rock fell from the ceiling as another explosion rocked the tunnels. I could hear the screams and snarls of ghouls from the same direction as machine-gun fire. I shot to my feet as Menerytheria swooped out of the floor before me.

"What's happening?"

"Lone Star patrol! Only a moment ago!"

I ran toward the sounds. The Stars would be equipped for combating ghouls and bugs. They probably had no idea what to do with one of my kind.

It was two floors up and several unsteady strides before I came to a junction leading to one of the surface entrances. I jumped back as a hail of gunfire ripped the corner I stood by. Looking around at the others assembled, I figured I had about eight sentient ghouls behind various barricades. Each was armed with some gun or another, several of them bleeding, but all determined. The entrance was littered with corpses, one armor-clad LS officer, maybe four ghouls. I knew three of them had been the feral ones. I couldn't tell who the last one was.

My eyes slipped into the astral for an instant to see what foes might be near. I shifted out of my body and around the corner. The three remaining LS officers by the entrance had cyberware. Maybe we had geeked the mage first. No way to know for sure, now.

Shifting my sight back to the norm, I wove my hands in their familiar patterns for combat, shaping my own personal interpretation of the spell most people called "manabolt." Raw magical force found barest containment in my fingertips, tainted black and violent violet by my ministrations, crackling with unforgiving power.

Needing only direction, I leaned my head around the corner and extended my fingers at the lead officer. The shard of black light flew toward him, striking him square in the chest. I leaped back before I could see the results, but his scream was unmistakable, even over the machine gun fire of his compatriots.

"How many?"

Needles had come up behind me, hefting his prized HK227. The transparent clip had red- and blue-coded bullets. AP phosphorous, then. Ouch.

"Two still active that I could see. Lots of armor, cyberware. I don't think I killed the one I hit. The other is dead."

"Drek."

I glanced back at him. Something inside him was screaming for blood, screaming for vengeance. He could see the corpses of his people as clearly as I. Vile, primitive logic vied for his approval: *we've lost four. We kill them all now, and it's even.* But he knew that would only bring more. Wouldn't it?

His eyes darted to me. He expected my opinion to be an enlightened one? I was caught between my identity crisis as a vampire, my amorous ex-familiar, and a post-apocalyptic war zone. He could have found better counsel.

But here I was. I looked back, and the fear in the air was palpable to someone who can taste such things on the astral. Not just ghoul fear, but human as well. That was something to bargain with. Then again, fear makes people jumpy, irrational. I felt like I was straddling a mechanical bull wearing a tac-vest full of nitro.

I shook my head. "We've gotta try for peace. That'd be a whole other kind of victory."

Needles looked pained by my words, but I could see he was thinking the same thing. Ah, how easy it would have been for all of us to surrender and just frenzy on them, revel in the tearing of flesh—

I banished those hated thoughts from my mind and looked at the ghoul corpses. None of them had burn marks or chemical stains. Plain ammo, then. Fine. I could deal with that.

I looked at Needles, who nodded. I concentrated for a whole instant, drawing forth strength from within to steel myself for the pain ahead. My skin became tougher, supernaturally hardened. I then stepped out into the hallway. The two gunners turned their rifles on me.

I felt the impact and force before I heard the explosions of their launch. I held my ground for a remarkable two seconds, not screaming as I felt the rounds perforate my body. I finally fell back, hitting the ground in a bloody smear. It oozed gray out of me, tiny swirls of those sips of human blood intermingled like oil streaks in water. Time had slowed for an instant, the high of my stolen soul-driven power keeping me alive, despite the massive damage. I could feel the holes closing even now, seconds later, but I remained still. I didn't need the two officers to feel any twitchier than needed.

"Hold your fire, hold your fire!" Needles screamed. The two Stars looked shocked they had just shot someone who didn't look like a ghoul. That moment of hesitation was what we were counting on. "We're willing to negotiate!"

The Stars looked at each other. One covered the hallway while the other reloaded. The larger, a burly man, was sweating. I could smell his fear from here. The other, a smaller woman with a weathered face and the bigger of the two guns, an LMG on a gyro mount, seemed like she had no intention of talking to flesh eaters.

Needles gave them one last chance. "We can and will kill you if you give us no other choice! Lay down your arms, and you'll be treated fairly. Fire again, and you'll leave us no other option than to put you down!"

A heartbeat. Two...

I heard one of their guns cock as the LMG started its buzzing fire again. I felt the bullets whiz over my face and then the sound of the gun jamming. I took the opportunity to sit up. Filled with the physical potency of my nature, I overcharged a spell that required no somatic components. My eyes met the man's as I cast the last spell in my repertoire. The mana morphed in my throat, burning it as the spell took a physical toll on me. Still, my voice was smooth as I called to him with mystically charged words of persuasion.

"Lay down your weapon. We're all friends here."

His eyes were wide, but he placed his assault rifle on the ground. She looked to him with a startled jolt, and stopped trying to fix her gun. It was enough time for Needles to run out and smack her in the back of the neck with the folded stock of his SMG. I didn't let my eyes leave the man's.

"Sleep."

He lay down on the ground and closed his eyes. Normally the "Influence" spell doesn't have that much direct power, but I was drastically overcharged. Smoke from my burning flesh puffed from my damaged lips as I rolled over, moaning. I swallowed thickly, the swollen tissue ruptured and bleeding, the hot coppery taste of burning blood sliding down my windpipe into my lungs. I kept swallowing, afraid to lose any more blood if I coughed. It hurt. It hurt bad enough to make my eyes water. Crying isn't easy for a vampire. Not the physical symptoms of it, anyway. I started to come down from my high, the world spinning and every wound on my body closing up but the one in my throat.

I'd forgotten to mention this earlier: physical drain from spellwork heals at the normal, human rate, not a vampiric regenerative one. I would be regretting this for some time.

I felt the soothing touch of a damp hand, and gratefully passed out.

I came to with a moist figure pressed against me, once again. Menerytheria floated up to her feet to look at me. I tried to swallow, found it much easier than I expected, and scratchily croaked out, "Is everyone okay?"

She smiled. "You were wonderful."

I took that to mean yes. It wasn't said in a consoling way.

I leaned up, despite her protests, and wished I could weave a healing spell for my blistered lips and tongue. I had let the drain happen, feeling my own energy sapped as I resisted its exhausting effects. I wasn't going to be running around for a little while. Still, there was a lingering aura hanging about me, something of Mene that clung to me and had accelerated my recovery. The burn had eased in my throat, and my lips were merely tender and swollen.

Despite the urge to roll over and go right back to sleep, I levered myself to my feet. I noticed they were bare as they touched the cold concrete. I saw a heap in the corner that was vaguely recognizable as my old clothes, now shredded rags. Even a feral ghoul wouldn't wear them.

I pulled the blanket around my shoulders, shuffling into aged tile hallways. I looked over to Menerytheria, loyally hovering right behind me.

"How long was I out?"

"No more than a few hours. Six, maybe?"

I nodded, then slowly shuffled to where Needles usually hung his hat to find him behind his makeshift desk. He smiled faintly as I plopped down in a chair across from him.

"Glad to see you're okay."

"Likewise." I smiled briefly. "How many did we lose?"

"Just the four you saw. Spirits damn it all...this will change things..."

"What?"

He fixed his gaze on me. "The pack won't like letting them go."

"What? For revenge?"

"It's not just that, Rick. They're hungry. Bug flesh is fine and all, but it's awful for flavor. You know that. It's just filler. Sometimes we luck out and find a corpse, or we eat what we kill when it's a gang or warlord. But this? This is live, fresh meat. The ferals are spending their time outside the cell, staring at the door, smacking their lips and drooling."

"Kick them away."

Needles surged to his feet. "Do *you* resist your hungers? Do you tell yourself, 'This makes me less human' whenever you drink?!"

My eyes narrowed.

He slumped back into his chair after a pause. "No. No, of course not. You don't have to. You don't have to maim someone, at the least, to get what you need."

I don't think he recognized the issues I was having, and had always had since my change, but now didn't seem like the time to engage him. Instead, I just let him continue. It was what he needed.

"You don't understand, Rick. It's not like it used to be."

"What do you mean?"

"These past few years...it's like the hunger has become sharper. We don't need to eat more, but the craving for flesh has gotten so much more insistent. Mouths salivate easy, and the temptation to go hunting for real human meat is always there, always at the back of your mind or right behind your eyelids when you go to sleep."

"Well, you guys have been without for a long time."

"That's not it! Other Infected are going through the same thing! Or—" His eyes swept me strangely. "—most of us, anyway."

"What?"

"It happened all at once, almost. Some kind of change swept through the Infected globally. Maybe it's some kind of magical phenomenon that inspired mutation, or maybe another astral push, a mini-Awakening like for Changelings, that knocked loose what it means to be any given kind of Infected. The sun is burning brighter and hotter, now, and the hunger is greater than before, and...I don't know. Ghost knows why. Maybe God woke up one morning and just decided to make it that much harder for us.

"You, though...I've heard vampires are changing, too, but you seem to be just like you always were."

Not always.

I shrugged. "Maybe being down in the river, cut of from everything, kept me sheltered from whatever is happening up here, too."

He nodded absently, distracted as he returned to his chair.

"The pack will protest releasing the Stars. They'll use vengeance as a cause, but it's backed by something really simple and hard to ignore: hunger. They'll claim the starving look in their eyes is nothing but hatred. The smarter ones have a hard time reconciling it, so they fall back on justification."

"And you?"

He paused. "I...I want to chew them up. I want to eat them while they're still alive. I want to feel it, and I want *them* to feel it." He turned his eyes on me with more soul than you'd expect from cyber replacements. "Don't you ever feel like that? Don't you just want to tear into them, let it drip around and flood over you?"

I knew exactly what he was talking about. "I don't let it go that far. That's pining for luxury."

He sniffed. "We've got a strange perception of 'luxury' then, chummer."

"No, really. Isn't the purest form of luxury just...waste?"

"So, you're saying the real luxury is...?"

"Not having to hold back. Not worrying about wasted drops or the well-being of your donor. Just... release. Lazy indulgence past what you need."

He thought about that. "So...you're saying I don't need their flesh? I just want it?"

I let him make up his own mind about that one.

The cell door swung open on rusty but solid hinges. It used to be a supply closet for the subway, with only a tiny sliver beneath the door for air. It was the same bare and sterile room I'd woken up in. The three LS officers looked away from the sudden invasion of light.

The largest, the hulking black man I had influenced, squinted at us. He tensed and shifted his weight. I looked to Needles, who signaled two of his boys to train their weapons on him. They even cocked them for the menacing effect. He settled back down, sullenly.

The one with the burn mark on his chest looked much better. Menerytheria had done Needles the favor of healing the worst of the damage. This officer looked older, wrinkles on his face and short, salt-and-pepper hair. I couldn't tell if his life was one spent frowning or smiling. The lady, also rather wrinkled despite youthful blonde hair, struggled with the old metal shackles chaining her up.

Needles snapped, and the ghouls ran in two at a time to pick up an officer and pull them into the narrow hallway, guns trained on them from a distance the whole way. They were led to the large chamber, formerly a flood reservoir, set up with rows of makeshift benches, like an auditorium. The ghouls of the pack, an impressive thirty or forty of them, including children, were assembled. The officers' expressions ranged from stoic to terrified. Who could blame them?

"I brought you here today," Needles said, the room picking up his voice enough for every ghoul in the room to hear, "to be judged."

The snarling cheers were ferocious, horrific.

"You are guilty of the slaughter of four unarmed, innocent members of our community. You also attempted to murder several other members of the pack, who, though not innocent in the eyes of UCAS law, are not deserving of the death penalty."

"We should have a jury!"

Needles turned to face the defiant older officer with the gray hair.

"Your insolence is amazing. Did my people get a trial, or a jury? Did they get a chance to plead for their lives before you cut them down?"

Needles paced before them slowly. The ghouls around them licked their lips in anticipation. "Above and beyond all of your other faults, however, you are guilty of ignorance."

He looked to the officers, who seemed confused.

"Your ignorance is the root of your actions. You see, if you were not ignorant, you would have recognized that this pack has not fed on metahuman flesh for over eight months."

One of the officers began to speak, but Needles cut him off.

"You would also have known that this pack does not engage in murderous activity. Nor do we protest when your Lone Star Security takes the credit for the insect spirits we kill, or fails to extend its protection to us. You would have known that the four ghouls you executed in cold blood were non-combatants, civilians. You would have recognized their innocence, and held your fire. If you had known these things, one of our pack would not be a widower."

He indicated a single ghoul near the back of the room, clenching and unclenching his fists.

"If you had known, one of them would not be an orphan."

A single, gray-skinned, bald child began crying, held tightly by another ghoul. I recognized the child the half-naked mother had held nights before.

"It's your ignorance that lets you righteously slay civilians. It's your ignorance that strips your conscience of its obligations toward our people. It's your ignorance that lets you group us all under the same aegis of guilt."

The crowd of ghouls closed in slowly toward the three officers. They seemed hypnotized by Needles, however. He turned back to them with his most human gaze.

"The penalty for this by any other warren would be death and consumption by the pack." The ghouls began to surge forward before Needles barked them off.

"The justice should seem self-evident: kill four of ours, we kill four of yours. Perfect and even. But we killed one of your number. You've left us with your weapons and equipment, which will be confiscated for the betterment of our community."

He looked to either side, at the ghouls who stood ready to rip the three humans apart. He spoke to them, then to the officers.

"Killing them fixes nothing. Their deaths will not amend them of their flaws. And punishment is meant to educate. That's how a good society works...I strip you of your ignorance, Stars. You don't get to leave here with the firm knowledge that every ghoul you kill is a monster. I leave you to live, to reflect on the innocents you murdered, and your comrades who will come tomorrow and the day after and after that, to kill more. I give you the responsibility to tell your superiors, your fellows, anyone, of how you were judged fairly, how you were shown mercy, by ghouls. Tell them how you were released. Tell them how they wept for their fallen and screamed for revenge. Tell them how you lived to bring back your dead friend, and breathe another day, whole and uninfected."

Needles drew close, pulling up one of the Ares Alphas we'd taken from the team. He cocked it, set it to full auto, and aimed it at them.

"But understand this: the next time I see any of *you* three with a gun pointed at my people, consider your lives and your flesh forfeit, because if you can't learn this lesson, then all you're good for—"

The gun clicked empty. The officers flinched. He tossed it to a nearby ghoul. "—is food."

I clapped slowly as he walked into the room. Needles looked exhausted, but smiled as he turned to see me.

"That was an awfully human thing to do out there."

"Don't you mean 'humane'?"

I shrugged. "Sure, that too."

He smiled a little wider, then sat in a chair. This had once been a break room for subway workers, and still held a table or two with seemingly-indestructible plastic chairs. It creaked a little as he sank into it, running his hands over his bald pate.

"What's got under your skin?" I asked.

He didn't meet my gaze. I pulled up a chair across from him and waited. "This will mean a lot more trouble than you think."

I would have asked him, but he got up and slowly strode away. I wondered what was swimming through his mind to take him down a peg after such an empowering moment.

I signaled the three ghouls with me to hold up, holding our breaths in the chill night as we headed to a Wall-Zone close to a Lone Star compound. Each ghoul carried a wriggling brown sack filled with the Star's finest, bound and gagged to avoid attracting any attention. Thankfully, the three, two men and a woman, were among the smartest and strongest of the pack. We'd make it, I was sure.

I could see the wall clearly, its floodlights steaming red in my thermal vision. Starlight made it bright as day anyway. But I had to be the spotter. The ghouls were blind to anything unliving, seeing shapes without definition unless it contained the spark of life. Seeing only in the astral was a natural hunting mechanism, but it must have made life for ghouls without cybereyes far more difficult.

I, on the other hand, could make out the details, the signs for entrance corridors in the wall and machine gun nests, while my compatriots could clearly make out the patrols moving back and forth over the wall, eyes alert for any sign of hostiles.

We moved forward, dodging from ruin to ruin. If we were seen, we could expect the first greeting would be a burst of gunfire. No sense getting caught or killed on a mission of mercy.

I looked at the three ghouls and wondered how they felt about letting fresh meat get away like this, but they seemed to be focused on the task at hand. Needles had hand-picked them. Now I was sure he had picked them well.

The fifty meters before the wall had been cleared to create a perimeter. Bullet craters pockmarked the few ruins left, testament to bug spirits staging an attack, or any number of predators, man or monster, wanting to hunt fresh meat on the other side.

We were huddled against a small bit of standing wall right before the barren space. Putting them in the middle of it would be fine. They could send someone over to pick them up. But there would be no running it from here.

I shifted my eyes into the astral, scanning for the presence of a mage on the wall. If there was anywhere an LS mage or shaman would be on duty, it'd be here, on the border of a territory of supernatural chaos. My real worry was that one of them would present a threat to our decoy...

Whispering her true name made Menerytheria materialize before me, smiling serenely, though I could tell she was excited to be helping out. She knelt with us, elbows on her knees, looking like an excited kid.

"You rang?"

I looked up at one of the two watch towers, pointing past it. "I need you to fly up past that nest, draw as much attention as you can. Lots of flash and swirl. Let them know you're there. But the moment you sense a real threat, get out of there, okay?"

She giggled with anticipation, her eyes lingering in gratitude for my concern over her well-being. Were kind masters so rare that I was such a catch? I signaled the ghouls to remove the sacks over the officers. Didn't need the wall guards to think they were bombs or something.

I nodded, and she sped off, trailing water droplets that hovered in midair for an instant before hitting the ground. I rose as the floodlights turned to track her, running with the three ghouls behind me. The officers were moaning and wriggling, but couldn't put up much of a fight. The time crawled and the meters seemed to pass slowly. No drawing on my vampiric abilities for this: this was pure adrenaline. It would only take one of those heavy machine guns raining hot lead death on us to kill us all, regeneration or not.

The already broken ground was littered with shards of glass and bits of noisy debris, making a stealth approach impossible. Whoever was in charge of this garrison, they were clever.

Fortunately, we were all wearing combat boots.

I stopped halfway to the wall, pulled off my tattered long coat, and laid it on the ground. The ghouls piled the officers there. My eyes darted to the spotlights as heavy-caliber fire chopped into the sky. Menerytheria was a small storm of distraction, leaving wet trails behind her as she danced through the sky, uncaring whether the harmless bullets passed through or sprayed around her. She still made a show of it, dancing about and occasionally clutching her chest as though mortally wounded, falling, then spinning back up to soar around again. I could hear the frustrated, confused cursing of the security gunners between their HMG bursts.

The tiniest twinge of intuition told me to dodge right while the ghouls ran straight back. It turned out to be correct, as a spotlight landed squarely on me. Throwing up a hand to block my face from any cameras, I ran faster. Gunfire peppered down around me, licking at my heels and throwing up bits of glass. I pushed myself, blitzing forward until I felt a round pierce my ankle. The sickening snap and burning feeling stunned me, I heard Memerytheria scream as I fell face first onto the filthy ground.

Not anticipating me going down, the spotlight passed me in a flash. In the instant of darkness, I pushed myself...well, sideways I guess you could say. I melted into an amorphous cloud, simple mist given will. Colors diluted and vision distorted as though I was staring through a dense fog, sound muffled as though I was wearing earplugs. As my unattuned clothes fell to the ground, I stretched myself in ways my physical form could never accommodate, spreading myself thinly over the ground, to present as little profile as possible.

Slowly, inching my way away from the light I felt on my ethereal form, I floated to an outcropping of wall. Pressing my misty self against it, I materialized, hands and cheek flat against the bricks. Pulling back, I knelt, letting my ankle regenerate as I whispered her name again and shivered with my nakedness.

A ringing of pixie-like laughter let me know I'd been heard, and she spun off into the ruins, drawing the bullets and lights away. I waited for a while, listening to the post-skirmish chaos of the watch posts.

Peeking around the corner, I saw the three officers were now lit by one of the spotlights. Reinforced doors hissed open, and six more Stars ran out in covering formations, just like in the trids. Two more followed with med kits, making sure they were real officers before they were picked up and led back through the wall. The spotlights formed a perimeter around them until they made it back inside, leaving me in the darkness.

I took advantage of it and gingerly walked off into the night, content with my good deed.

I opted to take the scenic route, feeling pretty invincible and willing to tangle with a bug if it felt the need to fight. It was a little surreal, strolling naked through the blasted ruins of the city I grew up in only seventy-five years ago.

Seventy five years...has it really been that long?

I didn't like thinking about my age; it brought up too many uncomfortable things. My family was long dead, whether by age or VITAS, with only a few of their descendants scattered about the UCAS. There was Gizelle, of course, but my close associations ended there. A few other distant relatives had proven to be a depressing discovery, few who cared to associate with the pale, long-lost uncle with a questionable career. But I missed my immediate family dearly.

More directly, I missed the trappings of my old life. I missed eating, socially and privately. I missed the feeling of comfortable, natural sunlight on my skin. I even missed the pain of a wound that took a week to heal. I couldn't go out drinking with my chummers, or sunbathe, or ever get cyberware. If there was ever a way to have kids, someday, they'd almost certainly be infected with HMHVV, whether they wanted it or not. And could I find someone to love who would understand my condition without being some kind of wacko? So much of the world was closed off to me. It just didn't seem fair.

And then there was what the virus demanded of me, in return...

I pushed those thoughts aside altogether, my face scrunching up with physical revulsion. I started running, making for the warren, hoping the painful sawing of chill wind in my lungs would distract me.

CHAPTER 6

TRUTHSAYER

The hissed, hushed whispers of discontented ghouls filled the silence for the next few days. Words like "traitor," "soft," and "weak" were bandied about in the long debates over Needles' release of what some considered good food, others guilty criminals.

For my part, I knew he'd done the right thing. He'd built good PR, and maybe swayed some minds. In the long run, that could save lives on both sides. But his eloquence had been wasted on some of the more feral members of the pack, and it was becoming more and more apparent that there would soon be a reckoning.

In particular, the widowed ghoul Barnes was one of the more outspoken of Needles' detractors. He was an interesting case. A well-bred and educated doctor before his infection, the transformation (from a late night bite at the ER, I was told) had left him still sentient, but possessed of a feral edge. He was one of the warren's "cooks," or people with enough knowledge of anatomy and familiarity with surgery to get the most out of a kill, wasting nothing usable. His wife, one of the younger born ghouls of the pack, had died during the Lone Star assault, and he'd been helpless to save her, trapped around a nearby corner by two other ghouls holding him back.

His persuasiveness wasn't just born of his well-spoken manner, but the fact that he was able to channel that with his feral senses to appeal to the less-cognizant ghouls. He went into vengeful detail about how he would have sliced them up while they still lived, and served their tender flesh to every ghoul in the pack. He spoke of how every member would have had a share, and some began to compare that to Needles' methods of leadership. Needles favored a few ghouls, like Pretty and Slim, with more toys and attention. I knew he did that to keep them operational in their respective roles in the warren, but some could not, or would not, see that. Barnes was, perhaps, one of them.

The tension became the two sides became palpable. Divisions between loyalists to Needles and Barnes's supporters were a physical thing, as ghouls split into little cliques in the hallways, casting suspicious glances at one another. I could usually tell who was who, since it was well known I was one of Needles' friends. His supporters looked at me with something like awe, while Barnes's ghouls growled or hissed quietly.

One day, as I sat down across from Slim in his gadget room, I could already tell the politics of the warren were taking their toll. His eyes flitted nervously from commlink to busted component, occasionally darting up to look at the Maria Mercurial poster. I waited patiently until he was ready to talk. Then again, if he got too distracted, he might forget I was there altogether.

Finally he focused on me, the smiles in his cybereyes not so smiling today. I tried a weak grin. "You feeling okay, chummer?"

He nodded, his lips pouting and his hands gripping the arms of his chair over and over. All of this must have been hitting him pretty hard.

"Anything I can do to help?"

He shook his head, eyes gazing at nothing, his thoughts elsewhere.

"You hungry? We brought in some more termite yesterday, I could grab you a slice—"

"Nah, nah, I ain't hungry. I don't usually eat that much."

"Don't like the taste?"

"Oh, I never taste what it *really* tastes like."

"Pardon me?"

"I slot a cannibal chip. I picked it up a while back, a reality filter for vampire wannabes and sickos, makes everything you eat taste like blood and stuff. Actually pretty close to the real thing, and far better than the bugs really taste. It's pretty wiz for my purposes."

"Huh... Yeah, I guess it would be. They can make all those soy paste meals taste like filet mignon for the wage slaves, so why not a little something for us, right?"

He nodded, still distracted.

"So... who am I meeting next?"

He halfheartedly held out the 'trode net for me, and loaded

up the file. The clean, white room manifested before me, and I noticed this one did not have all the charts and calculations. He was really distracted, then.

A dwarf in a human-sized trench coat, the excess pooling around him like robes, worn cargo pants, and mesh tank top appeared before me. No beard, going bald on top but the rest of his black hair was long enough to be tied back. His swarthy skin and aquiline features suggested his ancestors hailed from India. Funny, but I'd never met a dwarf from there before.

"This is Halian Focht."

A short list of data appeared before him as his profile began to rotate. I made out a pair of datajacks on his temple, and a few other bits of chrome on his skin. He didn't look like a samurai, but I had been fooled before. My money said he was a hacker. Given the aged-looking datajacks, I was willing to bet he'd been doing it since they were first given that title.

"Do we know what he does?"

"He doesn't have a SIN, if that's what you mean. No, he operates in the black. I did a little checking in the Shadownets and it sounds like he's an info broker. I don't know if that means he's a hacker on his own, or just knows lots of people, and passes on what he knows for a price."

"What's our pitch to him?"

"You mean why should he care about us? We get all kinds of weird tidbits about Lone Star when we steal or salvage their gear, plus we could pass on things from other contacts we're making. And there's always the chance we'll need some info at some point."

I nodded. "Fair enough. When and where?"

"Tomorrow, just after sunset. Seattle's Choice Coffee Shop in the NeoNET Zone of the Naperbrook subsprawl."

Pretty didn't guide me this time; in fact, I hadn't seen much of her lately. When I'd asked Slim, he said she was busy meeting with Edgar about fencing some loot. So I donned my nice shirt with my torn jeans and boots, and cleaned the synth-leather jacket so that it looked worn, but not destroyed. I figured fostering the "I could afford better clothes, but I'm such a rebel" look would match his own, and from what I'd heard, it was all the rage for the rich bratpacks that populated the squeaky-clean corporate subsprawls.

A trip down the sewers and ducts and a quick shower later, and I was on my way to the coffee shop. The neighborhood was much improved. I remembered the old days, before I was turned, when it had straddled the line between dangerous gang territory and popular hipster hangout. Since Chicago's population had surged outward with time and the Breakout, it had become a much nicer area, with higher security and well-dressed young students-cum-socialites.

It's my opinion that neighborhoods go through a growth cycle. At some point or another, a place becomes trendy, slowly driving out the riff-raff as expensive shops and high rent bring better security. It stays that way for a little while, as only people "in the know" live there, until good press gets *everyone* who wants to be cool to take up residence. Soon it's packed with too many people, standard shops move in, and it's no longer trendy. It becomes a boring little neighborhood where people sleep, but don't spend any of their free time.

From the look of things, this was a prime example. There were still a few trendy types, but it was clearly winding its way back into safe normalcy, with happy family businesses popping up to supply the average people filtering in. The sheer mundane nature of the setting, in addition to the safe feeling from the Lone Star beat cops, made this an ideal place for a meet. After all, who expects the shadows in calm, well-lit, upper-middle-class neighborhoods on a Monday night?

The coffee shop was a cliché, still clinging to the classic look of modern, sleek counters and decorations. Catering to a higher-income clientele, the place offered both soykaf and real coffee, ground right there in the store, filling the space with one of the most coveted aromas in the world. At least I could still appreciate the smell, even if I couldn't have a cup. Again, I marveled at how little some things had changed during my decade-long sleep in the river.

Halian stood out only slightly at his table, tuned into his commlink with a discreet datajack cable. He wasn't so rebelliously dressed, in a sweater and slacks. His age, as well as his slim build for a dwarf, reminded me of a harmless little college professor. It was a far cry from the street threads depicted in his picture.

I ordered a cup of cheap soykaf from the counter, and checked the room out while waiting for it. A few folks were enjoying their pre-bed caffeine infusion, but no one seemed out of the ordinary...until my eyes fell on a human, perhaps barely in his twenties, reading a hardcopy newsprint and casting suspicious glances over the top from time to time. He was angled perfectly to keep an eye on the door and Halian, and his scans always roamed over the other customers. He didn't have the shy or hungry look most young students have when cruising for a date or drugs, so I presumed he was Halian's backup. His gaze fell on me and lingered for an instant. I smiled back, and the paper shot up, his face buried in its sheaves.

I paid cash and coin for my kaf, despite the strange looks the barista gave me, and strode over to Halian's table. His eyes flitted up to me as I stood looking at him, clearing from whatever the commlink was feeding him. I smiled.

"Halian Focht?"

He was suspicious, but hid it well, giving me a discreet once-over before meeting my gaze again. His voice was soft, tinged with a faint Delhi dialect. "Do I know you?"

"I have a few questions I want to ask you."

"Are you one of my students?"

I somehow liked that he was, in fact, a teacher. This wasn't a coded phrase, and as I looked maybe 20, I could easily be mistaken for a college student.

"I'm just a seeker of truth. Information is power, as they say."

He smiled faintly, and gestured for me to sit. I did. He tapped a switch on his commlink, and suddenly my own AR started crackling. I shut my commlink down. Nicely done, jamming without making too much noise.

"I take it you are Mr...?"

"Crimson, sir, my name is Crimson."

"Good. I was starting to think you weren't going to show up."

"I'm sorry I was late, but my commute takes some rather unorthodox routes."

"No doubt. So, you contacted me on the Matrix?"

"No, sir, that was an associate of mine. I'm here on his behalf."

"And what have you brought for me?"

I assumed he meant information for sale. I figured as a businessman he might appreciate a mercenary approach. "That depends on how much you have to offer for it."

His face showed confusion for a moment before hardening.

KEVIN R. CZARNECKI   **83**

"Mr. Crimson, perhaps you do not understand what it is we are trying to accomplish here. The truth is not something that is the exclusive privilege of the elite and wealthy. Everyone, from UCAS citizens to the SINless to the rest of the people across the globe, has a right to the undistorted truth."

"About...?"

"Everything!" There was a manic light in his eyes. Nothing to scare me, but far more fascinating, genuine passion. It was a rare thing, in this or any age. I knew he was being honest. I could smell it on him, see it shining clearly in his aura. I also could see that this was a man who, though clever, was not prone to guile. Finding the concept refreshing, I decided to go with it.

"I'm sorry, Mr. Focht, I think I've misunderstood what you are about. I was given to believe you were an info broker. Was I mistaken in my assessment?"

Halian leaned back, considering me. I stayed steady. He had something to hide, that was for certain, but there was also something about it that denied malicious intent. No, this was a man with a cause, if I read him right. A man with a crusade who might be hunted down and stopped if he wasn't careful. And now he was wondering if I was a man who could be trusted with his secret.

He folded his hands on the table, considering his words before speaking. "Just what is it that you want, Mr. Crimson?"

"Well, at this point, I'm not sure what you have to offer, but I'll lay my cards on the table. I represent a group which would like to foster positive relations with you."

"What group would that be?"

"I'm...not sure I should tell you, yet. Some things should only be spoken of with those you trust."

"Indeed."

"However, I'm willing to reveal more if you are."

He smiled briefly, like a chess player who ruefully admires the move his opponent has made.

"I am... someone who brings the truth to the people."

"What truth is that?" I'd had my fill of religious zealots.

"Any truth. Mr. Crimson, you look like a man of the world. No doubt you've been privy to some circumstance or another involving wealthy or influential parties who did not want the actual nature of things discovered. So they spin-doctor it."

"Go on."

"Our world is, for the most part, run by massive, multinational megacorporations, complete with extraterritoriality. History shows us that governments have always moved to cover up their dirty secrets. And when every corporation is a government unto itself, how many more cover-ups do you think take place? Dozens, every day. Hundreds. Thousands. The spin-doctor is a profession that finds a lot of work, lately. And after they are done reweaving the truth into bland, digestible pap for the evening news, the regular Joe who makes the machine work has *no* idea what the world about him is really doing."

He leaned forward, the intensity in his eyes thrilling to behold. "Someone has to uncover that story. Someone has to bring truth to the populace at large. We deserve at least that much."

"And you're that someone?"

He sat back in his chair, scowling lightly.

"It is not an act of hubris, Mr. Crimson. Heroism is self-evident, in my opinion. This is simply a duty someone must fulfill. But, with those qualifiers made known, yes, I am one of those someones."

I smiled. I genuinely liked him. "So what can you offer me, then, Mr. Focht? Or is it professor?"

His scowl became a smirk. He nodded. "I suppose after this you can trace plenty of facts about me off the legal net, alone. Yes, I am a tenured professor at Columbia."

"A school for artists?"

"Do not underestimate the passion of youths in search of truth. Or their familiarity with broadcasting equipment and methodology."

"Touché. All right, then, I take it you operate *pro bono*? No money under the table to get you to paint the story just one shade off from true?"

"No, Mr. Crimson, I do not take bribes. I make more than enough money for myself with my regular job. And I am not just another link in the chain of misinformation. I am receptive to stories people have to tell, then I set about verifying their veracity."

I didn't ask how. He was obviously a data miner. Probably good, too.

"I suppose it's occurred to you that others might view your work as a way to slander their opponents?"

"Every job comes with some level of bias. I have no illusions about that. But then, the truth usually only hurts those who are guilty. I do not endeavor to influence people's minds, only supply them with the necessary information to make up their own. I will report any truth that's been hidden which I find, if it involves public matters."

"Then no personal secrets?"

He smiled. "No, no personal secrets. For example, I don't see why it would be necessary to broadcast that you are a vampire."

That took me by surprise, although I thought I kept my expression suitably deadpan.

The dwarf smiled. "Don't look so surprised, Mr. Crimson. The fact that your contact specifically told me to meet you after sunset was the first indicator. When you walked in, I noticed that you are exceptionally pale. You also purchased a soykaf that you haven't even touched since you set it on the table. Your blinking is sometimes staged, and it is only just possible to make out the tips of fangs and a red tinge around your eyes. The fact that they are blue, and natural, only accentuates that oddness. Of course, I might not have noticed those last two unless I was looking for them."

He had me in a pinch. Would it be safe to let him retain that knowledge? I'd long forgotten the spells to erase memories, and I had no intention of killing him.

He seemed to sense my inner conflict and chuckled. He reached across the table and patted my cold hands wrapped around the hot cup. "Your secret's safe with me. I've got a pretty good sense for people, and I'd judge your character as being basically beneficent."

"I might take that as an insult, considering my profession." I was still stunned.

He chuckled again and offered me an ARO with his information. "Whoever you represent, you've done well enough to inspire my curiosity. If they've a story they want told, and told honestly, I'll see to it. Until then, I hope we have the pleasure of sharing a cup of coffee again soon."

He strolled out, his so-called bodyguard trailing out after him, looking comically suspicious. No doubt a performance artist.

CHAPTER 7

DEATHS AND RESCUES

It was only ten o'clock, and I had all the time in the world to kill. Somehow, though, I didn't feel much like living it up. Low on cred, no fake ID, and the knowledge that I was recognizable as a vampire made me feel glum and self-conscious. I started to turn up my collar, whether against the season or to hide my features, but that made me feel worse, thinking it was as obvious as an opera cape.

I slowly walked back to the warren's secret entrance, hands jammed in my pockets against the chill autumn winds. It'd be snowing soon, and that meant some unpleasant nights ahead for the warren. Chicago winters were dangerous in the best of times, and everything the world had gone through had only made them worse. I made a note in my PAN to pick up some portable heaters or something similar the next time I was out with cred to spare.

I turned a corner and bumped into an ork so large I might have mistaken him for a troll. The sheer mass of his body bounced me back, and I started to apologize before seeing his two friends. One had a small bag filled with what I took to be novacoke. The other was handing him a chromed credstick. The one I had jostled slowly turned to scowl at me. Bald, a bandanna with gang colors on his head, and piercings through his tusks and ears. His eyes blazed at me.

"Sorry," I said lamely, knowing I was in trouble.

He turned completely to me, and I noticed the two behind him putting their hands in their coats, no doubt on hidden guns. Great. This was my nice jacket.

"Sorry ain't gonna cut it, *omae*. You best be bringing some'ting a little heavier den dat."

I like to think I have my share of humility, but I wasn't about to beg for my life to gutterscum. Besides, even if they *could* roll me, I had maybe fifty nuyen, if that.

"Look, buddy, I'm sorry. What else do you want from me?"

"Depends what you got ta give."

I rolled my eyes. I was done with guile. I felt like being me. I felt like being a real asshole. Go figure these three were in the wrong place and the wrong time. Just another story of the streets.

"All I got is troubles, chummer. Wanna share them with me?"

He flashed a chrome-toothed smile as he pulled a Remington Roomsweeper from his pants. Leveling it at my head with an awkward sideways grip, he lifted his chin as his grin grew even wider. His two friends pulled smaller holdouts, maybe a Streetline Special with a silencer and a Fichetti Security.

"No, *omae*, *now* you gots troubles."

I just smiled. Rookies.

I stepped closer to the ork, using his massive bulk to shield myself from his buddies. Sweeping my arm up to get his shotgun out of my face, I followed through with a punch to his unmistakable gut. He took it, grunting but not doubling over. The Roomsweeper boomed next to my ear, and damn near deafened me.

The other two also sprang into action, one stepping away to aim his gun at me, the other wading in on my left to drive a fist into my side.

I was too occupied with the shotgun-toting ork, and took the punch. These three were tough, to be sure. The one with the drugs was skinny as hell, but the other two gang members were big, burly types. I felt my kidney flare, and my whole back tensed at the impact. He must have had either bone lacing or brass knuckles.

My twinge gave the ork an opening to swing at me with a huge fist. My head snapped around, and I felt something in my jaw *crack*. I spit out a tooth, probably a molar, as he went to work on my stomach. It was too much for me to resist, and I took the punches.

I suppose I could have drawn on my reserve of stolen essence to take the blows, or get stronger or faster. I probably could have turned to mist. But something in me just didn't have the heart for it. The world seemed to slow with the pain, and I drew into myself.

There's nothing left of you, Rick. You're just a puppet. Hell, you're not even Rick, anymore. Just his shell, animated by a virus. Just a puppet with a hunger. You're not strong. You're not even weak...

You're dead.

"Look at dis little bitch! He's cryin'!"

The three thugs laughed heartily, taking a moment from their abuse to guffaw at me. I felt the wetness trickle down my face, felt my chest tremble with sobs eighty years in the making. I didn't hold it in. I didn't even try for dignity. I just let it flow. My moaning wail filled the alleyway, a screaming cry for my lost innocence and all the simple joys and accomplishments I could never know. I sobbed for my dead mother and stepfather, my sisters and brothers, my friends and acquaintances and memories crumbled away long ago. I let loose the anguish of missing all those years trapped beneath the cold, salty waves. I even shed a tear or two for Gypsi. I hadn't cried since I'd died. This was long overdue.

"Aw, Jonesy, will you shut him up?"

The ork named Jonesy took another solid shot at my solar plexus, and the air *whuffed* out of me. I squeezed out the last moan, and then started laughing breathlessly. The two grunts holding me looked confused, and Jonesy's face twisted into an enraged sneer as I looked up with my manic, bloodstained smile.

"Whassa matter, Jonesy? Ain't got the salt to keep hittin' me?" My words whistled through broken teeth and gurgled with blood streaming from my nose and mouth.

His fist flew at me again, knocking my head back in a whiplash of startling force. Even as I felt my nose break, I couldn't stop laughing. It got more and more intense, the more he hit me, until I was spitting blood with every hysterical snigger.

"That's the spirit!" I shouted with glee as he worked my lower body. I don't think he could understand why I wasn't passing out or dying yet. I'd lost track of time, but we had been here a little while. The boys holding me up started looking impatient.

"Look, Jonesy, he's psycho. Just finish it already!"

Jonesy walked up to me slowly, putting his left hand on my sore chin to make me face him. I spit a bloody gob in his face and smiled at his wince. He put his hand to my scalp, pulling back my eyelids so I could see his right fist as three spurs slid out from between his knuckles. With a long, slow pullback, he slammed them halfway through me, just piercing through my stomach to my back, almost two inches from my spine.

I guess it just wasn't my night to die. These slags certainly couldn't kill me. I'd just have to show them how it was done.

I looked up, my eyes placid, as I yanked my arms from the two thugs and stepped toward the ork, impaling myself even harder on the spurs. Something deep inside wouldn't let me resist drawing on my essence any more, and I felt myself becoming stronger. The virus in my veins knew it was about to be fed. Who was I to deny it?

Jonesy looked from the spurs piercing me back up to my serene expression. I put a hand behind his elbow and jammed the spikes in to his knuckle, stepping forward to draw him close. When his eyes were fixed on mine, I smiled broadly, revealing my fangs, already growing longer and regenerating from the cracks of so many hits.

"You wanna share my troubles, Jonesy?"

Grabbing his head with both hands, I pulled it forward and headbutted him with everything I had. His skull had nowhere to go, and I felt him slump from the impact. Dropping him, I let the spurs slide out as I turned to the drug dealer, who was screaming and wildly firing his Fichetti at me. He had no idea how to shoot, and I felt no fear, even as a stray bullet tore off the top of my left ear. Human length now, I felt the spot grow warm as it slowly grew back.

He screamed again, and I rushed him, driving a fist into his stomach hard enough to make him vomit. As he doubled over, I dropped an elbow on his neck, sending him to the ground. I stepped over his unconscious body and meandered toward the last one. He held the Streetline in both trembling hands. His eyes darted back and forth, as though searching for help.

"St-stay back!"

I smiled and held my hands out from my body, as though to ask what I could do. He whimpered and I shook my head, still smiling. My ear was completely healed now, and I could feel all my teeth in place, once again. I pushed on my jaw, and felt it *pop* into place. Sometimes regeneration left me a little stiff. The loud *snap* made him squeal, and I almost laughed.

Then he did something that stunned me. Looking around, realizing there was no way to escape, he dropped to his knees and, with a look of despair that haunts me to this day, put his own gun in his mouth and pulled the trigger. The shot rang with a hollow *pop*, the tiny bullet never exiting his skull. One eye jerked to the side, and he fell forward, slack face splashing into a murky puddle.

I was in a trance. I felt nothing. I *was* nothing. I strolled back to Jonesy, squatting over him and slapping his face to wake him up. His blurry eyes focused on me, and he let out a yelp loud enough to wake the dead. I dropped and pinned his arms with my legs, clamping a hand over his mouth and running one finger along his throat, feeling for the pulse. Fear, rich and sweet, radiated from him so thick I could smell it, a tantalizing tang. I stared down into his frantic eyes.

"You really want my troubles, Jonesy? You think you can handle *my* troubles?"

He shook his head in terror, and I felt something inside me become...aroused. It wasn't me. Even if I'd liked men like that, I wouldn't have liked Jonesy. But something similar, something akin to the thrill right before sex, stirred in me. I was compelled to drain him to the last drop, draw it out slowly and let his body lay undisturbed for a day or two, until he awakened.

The virus in me insisted, urged my open mouth down to his neck. My teeth pierced his throat, and the first taste sent me over the edge. Red blurs consumed my vision even as I consumed him, blood and soul. I let go and gorged.

It lasted an eternity.

I came back to my senses still crouched over him, his limp, pale body in my arms. I leaped away for a moment, noting the cuts on my clothing and blood everywhere. I glanced out the alley's mouth, but no one was coming. Maybe I'd misjudged the safety of the neighborhood, after all.

I quickly looted the bodies, grabbing everything. The drug dealer had a fake ID and a real one—I couldn't tell which was which—along with plenty of other drugs and a little cash. The others had a few weapons and a little nuyen. Jonesy had half a handle of synthahol on him. I would have loved to take a pull of it. If only he'd been drunk himself, I might have gotten a buzz off his blood.

As I picked up the Roomsweeper, I looked at the drained corpse. The eyes were frozen, the mouth a rictus of terror. I had to look away. I didn't have the luxury of debating whether I was a man or a monster, right now. But all the same, I knew Jonesy was now host to a parasitic, metamagical virus. Even now it was making inroads into his body and, presumably, the tattered remnants of his soul.... I didn't want to think about it.

"You wanna share my troubles, Jonesy?"

I flicked off the safety and aimed the gun at his head. If I took out the brain, he wouldn't change...

Something inside me railed against the thought of killing him. It felt like it was my idea, my prerogative. Instinctually, I wanted to make sure he changed. It was procreation, pure and simple. Rape, if you looked at it long and hard enough. The gun felt heavier, my vision blurred, a dozen little symptoms to unconsciously make it harder to fire.

I blinked, drew a deep breath, and with the same willpower that makes a chain smoker throw away a full pack, pulled the trigger.

I picked up the bodies, still benefiting from my strength boost, and tossed them into a dumpster with old newsprint stacked up. I crumbled each up for kindling, then emptied the bottle of syntha-hol on them. The dealer's lighter was last, making the dumpster a funeral pyre. I wasn't so concerned about the cops identifying the bodies as finding traces of me on them. Ritual sorcery had made police work a whole new ball game.

I picked up my lost molar and pocketed it. Splashing some cold puddles over the bloodstains would tamper with the link enough to keep me in the clear. Taking one last look, I ran down another alleyway and zigged about the city for an hour in search of a shower.

The drug dealer's money paid for a full hour of hot water and good soap. As I stepped into the booth, I placed an emergency delivery order for a small clothing store nearby to deliver some clean clothes in my size. Again, the dealer, Ronnie Chase by ID, picked up the tab.

I let the heat numb me. I hung my head and wished I had tears left to cry now, but the shower played surrogate well enough. The fact was, I was too pragmatic to linger over dead friends and family for long, no matter how well-loved. Life goes on, and in my place, they'd have to do the same.

Life, I mused to myself. *Is that what this is?*

I couldn't stop the debate now, as I wondered about the nature of an infected soul. True, the Human-Metahuman Vampiric Virus was mystical in nature, the more potently-infected feeding directly on what some called "essence," or the soul. It took root when there was no more resistance, and made the victim into a host. The question was: did the virus leave the last shreds, the core of your soul, intact and mutate the rest, or, like a perfectly-merged insect spirit, did it simply retain your memories and skills, using those to hunt more efficiently?

I had met with other vampires in the past, and debated the theories. One of them, Adam Pawloski, had said he was fine with the idea that his soul was gone forever.

"Why doesn't that bother you?" I'd asked.

"Why?" He laughed as though it were a ridiculous question. "My friend, I am who I am. Maybe that's based on someone else, but then, isn't that like reincarnation? Did you know that the elves of Tír na nÓg have this religious belief that they are all reincarnated after every death, and therefore, truly immortal? Is their previous life invalidated because they have a new one now? Is the current one guilty of taking something from the old one? Doesn't really change things for me, either way. Maybe I am who I was before, but I'm comfortable thinking I was born the night I was changed. I am who, and *what*, I am right now, no matter what I think about it."

I didn't think I could agree with him, though I knew it would be a comforting thought. Another vampire I ran with for a while, Tali, had gone the other route.

"Red, after getting infected, I spent ten years doing some serious soul-searching. That right there should tell you something. If it's an infection smart enough to completely optimize you for the purposes of hunting, only keeping enough humanity to help you blend in, then it would discard those kinds of doubts and fears that get in the way. Ten years. That's a long time, and I spent it coming to terms. That's who I am, and who I was. I remember everything. I still make choices just like before. It's just a change. You think orks and trolls didn't ask all those questions when goblinization happened? I'll bet they wondered if they were still *who* they *were*. But we know they're still the same people. Same thing for the ghouls who keep all their marbles after changing. We've all got different needs, now, but the bottom line is that we're still people."

I liked her theory well enough, and it even made sense, but on some level, it still gnawed at the edges of my mind.

A knock sounded on the other side of my shower booth. "Clementine's Nighttime Apparel!"

I cracked the door open and held out the credstick with a hundred nuyen on it. He slid a new pair of jeans, a burgundy tee, and a clean synth-suede jacket through. The deliveryman took the stick and looked at it. I could hear it being loaded into his commlink as I put the pressed laundry into a dry alcove.

"Nah, keep the change, man."

"Hey, thanks, chummer! Mind if I ask what happened?"

"I was dating a werewolf and she shit on all my clothes before throwing me out."

He laughed and wished me a good night.

Midnight came as the night crawled on. Still warm from the shower and enjoying the feeling of truly clean clothes that fit well, I was reluctant to surrender the feeling of normalcy by returning home just yet.

I was wondering what I should do with my newfound petty cash when my commlink signaled an incoming message. I flipped my display shades on and approved the transmission. Slim's Matrix persona appeared before me, looking remarkably like he might have if he wasn't a ghoul, but in noir black and white tones. Even the filter had bits of old-film scrambles to it. Pretty flash.

"Hey, Red, it's me, Slim."

"I see you. What's up?"

"Needles wanted me to call you. Pretty left earlier to meet up with Edgar to fence some of the drek we can't use from those Star slags. She was supposed to check in an hour ago, and she never misses those calls. Could you see if she's okay while you're out there?"

I sighed. I had a feeling Pretty was just being rebellious. "She probably just got distracted."

"No, no. Pretty is really good about calling up. She knows Needles'll get pissed if she doesn't, and then she won't get new clothes and drek. And, you know, she really is loyal."

I rolled my eyes. "Fine. Where is she?"

In the parking garage underneath an apartment building on Halsted, I listened intently to the silence. I couldn't hear anyone or anything but the slow drip of coolant from an old Yamaha Rapier that had seen better days. The three layers of garage seemed to go on and on, without a trace of life to them.

I finally noticed the faint scent of burnt rubber, and saw tire tracks from a parking space near a storage room door. I knelt down, slipping into the astral, fighting through the distant echoes of horror the city's spirit has yet to forget, tasting the air for traces of recent strong emotions.

–Anticipation. Excitement. Fear.
Confusion. Pain.
Pain. Elation. Pain.
Urgency.–

I was confused by the combination, but it filled me with dread. I could feel the trail lead to the door from the spot where the van had been parked. I quietly ran to it, listening through it. Nothing. Even with elven ears and vampiric fine-tuning, it was too thick.

I steadied myself and yanked the door open. Blood. It's always the first thing I notice.

The racks of cleaning supplies were knocked over, chemicals and buckets and the like strewn over the two figures within.

Edgar was slumped against the wall, his gray suit a mess from the bullet that had exploded through him, spraying the back wall with his innards.

Pretty lay beside him, her black blazer and skirt soaked with blood. On the floor, some of it was the blackish color of a ghoul's, mingling with Edgar's. I might have thought she was dead, but I could see the faint traces of life in the astral, hear the tiny, shallow breaths she unconsciously sipped. She was out cold, but alive.

I ran to her, ripping her blazer open. I didn't register the blood, or the smooth perfection of her soft skin. All I saw was the ragged bullet wound in her chest, the darkness of outer burn marks. It was just above her right breast, hopefully not piercing the lung. I didn't know enough about medicine to tell.

She stopped breathing.

I figured she was in shock, and shouted her name, slapping her lightly across the face. If I couldn't wake her up, it was hopeless.

"Pretty. Pretty! Don't do this... don't do this, Pretty! *Pretty!*"

I looked about, found a faucet for filling buckets and cupped my hands to splash her face. I laid her on her back and began pushing on her chest with the most basic understanding of CPR, counting as I did it to keep my cool. I held her nose and breathed for her. A coughing gasp after a moment of this brought her around, moaning in pain. I held her face close to mine.

"Pretty... Pretty, look at me..."

Her eyes looked into mine as I softly chanted the words to Influence her. *"Stay calm and relax. Do not worry, I will help you. Just trust me and let me help you."*

The moaning stopped and she calmed, her eyes gaining their shy, fearful look again. I was confused for a moment before I realized this *was* her relaxed expression. She was totally at ease. She was *herself.*

I dragged my gaze away from her wide, vulnerable stare and concentrated my will, fighting the chaos of the astral and drawing forth the energy, giving it the shape of a healing spell. The soft turquoise glow was like a balm on my hands, and I spread it on her wounds, gently pushing it into the bullet holes. I can never quite see into the area being healed, so I don't know if it kickstarted her regenerative system, or simply replaced flesh that had been lost, but it worked. The small slug was pushed out, landing with a *tink* on the concrete floor. Her breathing became stronger even as she stared at me, and the bleeding from the remainder of the wound, nothing but a bloody gash now, oozed slowly, controllably. I tore a sleeve from her blazer and used it for an amateur bandage. It would have to be enough until we got back.

Picking her up, I took her out of the closet. Setting her down gently outside the door, I went back in and used the rags and cleaning materials to clean any trace of her or me from the spot. No fingerprints, and the spilled blood was doused liberally with sterilizing solutions to corrupt them. I dumped out almost every labeled bottle in the room, heedless of toxic fumes. When I was sure the metroplex guard would only find Edgar's dead body and a great, big stew of cleaning supplies, I picked up Pretty and carried her out of the garage.

She moaned softly whenever I jostled her, keeping a brisk step and trying to look as casual as one can while carrying a wounded, semi-conscious woman. I had put my jacket around her shoulders to conceal any bloodstains, and whispered soothing words whenever she winced from the pain. "We're almost there," I told her, "we'll be home soon."

I got her as far as the derelict control room before I could go no further. Despite my healing, I was still out of shape, and puffing from both that exertion and my earlier violence when I set her down. The decades-unused, padded couch in the room was covered in dust, but I didn't have the patience to clean it before I laid her out on it. I locked the door and braced a chair against it. Somehow I got the feeling that leaving Pretty here as I went back for help would be a bad idea, but I didn't see how I could get around it. If only I still had—

I smiled and started to call her name before I hesitated. It was still a good plan, but I didn't like the kink of Menerytheira's jealousy toward Pretty. I remembered the old tales of genies who granted wishes too literally when they were displeased with their master. And really, I was no longer her master. She had no obligation to me. I'd just have to hope I still had enough influence to get the job done.

I spoke her true name and felt a tickle at a corner of my mind. It was her way of responding positively to my summons. In an instant she had flowed from under the door's cracks, starting with a smile like a Cheshire Cat and filling out from there. She started to speak before she noticed Pretty lying on the couch, and those fluid eyes narrowed.

"What is *she* doing here?"

"She needs help. I don't think I can leave her here alone."

"Why not?"

"She's hurt!"

"She got here okay."

I rolled my eyes and tried to keep my patience. It never fails to amaze how a being of seemingly infinite insight can be so childish, sometimes.

"I had to carry her here. It exhausted me. Now, I can carry her the rest of the way and cause myself a great deal of undue pain, or you can help me out and go and get some help to carry her."

"Why should I?"

I drew her gaze and held it for a moment. "Because I'm asking you to help me."

It was like something in her was melting, but she still looked angry. Then again, it might have been tears, but she flew through the wall and was gone. I only hoped it was for help.

After a half-hour, I was worried that she hadn't delivered the message. My Influence was still planted in Pretty, as she kept staring at me, quiet, peaceful. She looked like a deer near a trusted human, a creature normally ready to bolt at the slightest movement, but still and calm for certain exceptional individuals. I felt guilty that this particular suggestion was something that could have far-reaching effects. That's the risk of a Suggestion: for short-term goals, they wear off after the compulsion is accomplished. For long-term ones...the effects might be permanent. Oh, I could reverse them with a counter-Suggestion, but I was exhausted from the night (Was it only two in the morning?), and didn't have the focus necessary to whip up another mindbender.

I was about to get up from the rickety plastic chair and start off to the warren myself when I heard a rustling in the ducts. I pulled one of the pistols, the Fichetti, and aimed it toward the duct as I assensed for any bug spirits.

It was a welcome surprise when Needles climbed out and headed to Pretty with a medkit. I lowered the pistol and made way for the other two ghouls who had come with Needles. He turned his gaze to me, smiling.

"Good job, Red. Looks like you did all right with her wounds, too. A little food, medicine, and time, and this won't even scar."

He seemed to look closer at me, and his smile faded a bit. I wanted to ask what was wrong, but he motioned for his men to take Pretty back to the warren. He regarded me for a moment as I put the pistol back in my jeans. "Dined out tonight?"

My brow furrowed, and I wondered how he had known. "You're blushing, Red. You can't do that on bug blood."

I closed my eyes and slumped into the desk chair with a sigh. He walked over, looking down at me.

"Wanna tell me what happened?"

"With Pretty or with my fight?"

"Both."

So I laid out my whole evening. The meet, the mugging, my temporary loss of sanity, and finding Pretty in the closet with the dead Mr. Edgar.

"Edgar's dead, huh? Probably someone wanted what we were fencing. I imagine he was cleaned out?"

"His pockets were torn open. There wasn't anything left to find. I'll bet Pretty might have gotten a look at their license plate before they got out of there, but unless she has a photographic memory, I'm not holding my breath."

"Close, actually. She's got cameras in her cybereyes. It's where Slim gets the graphics for people she meets for those files of his. If she saw it, we can retrieve it."

"Well, that's something, isn't it?" I rose from the chair, pulling out the pistols and other gear I'd taken. "Here. You can use these more than I can."

Needles eyed the bags of novacoke with disdain, but pocketed them all the same. In the warrens, you used everything of value, and threw nothing away. He rose up from his haunches and eyed me.

"So, how'd it feel?"

I paused, unable to look at him. All my high ideals and righteous speak about sparing people, and look what I'd done. I was nothing but a hypocrite. Worse, I was nothing but a host.

"...Ask me after I try to sleep, today."

Turn after turn down the repurposed CTA tunnels, I found a stretch that was unoccupied. Alone, finally, I slumped against the wall and hugged my legs to my chest. Still feeling short of breath, I breathed slowly in and out. I didn't want to meditate. I didn't want to have to work for peace of mind. I didn't want to have to shut my eyes for it, but the dark didn't mean anything to me any more. I only wanted peace, with the same ease as anyone. Unfocused, my eyes stared at nothing, the pulse of blood and the echo of a soul not mine striking lightning in my eyes.

This feels good.

I squeezed them shut.

This feels natural.

Bit my lip.

This feels right.

The taste of my own stolen blood on my tongue only made me want more. Even now.

Even with a whole life in me, I still wanted more. And deeper, the implacable, unquenchable lust. Feeding was good and right and proper and what I had to do, and it felt more than right. It felt like vindication, or reason. It felt like the whole purpose of existing. And yet, the possibility of propagating, of infecting someone, drinking them in until nothing was left but the tatters of their soul for the virus to overtake, assimilate, rebuild, and reanimate into a perfect predator, it stirred me. Visions of a pack at my command, of companionship, sharing the kill and reveling in the hunt.

The ghouls were kindred spirits, but they didn't know how far a vampire's thirst reached. They absorbed some trace elements of metahuman spirit when they consumed their flesh, but they could find what they needed in morgues and chopshops. Surgery happens every day. People die every day. There would never, ever be a shortage.

Sharpening knives in charnel houses. Lesser beings. They don't know this pleasure. They don't know this pleasure.

They knew hunger, but they didn't know thirst. They didn't know what it felt like to take something irreplaceable, satisfy the debt inside that is the only real barrier to immortality, like filling an hourglass with more sand. Every turn of the moon, every shift of the blood, you could feel the difference, the move away from eternity. And somehow, infection made whatever an afterlife must be feel like a very cold, very dark proposition. There is so much more to lose when death is not an inevitability. Living forever, constantly dying...

There is only life. And there is only the taking of it.

And for all the power the virus offered, all the promise of eternity, it was...fear.

I unclenched my jaw. Felt the wound heal almost instantly as my fangs retracted, leaving only the memory of a sharp, coppery taste as any proof.

For a mage of my tradition, fear is the last sensation before oblivion. And the last thing I would ever be is a slave. Not to fear, not to hunger, and not to the parasite in what little was left of me.

CHAPTER 8

WINE, MUSIC, AND WONDERFUL ROSES

The next few days passed quietly. I kept my face out of things as much as I could, meditating and taking long walks by the waterfront. The nigh-ancient ruins of Navy Pier were aglow with stolen electricity, the old pumps of the Union purifying water for the people of the Corridor under the watchful eyes of well-armed guards. I stalked about its edge, using an old pair of binoculars to spy on the gang that had taken it over. I wondered if it was a temporary arrangement: as soon as Lone Star felt they were too much of a hassle, would they send some boats over to clean house? *Hell*, I thought, *if they fixed it, it'd make a great staging point for them.* By tomorrow, another attempt at a public contract might take root there, or it might be shelled by a rival gang, or the bugs might start a hive there. The map of uncontrolled Chicago territory changed on a daily, sometimes hourly, basis.

I learned I could still astrally project, but it was harder than before. Maybe it was from so much time spent locked in my flesh beneath the river, or just the corrupted influence of the astral in Chicago's city core. Without any resources beyond the Matrix (and research into circumstances as unlikely as mine was next to impossible, even when the spotty connections were strong enough for a search), I could only wonder if I was permanently damaged in the astral. All that time beneath the water had eroded my body and my magic, and there was no telling if I would be able to get it back to where it had been more than a decade ago. I toyed with those spells I still remembered clearly, stretching my abilities in the hostile energy of the city. There were times I could almost feel the fingers of ghosts clawing desperately at the weave of spells, maddened forever and crying out for help or in blind pain. The Shattergraves were my crucible once again, and time had only made them all the more dangerous. I cast my telekinetic nets and manabolts and felt my tenuous link to the other planes grow, feeling something familiar and yet different, learning to walk the path of magic all over again.

If there was one advantage, it came from my tradition. A pre-Awakening fusion of Black and Chaos paradigms, it drew on the piecemeal adaptation of the latter while thriving on the ecstatic order of the former. For me, magic was as much about symbolism as it was about forcing my will upon reality. The shuddering pleasure of ego was a heady rush, and a distraction every Black mage had to overcome, but it served well if tamed into an incentive to keep practicing, keep growing. Growing back into the man I had been, and discovering who I would yet become.

I reveled in sense of rightness and power suffusing me, opening my eyes to the string of broken masonry and concrete I held suspended all around me, slowly spinning them in a vortex of debris before launching them into the air. Only when I had released them into their course to fly beyond my sight did my vision blur. I swooned, steadied myself, and grinned. Not the vast exercises of power I'd once enjoyed, but I was getting it back, and was better at maintaining more spells at once than before.

I meandered back to the warren without any plan more complicated than grabbing a bottle of bug blood and sleeping the day away when I heard Needles talking in an agitated tone with Pretty, who sounded, if anything, like a petulant teen. I guess rest and protein salves really *had* worked well.

"He saved your life, Pretty."

"I didn't *ask* him to."

"Just what do you have against him?"

"I don't like the way he looks. I don't like the way he talks. I don't like his attitude, or his style, or his mouth."

"His mouth?"

A momentary pause. I leaned against the wall and inched my ear closer to the doorway. "Uh, yeah... the way he talks."

"Uh-huh." Needles sounded anything but convinced.

"Why do you want me to do this, Needles? Why do I have to owe him?"

"Because you do!" he exploded. "Didn't I try to instill some kind of honor in you? He risked life and limb bringing you back when no one else could. I'm still waiting to hear what bad quality of his is worth erasing that supposed good deed!"

The silence was laden with her sullen brooding. I couldn't tell if it was another act or her honestly being a teenage girl, ghoul or not.

I decided to walk away quietly. What did Needles want her to do for me? I immediately turned away the idea that he was asking her to do anything carnal. I mean, that just wasn't his style. Strangely enough, though, I couldn't think of anything else. It had been a *very* long time, after all.

I did my level best to avoid thinking of Pretty like that as I settled down on my cot with an old vodka bottle filled with greenish-gray ant blood.

I woke up early the next evening to find a folded slip of paper on my chest. I could just make out a trace of Pretty's perfume on it. Perplexed, I opened the note.

> *Rick,*
> *I haven't had the chance to properly thank you since Monday night. Maybe you'd like to come out with me for a drink? Meet me in the old control room around ten.*
> *Pretty*

Huh. So *that* was what Needles had asked her to do. I smiled to myself. He'd always thought of me as a playboy, a reputation I felt was undeserved. This was probably his way of getting me to go on a date. By his reckoning, what else could I want more?

Checking the time on my commlink, I found the signal scrambled beyond recognition. I ran for Slim's quarters.

I stepped in to find him, as usual, engrossed in whatever it was he was doing. What was so unusual was the sound of scribbling. He was hunched over his workplace, the area before him cleared, as though he had swept the clutter aside. The scratch of pen on paper was frenzied, stopping as I heard the nervous *tick* of his pen tapping on the desk, as though he was deep in thought. I think he was more nervous than usual. I waited until he leaned back from his work before diplomatically coughing.

He jumped again, worse than ever. I smiled and walked up as

he scrambled to hide whatever it was behind his back. I stopped, giving him his space, still friendly.

"You okay, Slim?"

He was breathing hard. "Yeah, yeah, I'm wiz...you?"

I held out my Meta-Link. "My commlink's busted. Think you can take a look at it?"

"Sure, sure, no problem." He reached out with an adrenaline-shaking hand and took it in filed fingers. I just got a glimpse of what looked like a handwritten letter, but I didn't ask him about it. He'd talk about it if he was comfortable doing so.

He swiveled around in his chair and popped the case off, poking about in its innards. Looking around, I waited a moment or two before cutting in, "Hey, I really just need to know what time it is. I'm going out tonight."

Slim's eyes flicked downward for a moment, seeing something I couldn't, probably a clock in his vision. "It's seven p.m." Then he paused in his work and looked up slowly, a thought occurring to him. "You're going into town tonight?"

"Yeah."

He turned to me with a light in his eyes that even cyber replacements couldn't conceal. "Could you do me a huge, huge favor?"

I grinned. He was so sincere. "Yeah, chummer, what do you need?"

He smiled nervously, almost a giggle, and turned back to his mystery letter. Folding it meticulously and placing it in a remarkably clean plastic envelope with address code chip, he handed it to me. "Could you mail that for me? The postage is there and everything, could you just drop it in a mail chute?"

"Who's it for?" I marveled that our resident hacker would want to send anything in hardcopy. Must be sentimental... or confidential. He blushed a furious blue, so I threw up my hands and backed off. "Okay, null sheen, chummer. I'll send it out tonight."

He sighed in shaking relief and grabbed another commlink off a shelf. He held it out. "This one ought to work fine." As I grabbed it he made a few AR motions from the busted one to the newer one. I knew he was transferring my fake ID. I thanked him and left with my strange cargo.

Only seven? I thought. *Plenty of time to get ready...*

I was climbing out of the ducts into the control room, taking care not to get my nice suit dirty, when I saw her.

Stunning would be a mild word. She was clad in a clingy, black cocktail dress with sparkling bits all over that set off the lights in her eyes, now almost black themselves, and streaked with gray. Her hair was done up with lacquered chopsticks, strands hanging down with precise frequency to look fresh yet elegant. I would never have placed her for a ghoul.

She strode to me, heels clicking on the concrete as she reached out to take my hand and lead me to the door. Something had changed in her. She was wearing a mask, but it was different than usual, somehow...

Our walk through the nasty little neighborhood was amazingly uninterrupted before grabbing a black cab to Naperville-Bollingbrook, and we made good time to a club on its edge.

The fruits of corporate pairings smoked Ares Black Labels in the neon and ogled the exotic clientele lining up to get in. A quick bribe to the bouncer got us through the door and sitting at a table on the upper level's VIP section, overlooking the writhing dancers below. The dim lighting and star-spangled blackness was a perfect match for her dress, and I was reminded of Club Penumbra back in Seattle.

"How did you pick this place out?" I asked.

"You don't like it?"

"Just curious."

She looked around at the ceiling, the dance floor, the denizens sipping their glowing drinks or moving in time to a remixed Shield Wall tune. "I feel like I can relax in here. Everyone who comes to a club like this wants to stand out. They put on their costumes and pretend they own the world for a night."

"And you've already got your mask with you."

She glanced at me briefly before returning to her observation of the dancers. "Look at them," she said. "See those retro-goths with the fang implants? Or the girl over there with the elf surgery, or the ork bouncer with the filed down tusks? You can see the bartender's scars from trimming down his SURGEd bone spurs. Everyone here's trying to be something they aren't. Everyone's trying to be someone else."

I followed her gaze, and sure enough, each was on the money. In fact, the more I looked around, the more I saw it. This was a SURGE bar, from the looks of it. Probably one of the last ones left in the city, now that SURGE wasn't such a vogue thing anymore.

Probably more of a poser club now. The more I looked about, the more the place seemed to be a poser itself. This was definitely ripped off Penumbra.

But Pretty seemed at ease, here. I contemplated her as she watched the dancers, wondering what made her feel more at home: the fact that so many people here had secrets, or that, being social outcasts of one stripe or another, they were more likely to know her pain, and accept her.

I got up and offered her my hand. "Care to dance?"

She looked at it, then me, uncertain.

"You do dance, yes?"

She smirked uncomfortably, started to offer her hand, then hesitated halfway. I wasn't sure which of us was more uncomfortable. I smiled and tried to laugh it off. "No, you're right, those shoes are too nice to dance in."

I walked down the steps toward the bar, mentally slapping myself in the head over and over for making things awkward. I was frustrated. How was I supposed to act around her? I hated it when people weren't straight with me outside of work, but I wasn't sure if she was capable of being straight with anyone, least of all herself.

I made my way past the vampire wannabes, somehow uncomfortable getting close to them, and ordered a couple of drinks, something that would look respectable. It didn't matter, neither of us could drink the stuff. It was more for propriety's sake. A flash of cash to the filed barkeep, and I was on my way back to the table. I felt even more useless when I found Pretty sitting with a bottle of what looked like wine on the table. The *Vino Sanguis* label caught my eye and I felt the old hunger stir in me again. I smiled and shook my head, taking a seat.

"The waiter's bringing us glasses."

"You might have told me," I said, putting a synth-whiskey sour before her.

"Then it wouldn't have been a surprise." I couldn't tell if she was honestly annoyed or just being coy.

Glasses delivered, she poured the too-thick liquid into each, quite full, and raised one to me.

"Here's to rescues. Thanks, Rick."

She had used my real name. I started to feel suspicious, wondering about this sudden turn of attitude. More than that, I could tell this was an act. I'd seen the honest her, and this was not it. She changed subtly when she put on a front, like a master magician slipping off one mask only to don another before their true face is revealed. But it was easy to spot, now that I had seen the real her. I guess my Suggestion had worn off, after all.

I sipped the glass and was surprised at the slight, dry bite to its contents. I hadn't felt that in almost seventy years: The tang of alcohol.

"You do know I can't have real alcohol?"

She smiled knowingly. "I did my research after you met with Ms. Jones. Seems *Sanguis* offers a tested vintage with alcohol. I guess they get it out of people who are sauced to the gills. Once it's in the bloodstream, it's palatable for our kind. Best part is that you just might get drunk off it."

Why the need to get drunk?

I sipped my glass slowly. This was uncharted territory for me, and I was in no mood for a hangover, or whatever the HMHVV-equivalent was. She drained hers quickly and giggled.

"So, you've had this before?"

She fixed me with a half-smile and a playful eye. "No, Rick, I saved my first drink for you."

Yeah, this was flirting.

I hesitated to pour another for myself, remembering the last time I'd lost control. She, however, seemed intent on making her first time getting drunk as memorable an experience as possible. Another glassful and she was already looking tipsy. Unsurprising, given her age and weight.

"Pretty?"

"Yes, Rick?"

"Why'd you ask me out here tonight?"

Another mask tried to slip on, but it didn't seem to make it more than halfway. "To thank you."

"Ah." I toyed with my glass, rotating it slowly as I spoke. I'd donned a mask of my own. "If you'll pardon me for saying so, that's not like you."

Her eyes narrowed, and she set her empty glass down, pouring another as she eyed me. "And what *is* like me, Red?"

"Did Needles put you up to this?"

"Why would he?"

"I'll bet you've been asking that question yourself."

"You've got some nerve."

"Don't remember Needles telling you to do something nice for me? Don't remember him twisting your arm to get you to make some kind of gesture?"

"Which you can't seem to accept gracefully. I can't believe this. I take you out for a drink, and you're throwing it in my face!"

"Oh, I never asked for a thank you, Pretty, and I wouldn't. Nor would I turn down a real one. But I can't stand when something that should be genuine, something honest, is so fake. And *that* is much more like you."

"So, just how do you think I usually act?"

I stopped fidgeting and drew my eyes to hers. "Belligerent. Arrogant. Superior. Condescending. Impersonal. Isolated."

I have no doubt she had the ability to fake crying. But this was not fake. Her lower lip quivered minutely as her eyes welled up with tears. She grabbed the half-full bottle and made for the stairs, stumbling down them as she upended it in her mouth. I got up and went after her.

Pushing through the crowd to go back out the door, the bouncer shaking his head at people leaving so soon, I caught up with her as she stumbled her way into Briarwood Flats, a wealthy neighborhood. I didn't know what I'd said to her, but I didn't think she knew I was behind her, so I hung back, hands in my pockets, watching as she kept drinking and walking along. We kept that game up for two blocks before she took the last gulp of the bottle and tripped, falling into a bed of red roses. They snapped under her slight weight, and she twisted just in time to land on her bottom with an "Oof."

I'd started running to catch her, but as I approached, I could still hear her sniffling. Her makeup was ruined, but she still looked angelic in the diffused moonlight. I came up slowly, crestfallen to see her so sad. I didn't want this. I hated her masks. I hated her defenses. But I think that made me cherish the girl underneath all the more.

"Needles didn't tell me to do this."

I squatted on my haunches next to her, staring at her as she picked rose petals off of her dress. Her eyelids were drooping with each passing moment as the alcohol slowly worked its way into her.

"He told me I ought to do something nice for you. 'Cause you saved me. An' I don't like how you make me feel...'cause..."

She hesitated, like it would be painful to utter the next words. There was no change of masks, this time. Maybe no masks at all.

"And he never told me, 'Take him to your favorite club,' or, 'Buy him a bottle of wine with your savings'. He just told me I ought to thank you."

I felt like the scum of the earth.

She hiccupped between sniffles, and I pulled out my hand-kerchief and wiped at her tears. Her makeup came off with it, and I drew that away, as well, revealing her simple, pale skin, still elegant by any standard. She looked up at me, her eyes having reverted to their opaline white now that she wasn't thinking about it. I might have kissed her, then...but it just wasn't right. Not like this...if at all.

I picked her up gently, like I had when I had carried her back to the warren, and placed the empty bottle in her bag as a souvenir. Her free hand toyed with a rose still in her lap.

"These are wonderful roses, Rick."

I carried her all the way back, stopping to drop Slim's letter at a mailbox, where the wealthy could still afford such archaic luxuries. As I walked I noticed Pretty was falling asleep.

"Pretty," I whispered.

"Mmmmm?"

"What's your real name?"

She smiled, gently and slowly, and snuggled into me slightly. "It's Marie."

I smiled and carried her home.

It was just past one when I tucked Pretty into her modest bed. I strolled back out, avoiding the envious glances of Barnes and his ghouls at my suit, my hair, and everything else that let me walk among the mundanes. It wasn't enough, though.

"Had a fun time with your joytoy, fanger?"

I stopped and slowly turned. Barnes may have had the clipped speech that indicated a good education, but his gutterslang was as rough to the ears as anyone's.

"That's not a nice thing to say about either of us. How is that supposed to make me feel?"

"Where were you?"

"Just went out for a bite to eat."

Barnes nodded, smiling knowingly, hatefully. He looked to the other ghouls fawning around him, some only barely able to comprehend his words, but hanging on them all the same.

"Look at the flush on his cheeks, boys. Fresh infusion look. I remember it. You get it when you have good, human blood pumped into you. Common temporary side effect of recent feeding in hosts of *Ghilani Vyrkolakiviridae* as the virus assimilates the new blood."

He turned his loathsome glare on me again, his lip curling up in a teeth-baring sneer. The others emulated him.

"Got nothing better to do than harass me, Barnes?"

"We've all got better things to do," Barnes snarled. "We'd be doing them if it weren't for our leader...and the slags he keeps close."

My hands were in my pockets, and I narrowed my eyes. "You can say what you want about me, behind my back or to my face. I'm giving you that. But you leave the others out of this. You got a problem with Needles? Try taking it up with him. If you can't appreciate the services and the risks Pretty or Slim or Pale or any of the others takes, then you're a shortsighted fool, and that's your problem. As for me...I just don't give a drek about you."

I turned around and started walking. I was ready for him to take a swipe at me, but he just snarled and stalked off, his entourage trailing behind him.

I was on Lawrence, debating spending the evening in an all-night Polish gypsy coffee house playing chess, when I got a call. The vidiwindow opened to show the kindly old face of Halian Focht.

"Good evening, Mr. Crimson. Is this a good time to be calling?"

I smiled. "Absolutely, Professor."

"Splendid. Perhaps you are about town?"

"I'm just outside a place with words I can't read on Lawrence. A Polish coffee house."

"Really? Have a seat, I'll join you there in fifteen minutes."

I ordered, watching the mounted trideo as the evening news played.

"...*In other news, the Chicago Metaphysical Institute was robbed late last night by unknown individuals. Professor Dougall made a statement earlier today indicating the Bhianchi Orb, an artifact on loan for study from the Dunklezahn Institute for Magical Research, had been removed from its containment vessel. Signs of illegal entry were apparent, and the CMI is offering a reward for any information regarding its whereabouts.*"

A picture of a stone orb carved with runes I didn't recognize appeared. *"While the Orb is known in certain circles to be a passive magical artifact, its abilities and function remain unknown. Lone Star has declined to make a statement regarding their investigation into the theft, saying only that they are optimistic it will be recovered soon."*

The timing was perfect. Sure enough, in the time it took for my untouched synthspresso to go lukewarm, Focht took a seat across from me, smiling.

"I'm glad you were in the neighborhood," he said. "Conversations are always better in person."

"Considering you have a pair of datajacks, I'd have pegged you for a net junkie."

He absently fingered his pair of dull chrome jacks and chuckled, running a figure eight between them.

"No, those days are behind me. After a time, you come to appreciate the old-fashioned comforts of reality."

I nodded, signaling the waiter to bring a cup for him. He smiled and shot it down, aerating to fully appreciate the flavor.

"You drink a lot of coffee in your profession, Professor?"

"I thought everyone did."

"I meant more specifically. Maybe trid-pirates need to stay awake more than standard news hounds?"

His expression soured slightly. "'Trid-pirate' is such an ugly phrase. I much prefer 'free journalist,' or someone who works for 'underground news.'"

"Doesn't strike me as being much more glamorous."

"Take a look at history, Mr. Crimson. You'll find that news piracy and free press, while sometimes going hand in hand, are two very different entities. The common legacy of the information pirate is the modern hacker, but the trid-pirate takes it a step further. You might consider them to be personal propagandists. The crazy man on the radio, the Humanis supremacist, and the ironic, hypocritical Luddite are hijacking common airwaves to spread their messages. These have been around as long as those means of conveyance have been common. Now, a truly free press...that's a far more noble endeavor. Remember World War Two and the underground newspapers in occupied Europe? Or Wanderly and Davitt here in Chicago?"

"I'm not so sure we live in such oppressive times."

"Do not mistake brand for scale. Perhaps the nature of the oppression is different, but it is no less prevalent or potent."

"I can't decide whether you teach history, journalism, or English, Professor."

He was stunned for an instant as I changed tack with a smile, but he laughed. "History, Mr. Crimson. An extended grasp of language is simply the byproduct of extensive education and reading. Journalism, such as it is, is a personal interest."

"I see. But how can I be sure, then, that your journalism is handled in an unbiased manner? What separates you from extremists?"

"I've been asked that question many times, my friend. And the more I've answered it, the more I'm come to realize that there is no way to gain trust but prove worthy of it. I am not a man of lies. It is simply not in my nature. But who could just take that at my word? No, I'm afraid you'd have to know me for some time, and see the proof that my news is genuine. All I have to offer is what I learn, and the oath that it is, to the best of my knowledge, unbiased and honest. It is really up to you whether you believe me or not, after that."

I shrugged. "Okay, fair enough. Please let me know when your next broadcast is. I'll tune in."

He nodded happily, signaling for another espresso.

"But you didn't just call me up for the conversation, did you, Professor?"

His eyes turned back to me, appraising me again. "No, Mr. Crimson, though I genuinely enjoy our conversations. Polite, but straightforward enough not to waste time. No, I asked you here for *your* story."

"Regarding?"

"Yourself. Given your condition, you more than most are a man of mystery. No doubt you've been around for a great many events, seen many great things. As a man of truth, perhaps you'd appreciate my interest in hearing firsthand accounts of history."

I slumped. This was the last thing I wanted to talk about. "Look, ah...you seem to think I'm...older than I am."

"How old are you? You seem physically no older than twenty, but as an elf, you might be older or younger."

"Well, I'm...sort of ninety-two."

"Really? What month were you born?"

"October. October twentieth, 1983."

He laughed. "Oh dear... I thought you might be a hundred

years older than that, or perhaps new to being what you are. I never suspected we were the same age!"

"You're ninety-two?"

"Oh, better than that, my boy, I was born on the same day!"

He found it hilarious as I sat, dumbfounded. It probably should have been reversed. "My, my, now I really *do* feel old, seeing you. But then, elves still age slower than dwarfs. All the same, it is amusing that I've been debating whether you were ancient, or still younger than me. Of all the possibilities I'd considered, *this* was never one of them."

I shrugged, still in awe. "No one bets on the edge in a coin toss."

He continued chuckling as I explained my limited experience of those years, trapped without air under the waves of the Chicago River. He sobered as the story continued. I felt somewhat sorry that I didn't have more of a tale to tell, given the time I'd had to come up with one.

"Oh, my boy, don't you see? Yours is a tale that's worth telling! How many others have had the circumstances you've experienced? I did a little info mining after our last conversation. You used to run the Seattle shadows, didn't you?"

I nodded, trying not to think about those times, happy though they were, initially.

"You saw the inside of the Arcology doing rescue runs. You did a few stints bug hunting before that. Tell me, were you a part of the group that revealed the White Heart Coalition?"

Again, I nodded. An amateur version of the Universal Brotherhood; the insect shaman in charge of it hadn't conjured a Queen yet. It wasn't too challenging to stop him. If only Dunkelzahn's will had been around that year, we might have collected a far larger paycheck for our time.

"You had quite a career. And then you vanished in 2063. Tell me, is Kevin Tripp your real name?"

I looked away uncomfortably. He really did know how to do his research. "Maybe you should be teaching journalism, Professor."

He leaned back, smiling gently. "I'm sorry. I am prying. I'm afraid it is in my nature, both boon and curse at once. If you care to tell this story, I'll appreciate it, but it would remain between us. It is purely *unprofessional* curiosity that motivates me."

I nodded. "All the same, you can call me Rick."

"And you can call me Halian."

I smiled. "I'd like to help you, Halian, and maybe someday I will, but in the meantime...I'm still trying to reclaim my life. It's a story without a clear end right now."

"Rick, when the end *is* clear, it's usually too late to tell."

I walked the Corridor's broken roads without lifting my eyes, more interested in my thoughts than the mapsoft directions. The crunch and spread of ruined pavement and endless debris faded until vanishing entirely, missing in the corporate enclaves. The fallen city core was recognizable by its darkness compared to the neon and spotlights of the subsprawl corporate zones.

The astral shifted even as the winds coalesced into physical forms. My fingers curled and the glow of a manabolt was already forming in my palm when I spun to face the new presence behind me, and the spell faded, half-finished on lips fallen silent.

Gizelle hadn't changed one bit since I'd last seen her. She was clad in a long real leather jacket and a Vashon Island sweater and jeans, her same pensive smile hiding a deep confidence, as capable of seeming cool and confident as I ever was and then some. Yet now, it was broken. The wind spirits faded back to the astral as she walked to me and threw her arms around my neck. Only a moment's hesitation from shock before I did likewise.

"Where have you been?" she whispered.

I laughed softly.

She had a car nearby, some newer model of Eurocar that somehow still hadn't gone out of style, with leather interior and a fully automated pilot program. We pulled back into the subsprawl and into a five-star Elysium Hotel. She led me to a private room in the rooftop cocktail lounge with a commanding view of the ruins of the city and the rare starlight of the clear night. I smiled at the memory of the last time I'd seen her, the view we shared then half a continent away.

When she had sat down, she leaned forward, resting her elbows on her knees as I did. "I thought you were dead."

I shrugged. "I was."

Her eyes narrowed. "Nice of you to let me know."

I laughed. "I was dead. How could I tell you anything?"

"Were the mobs really that bad?"

I sighed and began telling the story all over again. In the time it took, the waiter brought her all the tools and ingredients for her to start shaking her own martinis. She was three in by the time I finished bringing her up to speed. She grinned as she finished it, toying with the olives in the glass.

"Well, it was nice of you to call, even if you were playing it so mysterious. Seriously, 'a crimson name?'"

I shrugged again. "I was feeling mysterious."

"And you were still worried I was being watched."

I nodded. "It was stupid, I know. If there was any reason to think I was gone already, it was my businesses vanishing in the Crash."

"That's why I thought you were dead."

I sighed. "I didn't have very much say in it."

She stood up and began pacing the room. "I thought you were going to lay low, Rick."

"Going to Chicago is pretty much laying low. There's no radar to stay off of in the Zone."

"Blowing up insect spirits isn't very low-key."

"It's not. But when a friend calls for help, you respond. Doing anything else is a bad way to keep friends."

"But a bad way to stay alive."

"I'm still here, aren't I?"

"You are oddly selfless for a vampire."

"You're oddly calm around a vampire."

"I enjoy the novelty." She finished her glass and sat back down, her eyes fixed on the shaker, debating another. I seemed to be having that effect on a lot of people tonight.

"What about you, Gizelle? How has a decade—"

"More than a decade.".

"—more than a decade treated you?"

She shrugged, half-smiling as her gaze drifted out the window. "To be honest? I'm a little bored. The money is great, I've got more than I could ever spend. Stock options in multiples corps, savings, some stuff tucked away. I even get to take the occasional quiet potshot at Aztechnology for old time's sake."

"Sounds exciting enough."

She sighed. "Is it? Was it enough for you? I seem to recall you being awfully bored with the day-to-day life of retirement after the shadows. You seemed more...alive after taking down that blood mage. You hadn't looked that way since pulling those folks out of the Arcology."

I folded my hands, looked out the window with her at the crumbled ruin of the city where I was born. "Maybe retirement is better when you can kick back on a beach and sip margaritas. I wouldn't know. Night after night, blood only different by type. And they feel good, sure, but they lack in variety."

She chuckled. "They say retirement kills. But this is the first time in history people have had the possibility of life beyond a normal human span. Elves, leonization, infection, even e-ghosts, in a way. Everyone dreams of more time, but there is no societal precedent for it."

I nodded at the ruined city. "There's no precedent in history for anything happening now." I looked at her. "Maybe I should have just branched out. Learned Matrix programming or something, something challenging. A whole fresh start."

She poured her fourth and toasted me. "It looks to me like you've already got that."

I nodded, grinned. "You've got me there."

"How much of your memory was affected by the suspended animation?"

"Not much in the traditional sense. Mostly my muscle memory is scrambled, so I need time to relearn the physical things, and I was asleep for so long my magical skills, I don't know... decayed? I know exactly what I could do before, and how I did it, but the connection between knowledge and action is fogged." I reached out a hand to levitate a martini glass to my hand. "At least I still have the basics."

"And all the time in the world to relearn."

"Heh. Sure."

"What about the money and everything?"

I took a deep breath, slowly let it out.

She continued, "I could help you out. It's not like I don't have it to spare."

"I might take you up on that if things get rough, but right now, maybe a fresh start is what I need. I mean, I'm right back where I learned the shadows in the first place."

"Rick, Chicago wasn't a bug-infested hellhole when you learned the shadows."

"Yeah, but I was also a kid from the 20th century. I have a lot of practical experience to draw on."

"Fair enough." She drained the glass, exhaled, and set it down, finished. I had no idea how she kept packing them away, being so slim. Her aura said she was just a hint tipsy, but a mage as talented as she was could make her aura say whatever she wanted.

"What will you do?"

She smirked. "I'll keep doing what I'm doing. But if I get a chance…maybe I'll take a sabbatical into the metaplanes."

My eyes went wide. "That's hardly a vacation spot."

"If anyone has the connections to make it one, it's me. But it's been a while since I stepped out of my shoes for a long trip, and frankly, I could use the challenge."

"Aren't you at all interested in starting a family?"

She rolled her eyes. "Really? This old argument?"

"What?"

"It's what every professional woman hears at least once in her life. Or one too many times, at least."

"I'm asking for selfish reasons."

She paused, grew quiet. "Because you can't have kids."

"You're about as close as I'll ever have to one. Or ever will, the way things look."

"Mom used to talk about you, you know."

"Did she?" Gizelle never talked about this. Maybe she really was drunk.

"Said you had your hunches and your occult hobbies. She thought you were crazy, that you'd gone off and joined some cult or gotten yourself killed looking for myths."

"She was close enough."

"I don't know if she ever forgave you for that…until I was born."

"What?"

She smirked, touching her long ears. "A UGE baby like me. Everyone else was looking for scientific explanations, but she knew. She knew you were right. By the time magic started happening, she wasn't surprised at all. She knew what my imaginary friends were. You'd prepared her for that. And I think she was happy to know you were right. She wasn't as scared when she caught VITAS. She'd already set me up with the best tutors, found a way to scam life insurance to pay for an education in magic with her own death. I think…she made sure I was taught how to use it, that she was so proud of it in a time when most people were afraid. I think that was because of you."

She looked up at me, eyes focusing on the present again. "I

think I owe all of this success to you, in a way. Or maybe just how she thought of you. And I grew up learning magic because I was carrying on your dream. And then it turned out you were alive. After a fashion."

I chuckled. "Well, I'm proud of you."

She smiled, blinked sleepily. "Hmmm. Okay. I really, really need to get to bed."

I walked her to her room, only one floor down. A massive penthouse suite, warm cream and real wood I carefully avoided touching. As she plopped down in a seating pit surrounding a massive fireplace, she reached up to snatch my Meta-Link from my belt. A few twists and turns of the dials, and she tossed it back. "The rest of my contact info. Just so you don't lose it this time. Think you'll come back to Seattle?"

"Maybe. Probably. Eventually."

"Hmm. Well, when you do, stop being a stranger. You can start all over if you want, but don't leave everything behind, yeah? Family is about all you and me have."

"For the lucky ones, family is enough."

CHAPTER 9

FRIENDS, FAVORS, REVELATIONS, AND REVOLUTIONS

I returned to the warren to hear the roars of debate echoing through the old tunnels. I ran, reaching the audience hall to find Needles and Barnes in the middle of the chamber, surrounded by most of the pack. The division between the forty or so ghouls was clear, each standing on the side they favored. Right now the numbers seemed pretty even.

"You'd have us squatting in sub-human filth for the rest of our lives!" Barnes shouted. "We'll rot down here, feeding on bugs and cowering in the shadow of Lone Star flunkies! And for what?" His side of the room roared its approval.

"You want to live like a man, again, Barnes?" Needles asked. "You remember what it was like. Some of the people here never had the opportunity you and I had. I want give them that chance."

"At what? To ape being human? All you offer are human morals, which don't make allowances for cannibalism! Survival is about adaptation, and you don't seem to have any conception of what you've become, let alone how to lead others in the same position!"

"Don't question my leadership, Barnes!" Needles said. "I encourage anyone to come to me with their problems, but this is complete bullshit. You haven't been here for more than a few years. You weren't even a ghoul before that! If you can't cut it accepting what you are, keep those problems to yourself, or take them elsewhere."

"*I* cannot accept my nature? I happily prepare the meat for our packmates. I have embraced my nature more than you could know. I would embrace it more, if you did not keep us chained with ethics we've evolved beyond!"

"We can not walk among men again if we see them as no more than food!"

"Strange you would say that when you and your favorites always keep the best for themselves."

"What are you talking about?"

Barnes reached back and a ghoul handed him a wine bottle. I recognized it all too well. "Seems your little whore spent some time enjoying the finer things. Tell me, when do I get to put a little color back in my cheeks?" His crowd rumbled. "When do we get *our* turn? When do we get *our* share?!"

Barnes raised his arms, fingers splayed and claws sharp, and his side roared again, some snarling and gnashing their teeth. Looking between the groups, now, I could see that the mothers, most of the sentient ones, and the children were on Needles' side. Barnes had convinced most of the savage ghouls, or the ones who embraced their homicidal instincts, that they were being cheated.

Barnes tossed the bottle at Needles, who looked at it with confusion. Pretty had been telling the truth: he knew nothing about this. Barnes looked around to gauge the attitude of the room and spotted me. His smile turned cruel.

"Tell me, Needles, how much did we spend on that wine? Or pulling your vampire friend out of the drink? What was in it for the rest of us? Maybe you can explain why you and your favorites have dined on the sweetest flesh while the rest of us waste away on this mutant shit?"

Needles set the bottle down. His eyes were hard. "I didn't know about this, Barnes. I haven't tasted a human in three years."

Barnes threw up his hands in exasperation, as though talking to a particularly slow child. "You can do whatever you want, Needles, but you've got no right to tell us how to live our lives!"

Needles shook his head. "We don't have much choice, Barnes. You want to bring those damn Stars down on our heads, picking off innocents?"

"No one is innocent, least of all a pack of cannibals. It's what we are, Needles, much as you want to avoid that inconvenient truth. We have moved up the food chain. A human might call me a monster. I say I am evolved! Some of us don't have our heads buried up our asses, still clinging to delusions of humanity."

Needles's eyes narrowed. He flexed his clawed hands and spread his feet into a stable stance. A fighter's stance.

"If you're nothing more than a monster, Barnes, then you must be put down like one..."

Barnes slid a scalpel out of one sleeve and grasped the cleaver at his waist. Both sides hissed and snarled, advancing closer to the middle of the room. The children retreated to the far side, terror obvious in their pale eyes. For them, the astral was awash in color and intention, hate and fear they could see and smell and feel.

"Stop!"

Everyone looked at me, and the hissing stopped like the sizzle of a bomb fuse. Arms raised, palms open, I moved to the middle of the room. I knew I was at a disadvantage in my clothes, a suited man amidst rag-clad families, but I had no time to change.

"This is insane! You're going to fight over who gets to be leader? There's only forty or so ghouls here! That's including the children!" I turned to Barnes. "You want to make these children into killers, is that it?"

He grimaced. "It's what they are. It's what we *all* are, even you."

I turned to Needles. "And you want to have this fight here, amidst the civilians of the pack?"

Needles glanced back to see the half-dozen children huddled together. His scowl relaxed, but he was still ready to fight. "I'm not being presented with a lot of choices, Red."

I looked at both sides again. The ghouls were all angry, but it didn't seem like they were particularly enthusiastic about fighting members of their own community. Maybe this could all get talked down, but it was looking less and less likely. Besides, the seeds of discontent had been sown. There would always be a rift, now. Maybe it was just time to break ties. I turned to Barnes.

"You want to be top dog, Barnes? You think you've got the chops for it?"

He turned up his chin. "Look behind me, fang-boy. I've already got enough ghouls here to make a pack."

"Well if it's so goddamned awful here, then you should just leave. The Noose is still full of places to hide out and stay clean. You want to be a pack, then go be a damn pack, but don't you dare try to force anyone to come along."

Barnes scowled. "Why should I leave them here to languish under this tyrant?"

"Because it's their choice to stay, just as it's your choice to leave. And anyone else's. It was a human decision you made to become a leader. So let them be human enough to choose to follow you."

Barnes glared at me for a moment. "What if I feel like taking over here?"

I stared back at him. "Then I'll kill you."

He laughed, but I kept staring.

"Just you, Barnes. The rest can rip me apart, but you'll still be dead. Better that than you in charge, here."

We traded glares for a few moments, and I could almost see him calculating. He knew I could take him down, survive the onslaught of all his ghouls just long enough to deliver a killing blow. And the potent combination of a predator's mindset with a self-considered genius's ambition gave him a powerful survival instinct.

He looked back and forth to his side of ghouls, gesturing for them to back down. Throwing one last contemptuous stare at me and Needles, he spat on the floor, then strode out of the room with most of his ghouls in tow.

"How many went with him in the end?"

"Fifteen." Needles rubbed his hands over his face, exhaustion, and worse, resignation showing with frightening ease on his lined face. Sometimes I forgot just how old he really was.

"Well, that's not so bad, right?"

He fixed me with a tired, incredulous look. "Those were fifteen of my fighters and workers, Red. Fifteen. That's almost half. I've been left with a handful of sentient ghouls, most of them only partially so, capable of providing security. The rest are children and non-combatants. I've been left with the vulnerable ones. We also just lost our resident doctor and food specialist. And to top it all off, they have a grudge against us, and will probably go out and draw far more attention to the few surviving ghouls out here than we need."

He slumped in his chair. I couldn't bear to see him like this, bereft of hope. I'd made the wrong move. The more I thought about it, the more I realized it was a far larger problem being without them than with them.

"It could have been much worse," I told him. "What if it *had* come to fighting? You'd have lost a bunch of the loyal ones, and the surviving separatists would have gone on making trouble. You were going to lose Barnes one way or another. We can be thankful that it didn't get any worse than that."

"Worse?! We're sitting ducks now! Some bugs come crawling in here, and they'll have us all for dinner! Lone Star could waltz in any time it wants! All we have is an undermanned warren defended by children!"

I kept my gaze steady. "You want to leave, I'm sure we can find a way."

He fell back into his chair. "There is no other way. No other place. The world is full of ghouls, Red, make no mistake. You want me to take these people to Asamando? Maybe we can petition for membership to live in the jungle, like fucking Caribbean cannibal tribes. Maybe I could bring these little savages into the Tamanous family, huh? They could bring up their children in the company of chop-shop docs and murderers, like your friend Jones."

"Jones is no friend of mine."

He pulled out the bottle angrily. "Then where the frag did *this* come from?!"

I looked at it steadily, weighing my options. I hated to have Needles think less of me, but this was Pretty's home. She'd have to deal with the long-term repercussions of this, maybe at the hands of angry or jealous packmates. I was still the outsider.

"I'm sorry, Needles."

"Sorry?!"

"Look, it's not as though Barnes wouldn't have thrown his little revolution without it!"

"It made for one hell of a trump card, though!"

"What do you want me to say?"

"Nothing! There's nothing you *can* say to me right now. All your talk of self-control, releasing those Stars when...I *hungered* for them, Rick. I wanted to taste them. I've wanted it for so long, now. Sometimes I think I'd rather starve for a month and get a single taste of human flesh. But I held it together, knowing I had to set an example. It helped that I knew someone else who knew what it was like to hold off and find a moral way of feeding. And then I find you like to indulge in *this* shit!"

I almost told him outright that it was Pretty who did it, or that it was his urging that had led her to buy it. His friendship and respect meant everything to me. But he looked ready to cry, and that was something I just wasn't ready for. And I wasn't going to sell her out.

"I guess I'm just not the man you thought I was."

"I guess not."

The silence weighed on us, the moment stretching out, but there was nothing left to say. I left.

I sat on my perch above the ruins once again, taking deep, cleansing breaths. The late fall air betrayed the snow that was bound to fall in the next few days, but I didn't care how cold I was. My hair whipped about in the wind as I let my gaze slip into the astral.

The eddies and swirls of mana were weak here. I hadn't been taking the time to note my surroundings. Even though I could fight off Strain-III infection with chemical showers, my own regeneration and staying in the necessarily-clean warrens, I still spent most of my magical time in the cleanest areas, meditating and focusing inward to build up my mystical potential. I had thought I was far weaker than before, but as I studied the stunted magical energies of Chicago, I wondered what I might be capable of outside the city.

My gaze followed the slight glow of a line of power leading downtown. Historically, Chicago had been a hotspot for mystic energy, with several ley lines intersecting here. I always thought that was why the bugs favored it so much. It was almost certainly why the Strain-III was still alive. I could see the strange discoloration of bacterial infection all over the line, like blotches in a polluted stream. They choked it, feeding on it and growing stronger.

Experimental counter-agents Ares had dumped on the areas had given the lines a chance to grow back, but not enough to matter. The clouds of bacteria were visible in the astral, errant puffs of death for me and mine. It was fortunate they tended to group together in avoidable chunks.

That was partly how Needles and his pack had survived here for so long. With their dual-natured sight they could see the outbreaks, avoid the thickest clouds. Needles's know-how in medical technologies and procedure ensured they could treat early stages of affliction and prevent new ones. He'd chosen the site for the warren because it had fewer ventilation points, and he'd installed filters to keep them safe. It was one of the more menial, but no less important jobs to keep the warren as sterile as possible, stained but scrubbed.

Now I sat high enough to be almost safe. I studied the ley line again, trying to taste its echoes of power. They still stank of the bugs. Maybe they always would, after the taint such a huge hive would have left. Maybe they always had.

I felt her first, materializing beside me. Menerytheria was always brave to come out here like this. The clouds would eat her up faster than any of us, and there would be no way of stopping the spread by any conventional means, only passing through solid matter and letting the bacteria's physical form stick to the wall. But passing through a cloud completely? Suicide.

I glanced sidelong at her. She was perched beside me, trying to look like she wasn't watching me. Her movements seemed akin to Pretty's when the young ghoul had her sassy act going on. I didn't like what that portended.

"Enjoying the view?" I asked.

She didn't respond, only checked her liquid nails and hummed to herself.

"Something I can do for you?"

She seemed to sigh a little at that, but kept playing coy.

It was times like these that I wondered what spirits normally felt. Were they capable of being smitten while they were bound to someone? Was that, perhaps, the one emotion they could keep to themselves? How long had she been harboring feelings toward me? While she was my ally, or had they arisen as she combed the depths of the Chicago River searching for my body?

It didn't matter right now. I was in no mood for the additional complications of an unwanted romance. I was grateful to be rid of our connection in that moment, because I knew that thought would have brought her to tears all over again.

"Why did you leave Needles the way you did?"

Her words startled me out of my reverie. I turned to face her. She was maintaining her aloof posture, but her words still sounded the same as usual. I guess she'd only been *watching* Pretty, not *listening*. Thank goodness.

"He and I are having our disagreements. Every friendship does."

"Wasn't it Pretty's bottle of blood?"

"Just how do you get to know so much?"

"I'm never very far from you, Rick."

I sighed, rubbing my temples. My life was anything but ordinary. An ex-ally spirit for a stalker, living beyond the walls of a ruined city with killer bacterial clouds, bug spirits, and bandits, in the company of a gang of ghouls with their own sets of problems. Oh, and fresh out of hibernation vampire spike baby from the last century. At least I couldn't say I was bored.

"Look, Mene, I don't want to—"

"What did you just call me?"

What?"

"You called me 'Mene.'"

"Yeah, for short."

"What's wrong with the name you gave me?"

"Nothing. It's just long, to keep you safe so no one stumbles across it. I just called you 'Mene' in shorthand."

"My name is too long now?!" She seemed on the verge of panic.

"No! People give friends nicknames, special little mini-names because we spend so much time around them."

"Even special friends?"

"I... suppose so."

She squealed with delight and threw her arms around me, knocking me on my back. I was glad I was out of my suit. I started to push her off, but at that point, I was just too damn tired to bother. As she snuggled into me, I sighed and let her, running my hands through her liquid hair and turning my head to the side to watch the deadly clouds below.

I woke up the next evening in a quiet corner of the warren. I'd chosen the spot to stay out of the way, both to lower my profile and keep out of Needles's path. My Meta-Link was blinking, and I put on my AR glasses to find a message in my inbox. Slim's profile pic came up, and I opened it.

Red,

I didn't want to wake you up, but can you make another meet today? I've included the whole briefing for you if you think you can be ready and at the meeting point by nine p.m.

It was seven right now. I checked the attached address and knew I could make it with time to spare, if I hurried. I clicked the link to continue.

This is your contact.

The three-dimensional form appeared to the left like last time: a tallish man with scraggly dark gray hair and stubble, an earring, and a cigarette. He was dressed in the same worn but wearable style as my own synth-leather and jeans, so at least I could fit in easily. He was skinny, datajack at his temple, cybereyes, but realistic ones. And I could just make out the dedicated chipslot right behind the datajack. Either he liked his skillwires, or he was a chiphead. Those could change the game a little bit, one way or another.

Alan Ranes, age 36, occupation according to NooseNet is fence and Johnson, but word on the blogs is that he designs his own jobs. Comes up with the plan, finds the time tables for guards, passcodes, the works, and sells the whole package for a percentage of the take. He cut out the middleman by becoming his own fence. Since we've lost Edgar, we could really use a guy like this. He already has your picture, so he'll find you there.

A small video window opened. Slim looked like a shy neo-goth with his nervous smile and black-and-white-striped shirt, but I could tell he'd be a cute kid if he saved up enough for the surgery to look human like Pretty.

Now for my own favor...remember that package I had you drop off? Is there any way you might be able to pick up another tonight? I just found out it's been delivered to a P.O. box, but I can't pick it up. Since Pretty's staying in, could you get it for me?

A pair of checkboxes appeared, one labeled *yes*, the other *no*. When I looked at the *no*, funeral dirges played and a line of mopey 8-bit ghosts began pacing back and forth around the letters. When I looked at *yes*, fireworks flashed and little skeletons did a happy dance. I smiled and picked *yes*. The message continued.

Wow, thanks, chummer, you're a lifesaver! Here's the P.O. box address. Thanks again!

I jogged most of the way. Regeneration gives me a quick recovery time, and I was working on building back some of the muscle lost in my long sleep. I was heaving for breath by the time I made it three city blocks, but it felt good. Pain like this was something I controlled, something that meant progress. It was understandable and held no unpleasant surprises. I really needed that, these days.

It wasn't that far away, a small bar without a name on a cheap street in a bad neighborhood, which described most of the area surrounding the Zone. There were a million more like it all over the Corridor, holes in the wall barely lit by the glow of neon booze advertisements wired into solar battery packs and bundled glowsticks hanging over worn and patched booths. The cracked tile floor was littered with cigarette butts and bits of broken plaster and concrete kicked in from outside or fallen from the decaying ceiling. Old blues music played from tinny, blown-out speakers plugged into a commlink with no case nailed to the bartop. The smoke was thick enough to pick up the dim light and almost muted *the clack* of pool being played.

The clientele were rough around the edges, but I could almost taste the sense of community (among other things). There was something about the place that I just wasn't picking up on...

A hand slapped me on the back and I looked up to see Ranes, drink on his breath and a tall glass of synthahol beer in his hand. Ash from his cigarette fell onto my jacket, but it seemed like a waste of effort to brush it off in a place like this.

"'ello, boyo!"

Ah, that was it. Now that I listened, everyone in the bar, from the burly biker to the sixty-something way-too-skinny bleached-blonde ork bartender, had a thick British accent. Being a red-headed elf in this kind of place might get me more trouble than I wanted, but I opted to roll with it. Hell, maybe a bar fight was what I needed.

I smiled without showing my teeth and nodded in greeting, pulling out my best Hertfordshire brogue. "You Ranes?"

He nodded, his smile growing even broader. He pointed to a table near the back, waving at the bartender to get me a drink. She responded with a choice curse and complied.

We slid into the booth, thankfully far away from everyone

else, and had a good view of everything from the back door to the front. A wise choice of seating.

"So, you from the ol' country, then?"

"Not originally. My parents were Tir, but they got out before I was born. Grew up in the U.K."

He toasted me with a toothy grin. "Here's to it, then." I just smiled as he drained his glass, then shouted for another from the bartender. Her response was the same as last time. "Now that we've got all the pleasantries out of the way, what is it I can do for you today?"

The bartender brought our drinks over. Ranes slapped her on the ass, eliciting a glare as she walked away. "Nice bit 'o trim there, eh?"

I shrugged. "Sorry, chummer, I've got a solo-thing for Japanese girls." Total lie, my preferences were much broader than that, but it was none of his concern.

"Don't blame you, what with those uniforms and all. So, you were saying?"

"Rumor has it yer in the business."

"Everyone's in some business." He was playing it close to the vest. Couldn't blame him, given his game. This was the dance every runner did with every other professional the first time they met.

"Yeah, but I understand you got a way of providing others with jobs when they just don't know how to get work, themselves."

His eyes were alight, and he smiled coyly. "Well, I've been known to do an odd bit of matchmaking. Sometimes you've just got to find the right job for the right person, y'know?"

I nodded. "Well, for someone in my line of work, sometimes it can be tough to find the right kind of work. I'm a go-man, myself. I don't chart things out, I need a map. And I hear you're the man to find when a bloke needs a map."

"You run heavy?"

"Hell, term, I got a whole slew of friends. Just show me where 'x' marks the spot and you'll get your share of the booty."

"What kind of friends you got?"

"Bloodthirsty ones, usually."

His face sobered. "You mean that as a turn of phrase, eh? I don't want no truck with ghouls and banshees and whatnot."

Suddenly I was glad I hadn't let him see my fangs. I played to his prejudices. "Yer kiddin', right? Ain't any profit to hold when yer partner wants his share paid out 'a yer hide."

He laughed and nodded.

"So what are you in the market for? Just what kind of work do you do? Electronics? Firearms? Drugs?"

I shrugged. "I'll have to talk it over with my mates before I go making that call."

He smiled, slid me a small datacard with his info, and raised his glass. "Well, when you do, make that call to me."

"Will do." His glass held there, and I knew I'd have to down mine to seal the deal. Oh shit, but I hated moments like this. I kept my smile straight and raised my own, then downed it all in one long pull. Still smiling, I got up from the booth and made my way outside.

The moment the door closed, I ran around into the alleyway, feeling the brew sloshing around in my stomach like molten lead. My body wouldn't let it go any further, and soon it would retake that territory violently. I managed to totter behind some trash cans before it came back up, and I retched for long moments afterward. Like I said, vampires can't handle food or alcohol. Especially alcohol.

I stumbled through the back alleys, daring anyone to try mugging me, but was once again disappointed. It never fails. You want a rumble and a drink, and it's a silent night. You need to stay quiet, and all hell breaks loose.

I finally found the post office Slim needed me to stop at, still buzzing with Black Crescent package runners and guarded by young toughs. I washed up in the public restroom and paid the five nuyen to get my package. As it would turn out, it was another letter, this one in a slender white envelope. The return address was a girl's name, and as I looked at it closely, I could smell something on it...perfume.

Hmmm...

I headed back to the warren just before sunrise, my hood pulled up against the predawn light, quite done with the evening and longing to go right to bed. My stomach still burned, and even bug steak would have been a welcome replacement for what had been lost.

Slim was sitting at his workstation again, jacked in and smiling faintly. I was about to tap him on the shoulder when he opened his eyes. The cyber picture of a fanged smiley face was gone, replaced by dark brown eyes. They were remarkably humanizing. Hell, with a wig and some cologne, he just might pass himself off as a regular kid with bad skin, as long as he hid his teeth.

I held out the envelope with a smile even as his face formed the question. He happily snatched it and held it closely. I took the moment to depart. Some things are best enjoyed alone.

CHAPTER 10

ADVICE

Needles still wasn't in any mood to talk to me, but I forced the point, since I was the one doing the meets until Pretty was back on her feet. We sat in his office, tense as a cat and dog sharing a pen.

"Ranes is everything we've heard. Boxed-run man. Sells the plans and legwork for a gig. I'm guessing he'll work for a percentage of the take. Even if he doesn't normally, I can talk him into it."

"I'm sure you can."

I pressed on, ignoring his sarcasm. "We have to let him know what we're looking for, and he'll provide the job. The only question is: what do we need?"

"We need security," he said quietly. He was still getting used to being understaffed and so vulnerable. "We've got weapons enough, what we need is surveillance, security systems, cameras and motion sensors and the like. Maybe even some droned guns."

"Maybe he has a line on a warehouse that holds that kind of stuff."

He rolled his eyes. "How about we let our little expert make that call?" He'd never talked to me like this before. Then again, he'd never been this pissed at me, either.

"Fine. I'll take care of it. Anything else we need while I'm out? Ammunition? Kitty litter? Soy milk?"

He glared at me as I turned to leave.

It was only a few hours since meeting with Ranes. I doubted he'd be done with his partying, so I got back to Slim's room. Everything seemed as before, except...I could smell that perfume from the envelope in the air. I sniffed lightly and could tell it came from Slim's hands, maybe even his lips. As he turned to me, I noted a corner of the envelope peeking out from his pocket, close to his heart.

"Oh! Uh, hey, Red."

I smiled and took a seat. "You think you can call up Ranes and get another meeting tonight?"

"Uh, yeah, yeah...null sheen. Just, uh, just give me a moment..." He switched on his AR and moved his fingers to invisible keypads, dialing up a number and placing a text message. Then he pointed at me, and I felt my commlink vibrate with an incoming e-mail.

"I cc'd you a copy of the email I just sent, plus his response. I said it was you writing it, so you'd better know what it says."

"Thanks." I got up to leave. "Hey, uh, Red?"

"Yeah?"

"Can I, uh...um...can I ask you a, uh, question?"

"Sure." I took my seat again.

He moved behind me and closed the door, then started pacing about the room nervously as he worked up the nerve to continue. "You, uh, you're the kind of guy who gets a lot of girls, right?"

I smiled. "Not so much, Slim. Back before my last long nap, I only had one girlfriend in five years. And that ended pretty badly."

"Well, that's still more than I've had... technically."

"Technically?"

"Well... there's this... girl..."

"In the warren?"

"No, no...we met on a blog..."

Oh, drek.

"... she's really great! We started talking about games and music and all kinds of things, you know? She's really wiz! She's kinda like my best friend, you know? I tell her everything and she does the same back, you know? She's like..." He held his hands before him, as though trying to weigh invisible qualities to find the perfect descriptor, "... I don't know... she makes me feel like..."

"Magic?"

He snapped his fingers and looked at me, smiling ear to ear. "Yeah! Yeah, she's like magic! Fills me up! It's wonderful. And I think I make her feel the same way, you know?"

"Yeah."

"Yeah! And it's great..." His face fell. "...but..."

"But she doesn't know you're a ghoul?"

Well, I couldn't tell her that."

Where does she live?"

"Here in Chicago. I've got her address and picture and everything." He dug into his pocket to pull out the letter, revealing a small, hardcopy trid-photo of a blonde girl, a little sickly, but smiling and holding forth a bunch of lilies. She was clad in a white dress, green foliage behind her. It didn't look like digital editing, either. Under the lilies she was holding out, she'd handwritten "For you!" It was all pretty cute, and I found it romantic. She had to be about Slim's age, but wealthy and living in a corporate enclave by all appearances.

He slid the photo back into the letter with obvious care, as though it was something precious and fragile. My heart went out to him.

"How long have you two been talking online?"

"Two years, three months, eighteen days, twelve hours and fourteen minutes exactly."

"Well, that is a long time..."

"Do you—think she'd accept that I'm a ghoul?"

I sighed. "It's also a long time *not* to tell someone something as important as that. I'm guessing you use that little avatar I saw when you talk to her?

He slumped. "Yeah."

"Have you told her you are *not* a ghoul?

He hung his head. "Um...it never came up..."

"That's a no, then. Okay..." I ran my hands through my hair and exhaled slowly. "Okay, we can work this out. I mean, you're a guy, she's a girl, there's obvious chemistry... Stranger things than a human and a ghoul being in love and working it out have happened before."

He laughed and put up his hand for a high five.

"Wait, wait," I said, holding him off. "This won't necessarily end up happily ever after. I mean, we have to consider the possibility that being an Infected will scare her off."

His hand dangled in the air for a moment before dropping slowly. "I thought you said—"

"I know what I said, Slim. I said it's *possible*. But you've got to be ready to accept the idea that she'll turn away from you when she finds out."

"I've been saving up my money for a cyber-doc. I've almost got enough to pay for some cosmetic surgery. I can get my skin fixed, get some hair, file down my teeth, like Pretty does."

"Are you saying you wouldn't tell her?"

His eyes had a pleading, desperate look.

"Slim, she'd find out one way or another. Next time you're in public and have to dodge a Strain-III cloud concentration, or it's a sunny day, or you get spotted by a dog or mage, or you have to feed. She'll find out. And those are just the pleasant ways she might figure it out. What happens if you two become intimate? Just kissing her might infect her. Are you okay with her being a ghoul?"

He seemed unsure, but wouldn't meet my gaze. "I get along okay with it," he muttered.

"I'm sure you do. But you've got to make sure it's *her decision.* Judging by that pic, I'd say she's a rich kid. Probably has a weak immune system, from the looks of her. If so, she's even more likely to get infected. Maybe she's led a sheltered life, or grew up afraid of germs and getting sick. That'll make it harder for her to accept you. And if she *does* accept it, she'll probably have to give up everything she's ever known. Her family, school, friends, everything, and live here. That's a pretty permanent state of affairs."

Slim fell into his chair, the life drained from him, as though he might start crying. I felt bad, even though I knew telling him all this was the right thing to do. "Look, Slim, I don't want to tell you it's impossible, or that it's a sure thing. Everything in life is in-between. Just don't pin all your hopes on her, or give up altogether."

"So, what do I do?"

"Well, you need to tell her. But take it slow. If you want to win her over, start thinking about what you would have to offer her. I mean, what do you want to do someday? What's your dream?"

"Like in the warren?"

"Well, sure... is that where you want to stay for the rest of your life?"

"I... I guess I never gave any thought to it. I mean, where else could I go?"

"Oh, boy. This is the kind of thing that's handled outside the Zone. Look, there comes this point where you get old enough and want to make your own way in the world. Things are still pretty dicey for a ghoul out in the open, right now, but someday that'll change. You've got some valuable job skills. I mean, you are a wizard with commlinks and whatnot, you've kept this place going for a while, and you clearly have a talent for organization and research. I know all kinds of people who need those kinds of skills."

"Really?"

"Absolutely. Now, about this surgery. Do you want it just for her, or is it something you've been wanting for a while, now?"

"Well...I mean..." He shuffled his feet on the concrete. "Why should that even matter?"

"Because this kind of decision has long-term repercussions. You'll have to live with it forever. So is it something you want for yourself, or for her? Because in my experience, you have to make yourself happy before you can do that for anyone else."

"I think... I want to be able to go out there, in the flesh, and do things with people. I mean, the Matrix is wiz and all, and I'm not ashamed of how I look, but... I'm just so sick of hiding."

"That surgery's just another kind of hiding. Have you talked to Pretty about what it's like?"

"No, no, no one really talks to her."

"No one?"

"They think she's not one of us."

I thought about that. It explained a lot. Her isolation, even among the pack, and the attempts she made to blend back in, shifting her eyes looking like theirs when we returned to the warren. The quiet need for acceptance and love, and the hard shell she used to keep others from getting too close.

"What do you think?"

He answered without hesitation. "I think of her like a sister."

"Then why don't you talk to her?"

"Well, I'm not going to force her to talk to me. That goes both ways—she's not very enthusiastic about talking to anyone around here, either."

"Huh."

"But, what about Angela?"

"That's your girl's name?"

He blushed blue, nodding and looking down.

"Well, like I said, maybe you can make it work. But you've got to be honest. Every relationship is based on a foundation of trust. If you can't trust each other, then you can't love each other."

"What was your girlfriend like?"

I felt a stab in my gut that echoed emptily. Memories flashed through me without fanfare, a dozen happy and sad moments.

Meeting her at Dante's Inferno. Finding out we were going on the same run. The thrills that followed, on the run and off. Losing her in Louisiana. Finding out she'd been taken by Deus, remade into his slave. The final moment of her life when I granted her the only peace I could...

I shook my head. "Look, Slim, my relationship was...troubled, and certainly fell outside the realm of conventional dating."

He grimaced. "And what would you call mine?"

"Touché. Even so, they aren't comparable. Just...all you can do now is break it to her slowly, gently, and make sure she knows the score. If you really care about her, she deserves that."

He slumped. "Yeah, I guess you're right."

I nodded and got up, put a hand on his shoulder. "You'll get through this one way or another." He looked a little reassured as I got up to leave. "Oh! I almost forgot..."

He turned to look up.

"Did you ever get an ID on those bastards who stole our stuff and killed Edgar?"

He shook his head sadly. "No, no, she was in a hell of a shock the whole time, her eyes almost never stopped moving. And then she was shot. I tried clearing up the playback, but even if I pirated the software, I don't have the hardware necessary to translate it and get the job done. I'd have someone else do it on their system, but—"

"You never know who'll find out we're after them." I finished.

"Exactly. Especially in this town."

"Well, we'll be shopping for parts for electronics and stuff, soon. Probably enough to give you some real toys to play with. Let's see what we've got to work with then, okay?"

He nodded and got back to work.

I closed the door and hadn't gone one step before I was choke-slammed into the wall beside it. I struggled to ignore the instinct to turn to mist and locked eyes with Needles's infuriated glare.

"What the frag—"

"Where do you get off, Red?! What the fuck are you trying to do around here?!"

"What are you talking about?"

"First you take things out of my hands with Barnes, and I lose almost all the ghouls fit to guard around here. *Now* you're trying to convince my only tech specialist to *leave*?!"

"No, I—"

He let go, and I sagged against the wall, rubbing my neck. His dual nature subverted my regeneration. He really could hurt me. He started pacing in the deserted hallway.

"What the frag can you say, Red? I heard you talking. What does he want to do someday? You think he can make it on the outside? You think any of us can?"

"Plenty do."

"Oh, don't give me that drek! You and I both know that's the exception, not the rule, and pretty rare at that."

"Maybe that's for lack of trying."

He rounded on me, stepping right up in my face. "You think we can all just blend right in and become upstanding members of society, just with a little surgery and acting? Rick, most of these people were *born* ghouls. And you can't get the surgery until you stop growing, *if* you can find a doc willing to operate on a ghoul in the first place! But you grow up a ghoul. You want to just try erasing that and plopping them into a new life overnight? It can't happen. It can't work!"

"There are people down here who could have a more normal life."

"You think things are bad here? You remember Cabrini. It was a nightmare, no matter how good the intentions. No matter what Tamir's sacrifice bought us. And what about the ones who get twisted, who can't operate out there, can't ever be normal, no matter how much plastic surgery they get? They just get left behind?"

"Some ghouls try to make it work. You know about the Seattle Necroplex. No one got left behind there." The Seattle Necroplex was a sort of massive mausoleum where, unbeknownst to Seattle's greater population, ghouls consumed the remains of those interred. The owner, Adam Shepard, was a cosmetically-altered ghoul who made sure the other ghouls got taken care of and stayed in their own space. Many of them had been put to work in city sanitation, safely away from people to work and live in peace. Almost no one knew their trash was collected by ghouls.

Needles rolled his eyes. "It's not that simple, Rick, especially here!"

"Then leave, Needles! If it's so goddamn rough out here, head for greener pastures! There's territory aplenty for you and yours out there! Maybe you are attached to Chicago, but you've gotta think about the *now* and the *future*! Join another pack, head over to Long Pig Farm, make a connection with the Ghoul Liberation League. Do something bigger than locking yourselves down here to rot!"

He turned away, scowling. "You just don't get it."

"No," I said with a sudden flash of insight. "No, I think I do. This isn't just about what's best for the warren or the pack. This is about what *you've* built here."

"What?"

"You've invested years into this place. Hell, more than twenty years. Most of the ghouls here aren't even that old. This isn't just about the ghouls, or Chicago, or memories or anything. This is about Sara's dreams. This is about making it work."

"That's bulldrek."

"You've spent so much time here that you feel like it's going to be a waste if you leave it behind. And you can't even see the writing on the wall. The corps are coming. All too soon they're gonna come back and reclaim the city, rebuild it from the foundations up. You think you'll be entitled to squatter's rights? It'd be cheaper just to tell some Zone gang you're here and wait for somebody to collect the bounty."

"Shut up."

"This is your ghoulish little Camelot, and you'll trap everyone inside and take them down with you before you let it crumble—"

"I said shut *up*!"

He swung around and decked me on the jaw, hard enough to send me reeling. I stumbled and caught myself, holding my mouth as I got back up and looked him in the eye.

"Needles, this is just a place. The real legacy you're leaving behind is in your pack, not your warren. Sara wouldn't have wanted them buried down here."

He heaved for breath, rage and hate and bitter impotence written across his face. I turned and walked away.

The thin lining of my faux-leather jacket didn't do anything against the cold, but I jammed my hands in the pockets just the same. Once more, the metahuman predators of the Zone knew better than to approach me, and I let the raw cold of the air keep me stalking toward the markets in the northern Corridor. Gravel and broken glass gave way to mere cracked and overgrown pavement, the footing steadier past the crumbled ruin of a great ferrocrete containment wall.

There was little enough to say to Needles's anger. It was understandable why he would resist change when every previous one in his life had been for the worse. Sara's death, his infection, the collapse of Executive Order 162 and return of bounties on Infected, the Bug Breakout and the Bomb, the walls, and even their fall all kept him off-kilter, constantly adapting to survive new situations and never profiting by it. His tactical training as a DocWagon HTR had set him up to be reactive instead of proactive, and it limited his guidance of the warren.

The bazaar avenue hung with strings of bioluminescent pods, charged with gathered light during the day and casting just enough residual glow for low-light to work perfectly. The smells of woodsmoke and ozone drifted in the cold breeze, The stalls lining the path jutted out unevenly, overhung with rustling plastic tarps or colorful, faded second-hand blankets. Plasboard countertops held all kinds of knickknacks, salvage, and other objects of limited value. The expensive things, the meaningful things, would be locked up somewhere behind the counter where magpie hands couldn't snatch and run. Medical supplies, weapons, survival rations, purified water. But what I was looking for could be found in front of a dilapidated, repurposed garage with a bubbling hiss coming from within.

The proprietor of this small bit of industry, an ork wearing a cowboy hat and a faded tank top with a depiction of the Buddha under a threadbare and stained blue parka, woke from a light doze when I cleared my throat. He swung his boots off the stall table and nodded as I made my purchase. He bagged it up in brown polka-dot kitchen curtains, tied it with a zip cord, and happily accepted a payment of two grams of novacoke.

What was worse was the responsibility Needles laid upon his ghouls in return for what he took on in their name. They were his surrogate family, the second chance for what he saw as his failure. He had taken a group of people and used them to fill in the hole left behind where his love and humanity had been. He'd lost so much that losing any more would be inconceivable.

The only thing to do was to fight me, and whatever other powers tried to upset the world he had built. And right or wrong, he was my friend. And I owed him.

Hence the six-pack of home-brew tucked under my arm, packed in a homemade carton lovingly stamped with a crudely drawn ork woman wearing nothing but a cowboy hat and a tusky smile.

The trip didn't take very long, and I was thinking of how to phrase my apology as I walked into one of the utility entrances—

—and bumped right into Needles.

My hands glowed with a manabolt even as he bared his teeth and nails before we recognized one another. As quickly as it started, my chant and his hiss halted, and he took in the sixer under my arm while I noted the cooler he had been sitting on.

He smirked at me. I returned it.

At the lake's edge by Belmont Harbor, along a concrete outcropping that stands on the water, there's a spot where grass still grows green and the trees, if a little sparse, hang with rustling leaves in the Michigan wind.

Amid this is a single park bench which has inexplicably survived all that this city has gone through, and Needles and I sat there in that slice of displaced serenity, sprawled comfortably looking at the midnight waters. The moon was bright. Chicago was one of the only cities left in the UCAS that wasn't perpetually shrouded in smog, all her disasters ironically giving her enough of a break from industry to clear the skies, and if you listened for the distant subsprawl traffic and noticed the total lack of Matrix coverage, you could hear an echo of Chicago as I still remembered it.

Needles had cut a deal with a blood runner from the Black Crescent, and the cooler was filled with eight chrome cylinders of metahuman blood, still fresh and warm from their donors. The six pack of microbrew in its home-made plasboard carton sat at his ankle, and we were each three bottles in.

Popping the tops, we drank in silence. He was halfway through his drink when he spoke.

"If you could go anywhere, where would it be?"

"Hmm."

"Not for settlin' down, but to see."

"I've been a lot of places."

"Well, what's still on your list?"

I thought a bit more before answering. "I've never been to

Rhine-Ruhr. It's not what it was since '55, but I've always wondered what it would be like to see a functional anarchist society."

Needles smirked. "You've been in the Corridor. You know exactly what it looks like. People come together, make a community without selling out."

I shrugged. "Still. Must be a lot to be learned, even now. How it worked, why it didn't. How about you? Any place in mind?"

He was silent again, watching the black waves, the bottle rocking back and forth in his fingers as he rested his elbows on his thighs.

"I'd have seen Massachusetts."

"That's where Sara was from, right?"

"...yeah. Where she grew up."

He was quiet. I didn't press him. After a moment, he began again.

"She always talked about what we'd do when we were finished with the Cabrini Clinic. She wasn't the complaining type, she'd never say one word against it. She thought it would make her seem ungrateful for how good her life had been, and for the opportunity to give back. But she was a person like anyone else, and it doesn't matter how much good you're doing, sometimes you just have to let go. Think about what you'd like. And she would tell me about Lexington where she grew up, and Cambridge where she went to school. She'd go on and on about big family dinners and how her folks would make a big feast. Her dad would try to scare me by sitting the two of us in his study looking over a pond in their yard. I have this imaginary scenario in my mind of what it would look like. She told me so many times, I psyched myself up for it. Prepared for the bourbon and the hunting rifles over the window meant to scare me. Prepared to stand my ground and play it cool and confident without being arrogant or standoffish. I mean, I didn't go to some Ivy League school, but I'm a physician, I made good money helping people. And how was a hunting rifle gonna scare me when I carried an SMG and pulled bleeding patients off the pavement in the middle of a firefight? Still scared me, though. I was so ready for the quiet fight with the would-be father-in-law. I could map out my exits, she'd talked about that house so much. All wood paneling and whitewash. Classical Colonial style. Big house. And we'd go in the Fall for the leaves and the season, and that... was when I was going to ask her to marry me."

He took a long pull from the bottle, finishing it and throwing it out into the lake.

"It didn't matter if her folks approved, but I think I could have won them over. And I think they'd have done anything for her. And if I could leave this damn city, if I had the luxury of something approaching a more normal life and I could take a vacation, I'd make a pilgrimage out there. I'd see that house, at least, and see if it looks like it did in my dreams."

"What about her folks?"

He chuckled bitterly. "I was a man back then, Red. I was people. I had a future like anyone else's. I don't think her parents, if they're still alive, have any interest in the man who failed to protect their daughter. And I seriously doubt they want to be reminded of what she became when they look at me."

"How about your family?"

He sniffed. "What family?" He turned to look me in the eye. "Sara was my family. This warren is my family." He turned back to the water, his thoughts his own once again. I tilted back my bottle, finishing it before it could coagulate.

"Sorry."

He nodded. "Me, too."

My eyes drifted back out. The full honey moon on a calm, black lake. I'll see this night again as I die. Whenever that night comes.

"Glad you got back to me so soon, boyo. I might have given this little plum away to someone else."

Ranes waved a folded piece of e-paper between his fingers as we sat in a new bar, seemingly cloned from the first. That didn't say much: a lot of bars, cheap and pricey, were cut from the same cloth.

I kept my eyes on his, careful not to register too much interest for the plan he held or disgust for the beer before me. "Well, my crew's eager for work."

"And I'm eager to see my fifty percent share."

My brows bounced in surprise. This was the part where we negotiated. It was a smooth transition.

"Fifty? That's a pretty steep price. We've got a lot of mouths to feed, and it's not as though we can afford to move too much."

"You don't have to move too much to get a big profit when it come to electronics, boyo. Haven't you heard? Smaller is better these days."

I smiled. My supposed letter had let him know I was interested in electronics. I was glad he'd come through. "Just what kinds of electronics?"

"Commlinks, hardware, drones, some cyberdeck components, even."

"Pretty diverse."

"Shipment comes in fresh tonight. They put all their worry into transit. Security relaxes a bit after it first arrives, if you know how, when, and where to get in." He waggled the hard copy invitingly.

"Still, fifty...pretty steep."

He started to pull it back, his smile fading.

"Unless, of course, you can prove it's worth my while..."

He smirked at the challenge. "How much carrying capacity can you manage?"

"No more than one trip, a midsize moving van. Of four operatives that are along, two would have to ride back in the van."

He nodded, not asking why.

"I predict your take at well over seventy-five thousand UCAS after fencing."

"And you know a fence?"

He smiled. "I *am* the fence."

I smiled back. "Good. Then either you waive the usual fence's take or the percentage comes down. What say we call it fifty percent of the initial take, and you fence what we don't want to keep free of additional charge?"

He looked annoyed at the idea of giving up profit. I persisted. "It makes things a lot rounder in the end. You want half of what's in that van? We'll be the ones risking health and freedom to fill it up. Make it worth the while to do so."

"All right, all right." He threw his arms in the air and shook his head, tossing the paper my way. "All my life, never had anyone give me so much grief."

I highly doubted that. "How will you know how much we took?" I asked, keeping him on-topic.

"My sources can let me know just how much is missing from inventory as of that week. I'll know when a large score goes down, and take my cut accordingly."

I unfolded the electronic paper to see a fully detailed map of a distribution center for Black Lotus Software, one of Mitsuhama's moneymakers. That didn't bode well as far as security went: Mitsuhama was famous for their "zero-zone" security measures; zero penetration, zero survival. MCT guards are trigger-happy, and automated security is among the best. I considered it. Infiltration would be tough, but if we could subvert the building rigger who would no doubt be in control of security, we could take control of the facility for long enough to grab what we needed and make off before they could get any records or bring any backup.

Further down, there was a full workup of duty rosters and shifts, entry codes and primary login usernames and passwords. I looked up at the smug Ranes.

"Okay, I admit it..." I said grudgingly. "This is worth fifty percent."

"It's a simple grab job. We have the codes for the doors and the local systems. There might be a security mage unless we attack tomorrow night, when he has the night off. I can handle their wards. We know where and when the guards will be for the next week. There's only one or two at a time to start with. It's mostly drones on site. We'll also know where the cameras will be. All we have to do is get in fast and shut up their security rigger. We drop Slim in to take over the system and stop any messages for help and erase any record of us. Tap out the guards and we've got run of the place for at least as long as it'll take to load up a van. We load up some gear and drones and get out of there like it's a third Crash."

Needles, Slim, and Pretty sat in Needles's office, listening to me lay out the plan. It was hard to read any of their faces. Pretty was her usual masked self, Needles was completely focused on the plan, but still fatigued by his worries, and Slim seemed thrilled at the prospect of going out into the real world. The four of us were each bringing something to the game: Needles had combat experience and was still strong enough to muscle things into place, as well as being a decent driver. We'd need Slim to do our hacking and pick out the stuff worth taking, and while Pretty and I could both provide a face for the group. I also had my smattering of magic and more than a few runs under my belt.

Pretty looked over the maps. "What kinds of things does the place usually lock up?"

"The warehouse is a primary distribution hub for Mitsuhama. A kind of storage bottleneck before it gets divided and sent to other concerns, primarily Black Lotus. There'll be a lot of different things there, but the newest shipment will be easy to spot and still ready for movement right up front. And this shipment is exactly the kind of gear we need."

"How do we get into the security room?" Slim asked.

I pointed at the map. "I figure spoofing our way in is the best option. MCT riggers use closed circuits for their security rigging systems, standard for corporate layouts, so there's no way to hack in from the outside. Since it looks like they'll have gas traps, we can bet they'll have some filter systems in the air ducts, so I won't be able to mist through. What we *do* have, though, is the door code for the security room. If we can get in as, I don't know, something they'd trust, we could make our way to that room and disable the rigger. We dash Slim up there and he takes control of things. With so few guards, Slim can use the drones to take them out, and we'll be in control. Slim can use their own security setup to isolate and gas guards."

Pretty cut in. "How do we know who they'd trust?"

"Oh, oh!" Slim jumped up and down in his seat. "We know the address to the place. I bet they order food or takeout or something! We could find out which restaurant is the one who delivers the most and make a surprise delivery!"

I shook my head. "It's a nice idea, but they'll be ready for a 'random delivery' ploy. We'd have to know *exactly* what place they order from and when, and take their place."

"I could bug the area, intercept incoming calls and be ready for it when it happens. All we'd have to do is wait for it."

"You're talking about bugging lines they monitor, assuming one of them doesn't place the call privately. Then, we'd have to intercept their route of transit, meaning hacking into the city auto grid systems. *Then*, we'd have to hope they don't know the delivery people personally or something, and that we'd fit into their outfits, anyway."

Slim slumped in his chair. I tried to encourage him. "Hey, those are good ideas, kid, we just need to look for more options."

"What about masquerading as MCT personnel?" Needles asked. "We could intercept one of their shipments coming in or show up as inspectors or something."

"No good," I said. "They'll be monitoring their shipments closely via satellite, rigging, et cetera. They'll be ready for that. We'd need to show up as surprise personnel, which means getting our own uniforms." I looked to Pretty.

"No," she said. "I can't make them, I just don't have the materials or the time. And with Edgar dead, I don't know anyone who can get us some quickly enough."

"Okay," Needles said, "what about a simple assault?"

"Definitely not. They'll call for backup instantly, plus we'll have drones and autoguns on us before we have a hope of escape."

Pretty spoke up. "We *do* have some other uniforms. Lone Star and various civil servants. Maybe we say a criminal has fled into their grounds and we need to pursue?"

I thought it over. "Not a bad idea. We could stress that time is of the essence, and that if they don't comply, we'll be forced to lodge a complaint against them for impeding the apprehension of a suspect."

"Yeah, yeah, that would carry some weight here. Lone Star is the main police force, so MCT isn't gonna want the trouble they can bring down on them." Slim nodded.

"I like that one," Needles said, "but it might not get us any further than their front door. After all, they've got drones and cameras everywhere. They'll just flip through and tell us they don't see him."

"But they might let us in the security room if we insist on seeing through their cameras."

"Ah, you're forgetting, Red, things have changed since you've been away. They could just send us pics to our commlinks."

"Wait," Slim sat up. "Wait, you said they'd have to beam them to us?"

"Yeah."

"They'd have to establish a connection to the commlink. That's our way into their system! I could lock out the rigger from there once I was hacked in. And since we have the codes, I could do it real quick!"

I cut in. "Can't they cut off the connection physically?"

"If they have enough time, but I could be in full VR. Lightning quick! I'll program and copy a bunch of agents onto separate commlinks with me and have them all connected into the main line. I send them in to rush the system and lock him out! Then they don't have time to contact Lone Star to verify us, either!"

"Have we got the hardware for that? That's a lot of processing power and bandwidth."

"Oh, for this, I'll take our best along and run it hot enough to melt! I mean, we're going in to replace most of this stuff, so we might as well use it! If I overclock it, we'll probably break some of our gear, but I think we can get in. At the worst, I can have the agents act as viruses and clog up their rig enough to keep him busy. Scramble their IFF codes or shutdown or something. We can rush the room and get in, take out the guy in the chair. Then it's all ours!"

I looked to the others. Pretty looked impassive, but Needles shrugged. "What have we got to lose?"

I nodded. "It's a good plan, Slim. Let's make it happen."

CHAPTER 11

HEIST

Opting to go for the night when they'd be without their security mage, we got moving as soon as possible. Slim spent every moment programming his agents. It turned out he had all kinds of them, built in his spare time, so he altered their code for various purposes. Some were made to keep ICE busy, while other were designed to stealth their way past and subvert routines. The majority were designed to unlock the doors, disable cameras, and subvert the IFF on the drones and autoguns. Slim said he didn't know how good their rigger might be, so it was better to assume he'd be too good. On that assumption, he designed his system assault to keep him busy until we could physically get to him.

Needles sat in the armory, cleaning and loading every Ares or Lone Star weapon they'd salvaged over the years. He always had a few ghouls nearby, to show them how to handle and care for a gun. I realized this was not just as an investment into the future security of his warren, but also in case he didn't make it back.

Pretty spent her time alone with a needle and thread, subtly altering the uniforms until they fit as though they were made for us. Then she went through her collection of wigs and makeup, finding ways to make Needles and Slim look more human, and the two of us less conspicuous.

For my own part, I reviewed the plan again and again, meditating the rest of the time. I had to marshal my strength for this. I was sure I would survive, somehow, but it paid to be cautious.

I sat in a large drainage pipe far away from the group, poring over the electronic paper repeatedly to see if any new revelation would spring at me. I was so absorbed I didn't hear Mene appear.

"Why am I not coming along?" she demanded, hands on her hips.

I looked up. No need to ask what she was talking about or how she knew.

"Mitsuhama sites are filled with wards. I don't want to take the chance you'll get caught in one I can't free you from."

"The ghouls are all dual-natured. They'll get caught in those wards just like I could."

"But they have a physical component. Worse comes to worst, I can pull them out by force. What if you get caught in a flytrap that's too strong for me?"

"I can look out for myself."

"I don't doubt it, but that's not the issue. I don't want to lose you."

"I found you, Rick! *I* found *you*! I know what I'm doing! Why do you insist on treating me like a child?!"

I sighed. "Most children can't cast spells or flow through matter. But you *are* still that age, Mene. Besides which, I have another job for you. Something I think only you can do here."

"And what's that?"

Dressed and armed like Lone Star Fast Response Team troops, we left the warrens as soon as the sun set.

Needles and Slim didn't look half bad in their wigs, both unobtrusive brown cuts. Filed nails, polish, makeup, and dentures hid most of their ghoulish features, and both had cybereyes that could look human. The final effect was enough to fool someone who wasn't looking for it.

Pretty was wearing a platinum blonde wig and had dyed her eyebrows to match. She was stunning, but I hesitated to point it out. My own black wig pinched my head, and I'd had to shave my goatee and color my brows as well, but the effect was marvelous.

We quietly headed across the street to a garage the warren garage where the warren occasionally kept a car or two. The van I had heard so much about proved to be something of a disappointment. A rundown Gaz-Niki Legacy family van, with rust-corroded rims and windows thick with dust. I was suddenly wondering if we'd even make it out of the garage.

The door squealed alarmingly as we cracked it open. I peered inside. The bench in back had been removed, leaving only the passenger and driver seats. Needles threw on an old trench coat to hide his uniform as he drove the dilapidated van, and we piled in back, silently going over the plan. Slim readied his chain of commlinks, each carefully linked via fiber optic cable and carefully packed all over his person, in a backpack, and in pockets and pouches. In his hands he cradled a cyberdeck that looked more like a pile of optical chips and wire than the constant companion of any decker.

The ride over was mostly silent. I think Pretty and Slim were scared. This was like nothing either of them had ever been a part of, to my knowledge. Brutal as the Matrix might get for Slim, it's quite different from real combat, and I didn't think Pretty knew much more than how to point and shoot when it came to guns. I knew Needles could take care of himself. Keeping the other two alive might get tricky, however.

Needles called back to me. "How did you get your stalker spirit to stay behind? I didn't think she'd let you this far out of her sight."

"I told her I needed someone to stay behind and keep watch over things. She made me promise to summon her if I really needed her, though."

Needles chuckled.

The trip was rocky over the ramshackle roads of the Corridor to the O'Hare subsprawl. Finally, we stopped in an alleyway between a pair of empty office park buildings. Only two short blocks away was our prey, a squat but imposing warehouse filled with treasure. Unlike most corp-owned businesses, this one actually had its primary brand name on the side. The big, stylized "M" stood proudly over *Mitsuhama Distribution* in smaller script . As we slunk through the last alleyway, I slipped into the astral and got a look at the building.

Here, further from the scars of the past, it was much easier to see things clearly. The cold, dead surfaces of the streets and buildings betrayed no outer astral surveillance, no bound elementals or watcher spirits. Reaching out further, I could feel the hint of bound power within, probably wards. I'd be ready.

I nodded to the others, and we sprinted across the street toward the warehouse. "Where'd he go?!" I shouted to the others, beginning our guile.

"No sign, leader." Needles responded, swinging his rifle about.

"Base, Base, this is Tango, we have lost the suspect, we have lost the suspect, over." Pretty spoke clearly into a pretend mic.

The ruse sent us running all over the street. Pretty kept listening to her fake line as we spread out in a close-fire formation. She nodded, and looked up at me.

"Leader, Eye-in-the-Sky reports suspect movement north toward the MCT building."

I threw a look toward the building and slung my shotgun. Taking a deep breath like a corp goon about to deal with a rival corp goon, I signaled the others to round up and keep their guns down as we headed to the door beside the main garage. Pushing the buzzer, I made a show of being impatient and nervous in the cold December air. According to the intel, there were enough automated defenses for there to be only four security guards on duty tonight, along with the security rigger. A speaker grille grated a voice at us.

"Identify yourself."

Slim held up his badge taken from the Lone Star patrol. A fiberoptic cable connected to it, running down his arm to his primary commlink. Security badges usually have a small transmitter in this wireless world, allowing others to scan them for verification. Slim had used a basic forgery of the info to keep them looking at it for the valuable seconds it would take to establish a connection and place self-replicating viruses and agents in their system. In basic terms, his badge was a transmitter dish for viral hell.

"Lone Star Chicago Detachment 248 Tango, in pursuit of armed suspect. We have reason to believe they have entered your facility grounds."

"We haven't seen anyone."

"The perp is a Rat shaman. He is known to use stealth enchantments. Can we speak with your on-duty security mage?"

There was a pause. No doubt they were nervous about the possibility of a criminal on the grounds the very night they were without their mage. I suppressed my grin as the voice came back, hesitant. He sounded new to the job.

"Our mage is off-duty tonight."

I adopted a stern tone. "In that case, we'd better use our own. I'm formally requesting immediate access to your facilities."

"I'll have to send for authoriza—"

"We don't have time! He'll be gone by then. I'm sure you don't want to be held responsible for impeding an official Lone Star operation. In fact, this could be constituted as aiding and abetting the suspect."

The silence spoke volumes.

"I'll take personal responsibility for any damages caused, but we have to get in there *now*. Who knows what he'll do in there?"

Only a brief pause before the maglock buzzed, opening into the warehouse and loading dock. Security cameras and a pair of auto turrets were swinging to and fro, searching for a target. The security guard couldn't be over twenty-five, another kid trying to make a buck. I felt immediate pity.

"Please conduct your investigation quickly, officers. This is all highly irregular."

I smiled reassuringly, signaling Needles and Slim toward the stairway that led up to the break room, office, and security hub. Another signal to Pretty set her to watchfully sweeping her rifle across the room, looking diligent.

"Don't worry, sir, this will be handled as quickly and professionally as possible."

The guard nervously nodded before holding a hand to his ear. My hand tensed on my shotgun.

"This Rat shaman, is he any good with computers?"

"Why?"

"On site security is reporting an intrusion into our system."

I almost laughed. This poor kid! You *never* let these things slip. Then again, he should have known that we were, logically, the first suspects when something like this happens. Still, it would make things easier for us.

I nodded. "He uses a commlink full of agents and viruses, spreads confusion to cover his movements when he knows he's been seen. Can you use that to get a lock on his location in here?"

"Uh, it's a closed circuit system. He'd have to be in the security room, or..." His eyes lit up. "He'd have to wire in over this way!" He pulled his pistol and started running to a corner of the warehouse. Pretty and I followed.

We were halfway across the open expanse of the loading dock when I heard a muffled set of gunshots over the earpiece, followed a moment later by Needles' voice.

"Security Room secure. Drones and cameras disabled. Take out your little friend." Pretty aimed her assault rifle in a random direction and shouted, "There!"

The guard turned to look, and I swung the butt of my shotgun at his head. Hard enough to knock him out, but not kill him. I really did feel sorry for him.

Pretty actually smiled at me as we ran to the Security Room. An obese man was lying on the floor amidst a spray of rubber riot pellets, unconscious and wheezing. Needles stood over him, heaving for breath and drooling a little.

"Needles... Needles!"

He started and looked over at me. He nodded, clearing his head. "I'm fine...I'm fine, just hungry."

I nodded. Slim slipped into the control chair before a bank of monitors, plugging his gestalt system of commlinks in.

"Drek!" he shouted. "My agents didn't get to him before he sent out an update on their situation. I'll try to bull them long enough to keep reinforcements away, but we'd better hurry!"

Pretty sprinted back down the stairs to get the van and bring it in. I crouched next to Slim as he connected his cyberdeck and went full VR, plugging into the security rigger's system to adopt his persona and try to bluff Mitsuhama.

"Slim, try to pull up an inventory. You've got to tell us what to grab and where to get it. Open the door for Pretty when she gets back. Also, don't forget to erase any records of us. Erase the whole day, just to be safe. Find out if the goods have tracer tags, just in case, and keep us updated with the reinforcements' ETA."

His body seemed to roll its eyes as his voice emerged from speakers in the bank of monitors. "Is that all? Want a massage while I'm at it?"

I grinned wickedly and ran downstairs to see what looked good to line my own pockets with before Pretty got back.

I took the steps two at a time before jumping to the bottom. I love the kid-in-a-candy-store appeal of a robbery. My eyes scanned over row after row of boxes. Sorted by type and labeled in complex numerical strings and bar codes, I had no idea what might be in any one of them. I had hoped we'd have more time to sort through things, and I usually like to keep things neat and professional, but help was on the way, and robberies have a tendency to get messy.

I pulled a knife and started cutting boxes open. I figured each stack would be sorted into different product, so I moved on, box after box, so that I knew what to look for.

From across the room, a double door buzzed as locks activated. Muffled pounding and shouting came through as a faint hiss sounded. The noises subsided and my commlink crackled with Slim's voice. "Two guards knocked out. The third is locked in the john, but I'd still hurry."

By my third box I'd hit paydata. A dozen smaller boxes labeled *Soonan Simsense,* with a picture of a sleek sim unit. I pulled it out of the box and jammed it and its various manuals and peripherals, into a pocket. Moving down the line, I found boxes of sim chips for foreign languages, entertainment, and music. I grabbed handfuls and kept moving. I was about to slice open another when Slim's voice came though on my commlink.

"Red, move seven boxes to your left. Needles, get the ones on your right over to the garage door."

I did as he said, coming to a stack of boxes, each labeled for distribution to separate stores. I sliced one open and nearly whooped for joy. Inside, carefully insulated, were half a dozen midrange commlinks, probably worth about 2K each. I grinned at a nearby security cam, knowing Slim would see it, and started loading them near the door.

Four boxes of those and whatever Needles was grabbing. Slim directed us around the warehouse, grabbing two more smaller boxes, another four that were heavy as hell, and then two that would easily take up a quarter of the space in the van. Slim then asked if there was anything we wanted personally.

"Microsensors, Slim. We can use those for a dozen little things."

I found them two crates over. Button-sized up to handheld wands and scopes, they were exactly what we needed. I grabbed another two boxes, snatching up smaller boxes for sensors of every kind. As I did so, I saw Needles grabbing some of the boxes of chips and simplayers I had been at earlier.

The garage door opened, and Needles and I dove for cover, guns ready. Pretty's superior grin made me feel like an ass as I loaded our loot into the back of the van. Needles climbed in back, hauling things forward and stacking them as well as he could to fit it all in. Pretty got out and ran to help.

Slim's voice came over the commlinks. "Trouble. I can't fool them any longer, they're sending someone over to check on things. We've got forty-eight seconds before a satellite is in position to scan the area. We're out of here by then!" A small countdown timer appeared in my HUD.

The lights flickered as Slim came bounding down the steps,

sides heaving as he panted. I shakily started tossing boxes into the van.

"Thirty seconds!"

I threw one last box in and shoved Pretty into the driver seat. Needles jumped into the passenger side. Slim looked in back. "There's no room!"

I grimaced and grabbed him, shoving him flush against the boxes before slamming the van doors shut.

"Go!" I shouted. "I'll get out on my own, go!"

Pretty's eyes in the mirror showed a moment's hesitation before she slammed the gas, sending the van skidding into the night.

My eyes flicked down to my PAN.

00:00:20

Fine.

I blitzed out the open garage door. This was an industrial district, not many public places to hide out.

00:00:15

The doors were all flush with the walls of other warehouses, each most likely with their own security. The streets were long, and it would be a while before I made it to a residential neighborhood to blend in to...

00:00:10

I looked up at the sky. Somewhere up there was a satellite that was about to zoom in on me. There was no way for me to hide. I didn't want to mist form or I would lose all the gear, and being naked in the midst of a corp town post-run was a horrible idea. I was royally screwed. My head slumped...

00:00:05

...and I saw I was standing over a sewer grate. I drew forth my essence, willing it into strength and snapping the lock in a second. I jumped down, falling into shadows...

I landed with a splash in fetid darkness, the smell of waste. Switching off my commlink, I slid into a pipe large enough to hold me and waited.

Screeching tires above set my heart pounding. I double-checked that my commlink was off. Voices, Japanese and agitated, echoed dimly down. I tried to make out what they were saying.

"What happened? Why is this door open?!"

"Weapons ready, something's wrong."

The rest of it was too fast and complex to follow. I thanked my lucky stars to be without a SIN and untraceable, and turned around, crawling through the pipes in one direction until I felt safe.

My worn trench coat over my LS uniform, I traveled to our meeting point. Deep in the old Containment Zone, in a vault beneath an old Washington Bank, Slim had spotted an area completely dead to the wireless net. The walls were charred black from a firebombing years before, when Knight Errant had cleaned out a small bug nest. From the abandoned looks of things, no one had taken up residence since. I climbed out of an air duct into the basement and met them there.

Slim and Needles were unpacking boxes as I entered. Neither saw me.

"Rick!" Pretty ran up, then stopped short, uncertain before becoming impassive. "You got out. Good."

I smiled and turned back to the others, who had stopped to look at us. Slim grinned and went back to checking a roto-drone with a bug scanner. We'd chosen this place so we could find and disable any tracer RFID tags before bringing the swag back to the warren.

"How'd we make out?"

"Two drones, eighteen midrange commlinks, four on special order with attached bundles, three crates of linguasofts, tutorsofts, and music/media, sixteen sim modules, twenty security cameras, and four full-range sensor packages. Two more dedicated medical sensor packages, and enough spare commlinks and mainframe parts to wire up the warren for Christmas." Slim was grinning like an idiot as he listed the haul.

"Not too bad," Needles said.

"What were those four on special order?" I asked.

Slim reached into an open box and pulled out a slim, sleek commlink with a smaller box. "The Fairlight Caliban, crème de la crème of commlinks. Plus it's been wizzed out with upgrades straight from the box."

I opened up the smaller box. A pair of earbuds and a contact case fell into my palm. "Stuffed to the brim with enhancements. Not amazingly expensive, just hard to put together. The commlink's full of sensors, too. I think these four were for a special customer looking to do some surveillance or something. They're clean." I smiled. "I'm keeping this one."

We stepped out of the ruins an hour later. Slim had discarded all the packaging and gone over everything with his gear, even using one of the Fairlights to double-check. A few bugs later, and we were on the way home.

An hour's worth of tunnel navigation brought us and our very heavy prizes back to the warren. No sooner had we passed through one of the reinforced sewer hatches than Menerytheria manifested before me, looking for all the world out of breath.

"What, what is it?"

"North surface entrance. One of Barnes's gang."

We dropped out gear off and sprinted for the north entrance, a basement in a dilapidated house. Mene stopped at the door, holding the others back.

"What?"

"He's covered in Strain-III. I couldn't touch him. Alice and Smooth are getting clean suits to pull him into the showers."

"How long has he been there?" Needles demanded.

"About five minutes. Just before you got here."

Just then a pair of the mothers pushed past in yellow chemical suits, holding another between them. I followed close behind as they walked up the stairs into a blown-out living room. The ghoul was sprawled on an ancient couch. I remembered his name was Goolah. I opened my astral sight and saw he was covered with the bacteria, eating into his blind eyes and growing in all his joints, under his arms and between his legs. He moaned with incoherent pain, opening his mouth to take wheezing breaths, glowing in the astral with Strain-III particles. They sprayed him with anti-bacterial solutions, praying they could stem the growth before it got too far out of control. Once he was doused, they swabbed his arm and pressed a needle in, depressing a cocktail which would hopefully clear out internal infection.

Needles shouldered past me, gas mask on. He bent down to the writhing ghoul, who seemed to recognize him beneath the mask, and pulled close.

"Barnes hurt," he rasped out.

"What about the others?"

"Take... Bugs take. Gone to hive."

"Where?"

"Hive..." Goolah swallowed thickly. Predatory, to be sure, but definitely one of the simple-minded ones.

"Where is the hive?"

Goolah seemed to think for a while, coughing up blood in thick, discolored globs. "Cermak. The hot place."

Needles nodded, ran a gloved hand on the ghoul's brow, whispering thanks and praise. Goolah smiled, then the two suited ghouls picked him up on a worn stretcher, and headed for the chemical showers and makeshift sickbay. Needles pulled off the glove and tossed it to the two ghouls to be decontaminated, as well, making his way back to us.

"Think he'll make it?" I asked.

"Yeah, yeah, he's got a better chance here than anywhere," Slim said with hope. "We've got so much practice at this, after all."

I nodded. I didn't want to burden him with my opinion of his chances.

"So what's the plan?" Pretty asked Needles. Needles looked at her steadily for a long moment.

"We go after them."

"Even after Barnes threatened you and the others?" Slim asked.

"We don't leave our own behind. Most of them are just too hungry and stupid to know any better than to follow him. As for Barnes himself..." Needles paused. "We'll just have to see how he feels about life on his own."

"We're gonna need more guns," I said.

We ran to the armory, loading up on all the equipment we could carry. Hardened armor jackets, Ares Alpha assault rifles, Predators, flash-bangs, most of the good stuff was what we took from the Stars, but some assorted bits from Knight Errant, warlords and insect shamans had made their way into our packs. A few serrated knives and a sword from the Bloodcats gang, several quarts of insecticide in two jugs and various bug bombs, and a pack full of plastic explosives scavenged from a demolition/reconstruction crew site. Going into a hive usually meant an opportunity to do some real damage against honest-to-spirit monsters, and what better method than high explosives?

"We got enough?" I asked, racking the slide of my SPAS-12.

"We'll just have to find out," Needles replied with a sinister grin, hefting a pair of Ares Alphas.

CHAPTER 12

HIVE

The Chicago Zone's shattered nature made it hard to travel fast. It hadn't been a picnic when it had been in one piece; now it was a nightmare. A hour's fast march gave us plenty of time to recognize that we were probably too late to save anyone. After all, a sick, half-starved ghoul had staggered to deliver the message. How long had that taken? How much longer could any survivors hold out? I pushed that out of my mind and pressed on.

We looked like a Lone Star Fast Response Team team hustling across the ruins, still in the LS uniforms and now wearing gas masks and wetsuit-like contamination rigs. Thankfully they came standard with the LS FRT uniform in Chicago, protection against gases, radiation, and Strain III for those unlucky Awakened patrol members who were still stationed here.

"Something about this bothers me," I whispered to Needles as we trotted along a stretch of dilapidated roadway.

"What, just one thing?"

"Seriously, now. The Cermak Blast created one of the world's most famous mana warps. All those bugs dying in the midst of so many investitures, plus the massive ritual and the nuke..."

What's your point?"

"Needles, a dual-natured creature like a ghoul or insect spirit shouldn't be able to survive being in a mana warp. It ought to kill them, the closer they get to the center."

He looked at me, confused. "So how could they be there?"

"Exactly." I shrugged, worried. "If there really are bug spirits at Cermak, I have no idea."

"And what about us? Won't the warp hurt us?"

"It'll probably scramble magic, but the fact is the bugs aren't minding it. We ought to be—"

"Boss!" Slim hissed over the intercom.

"What?"

"I've been monitoring Lone Star frequencies since we left on that job. They just deployed two squads to scout the Cermak area, and are mobilizing a full platoon to follow on their order."

"Why?"

"Dunno. Maybe they're after the bugs."

"Good thing we're wearing the uniforms," I said.

"Unless they recognize the modifications," Pretty said.

We didn't talk about that afterward, and doubled our pace instead.

From the outside, the hive didn't look any different from any other dilapidated building in the city. Sure, it was more demolished than most, being the center of the infamous Cermak Blast more than twenty years ago, but it also had the dubious distinction of being the site of the world's largest recorded hive. For whatever reason, they kept coming back, even with the residual radiation and Strain III floating around.

"Over here!" Pretty called out from the burned-out husk of what might have once been a Chinatown market. We stepped over the charred remains of a wall and into an old kitchen. She stood over a sewer hole. Needles and I pulled it up, revealing a dark pit going two meters down.

I shouldered my shotgun, holding my hands out and reaching out with my senses as I opened myself to the astral. I stretched further and further—

–Chittering, squirming, writhing, clawing, build, build build feed growCHANGETHEMALLfeedreproduceEVOLVE–

My two eyes opened as the third closed. I was on my back, with Needles holding me and shaking me back to consciousness.

"You okay, Red?"

I gasped for breath, wiping the sweat off my brow and nodding. "What was down there?" he asked.

"Trouble," I said. "Bugs, that's for certain. Termites, if I had to guess. Probably only one queen, I only heard the echoes of one set of orders. But..."

"But what?"

"I heard something else down there, too. Something that wasn't the bugs, but...it was wrong. Twisted."

"Twisted?"

"That's the only way I can describe it, Needles. It wasn't natural. Even for bugs."

Needles looked down into the hole. Somehow it seemed deeper, now. Darker. I had wanted to know if this was the way to find survivors. Now all I was sure of was that it was a certain path to Hell.

We dropped down, guns ready. Needles looked both ways, then addressed each of us in the narrow sewer corridor.

"Okay, Red, you and I are point. Slim, you're in the middle, keep monitoring transmissions to see how far the Star is, and try to get us a map of the sewer system down here. Pretty, bring up the rear. You see anything that isn't human or ghoul, you just start firing until you run out of ammo. One of us will come back help."

"What about the FRT squads?"

"Let's try to work with them if we can. No need to fight on two fronts if we can aim all our guns at the enemy."

"So, just pretend we're one of the squads?" I asked.

"Exactly."

We started moving, keeping our pace as rapid as possible while maintaining stealth. Slim pulled up the old maps from before the Bug City incident, and transmitted them to all of our 'links. The labyrinthine layout was only so helpful, as some tunnels had collapsed. I checked the sensors on my new commlink, noting the slow rise in radiation. Strange. After all these years, the rads should have dispersed, even here at ground zero. Bio-sensors indicated no Strain III concentrations. That made sense. The bugs would never make a hive where they'd get eaten up by Ares' pet bio-weapon. I noticed the breeze blowing from down the tunnel, and suddenly I didn't need to assense, or even a map to know which way to go. I started walking faster.

"Red, where you going?"

"Isn't it kind of funny how there's no Strain III clouds down here?"

"Maybe it just never settled down here."

"It'd try to seek out something as astrally active as a hive. But you could keep it out with simple airflow. Don't you feel that?"

Slim pulled off his mask and felt the wind on his face. "Yeah, yeah, I see what you mean. And that smell..."

I knew it all too well. Familiar, organic, reminiscent of yeast. It would get stronger the closer we got to the hive.

"This is the right way." I said. "Let's get moving. Slim, keep track of our path. Odds are we'll need to get out of here in a hurry. I don't want to get lost because of a wrong turn."

"Already on it."

Another few minutes went by before I felt a sick, twisting feeling at my center, making my head spin for a moment. The collective groan I heard over the intercom let me know I wasn't alone in my assessment.

"What the drek is that?" Slim asked.

"Mana warp," I said. "In a place as Awakened as Chicago, *and* in the middle of a massive bug hive, that nuke twisted the astral something awful. Seems like it recovered a bit, since we made it this far in. It used to be much worse."

"Ugh," Pretty moaned. I could sympathize. It could only get worse for them. Unlike me, ghouls don't have a choice about switching off their perception to the astral. Dual nature in a mana warp is a slow torture. I turned to Needles, a silent question.

He met my gaze, refusing to let the discomfort get to him. "We move on. We're not done 'til we're done."

Deeper and deeper we went, far deeper than the blast crater and into the oldest parts of the city, the smell growing stronger. Slim and Pretty were moaning quietly from the stress of the warp. Needles bore it stoically, though his movements were stiffer now. Were it not for the equal disadvantage the spirits would suffer, I'd have said we ought to go ba—

Suddenly, the twisting sensation stopped. The others straightened up as they passed me, looking in wonder at the sudden change. I took a step back, and the twisting returned.

"What is it?" Needles asked.

"I'll be damned," I whispered in wonder. "What?"

"The warp...it ends here. Further into the hive, the warp has been...completely healed."

"What?" Needles look more confused.

"Don't you get it? The warp is enough to stop casual astral scouting. It'll stop astral bacteria like Strain III from getting in. It'll dissuade ghouls and mages from coming close. But it's just a shell. Don't you see? They've cloaked their *entire hive* and kept it safe! Like the eye of a hurricane."

"Can they do that?"

"I've never heard of it." I stepped out of the warp and saw with astral eyes. Sure enough, I could actually *see* the twisting, rippling distortions in the mana field, and behind me... deeper within the hive...

...*FEEDGROWREPRODUCEMUTATE...*

I pulled out before it could overwhelm me.

"What is it?"

"Something I've never seen before, Needles. I don't know if anyone ever has."

"I don't like this," Slim said, his voice quivering.

"What's to like?" Pretty asked bitterly.

We headed deeper in, until our boots started squishing on something. I activated a small light on my shotgun, and in the faint glow my elven vision could see the details of organic mush all over the floor. The smell was almost overwhelming, a blast of hot, fetid rot in my nose, but I kept my mask off. In the thermal spectrum, everything was dimly red, humid and awful, far beneath the dry winter night above. Skittering sounds came toward us, and I thumbed the safety off. I dared not assense for them, not in the belly of the beast...

The first came crawling along the wall, climbing hand over hand with frighteningly fast, jerking motions. In the dim light I could make out chitinous growths all over its body, and I took a moment to reach within and draw the strength of my stolen spirit into my reflexes. My shotgun came up in a flash and I shot, pumping the foregrip as fast as my mind could comprehend doing it, time slowing as the precision grew. The slug smacked it in the shoulder, bringing it to the ground with a wet *thump* and a distorted scream. I advanced on the lashing form and shot again, and again, until it stopped moving. It gave one last, hissing gasp before dying.

"Shit."

Needles moved forward, covering the hallway as I knelt over the corpse. "Red, what the fuck are you doing?"

"There's something wrong with this bug."

"He's right," Pretty said, looking down at it.

The chitin growths were more pronounced than usual. It had once been a human, that much was apparent. Probably a male, skinny and Caucasian. The eyes bulged unhealthily, and long veins of discolored blood looked more like lesions all over its body.

"It looks diseased," I said.

"Even for a bug." Slim chimed in.

"But more than that... Termites don't build their hives underground...but, except for these mandibles, it really looks like a Termite."

"Hey!" Needles hissed back to us over the comm. "We can dissect it later, but now is not the time, people!"

We got up and had our guns ready. But the bug stuck in my mind. It was different. Far different from any other I'd ever seen. And that worried me.

It was too quiet, with only ragged, nervous breathing and the squish of our boots in the muck as we went deeper. It was far, far too easy. I could feel us drawing closer to the center of the hive, even without astrally perceiving. Drones and warriors should have been attacking en masse to prevent us from getting any closer, but the place was silent as a grave, with only the steady air current from ahead, like the exhalation of a great beast.

Finally, a pulsating, soft red glow from around a bend told me we were close. The rasping sound of many creatures breathing echoed around the corner, along with a sickeningly loud heartbeat. Beneath it I could hear dozens more, each in time with the primary, throbbing in horrible rhythm.

I took point, stepping around the corner to gaze into a nightmare.

The chamber might have borne scars from the old Cermak blast, were it not thoroughly coated in the hive materiel. Termites love to build hives. It was massive, a cylindrical room that went up and down from where we were. From the pipes leading in, I could only assume it was a huge septic tank or sewage reservoir for the city. Tiered protrusions of organic matter extended out toward the center, each holding fleshy orbs with faintly writhing human shapes within.

Eggs. Dozens of them, each containing some poor, doomed soul. Termite flesh-forms crawled along the walls, tending the eggs and spitting out more matter, building more tiers.

The ring around our level was suddenly host to dozens of warriors, chittering menacingly and clacking their claws. I raised my shotgun as the others brought their guns up—

"Stop!"

The voice echoed up to us, and the flesh-forms backed off. The only human who might command the bugs would be...

I looked over the edge into the pit. A massive, bloated termite queen craned its bulging, distorted head up at us. Two men stood to either side of it, one more pale than any ghoul I had ever seen, and thinner to boot, the other covered in armor and adornments formed from bits of bug chitin and termite building materiel. I didn't dare assense them, or even speak. I knew we were in *way* over our heads.

"Welcome." The insect shaman opened his arms, as though to embrace us. "Welcome to Heaven."

The other man chuckled at this, wringing his hands as his gaze roamed over us.

The Termite shaman spoke again. "Please, come down here. Make yourselves comfortable."

Strong hands grabbed my gun, wrenching my arms behind me. I heard the others struggling, and struggled to see them. The termites had come right out of the woodwork, grabbing Pretty around the waist and snatching her gun away. Two seized Slim's wrists and squeezed until he dropped his pistols, exclaiming, "Ow ow ow!"

Needles was backed into a corner, Alphas aimed at the three advancing beasts. I looked to him and shook my head. He struggled for a moment, finally relaxing his grip and dropping the rifles. The termites grabbed him, firm but oddly careful. I knew I could escape quickly by turning to mist. I could even make a break for it, head for the surface... but what of them? No, best to keep that ace up my sleeve for now.

They lifted us off our feet, carrying us straight down the wall. Floor after floor I saw corridors leading off into the sewers, the access tunnels that had served the city for decades even before the Breakout. They led everywhere, some probably past the containment zones. The sheer number of eggs indicated they had been here for some time. Maybe this was the reason LS was so ready to go to war. Maybe bugboy had staged a massive kidnapping.

Toward the bottom I could see more cisterns, ten feet deep with open tops. Inside I could make out a few ghouls curled up, shaking and scared. Feral, cannibalistic, and predatory, even the simplest-minded ghoul knew to be afraid in a place like this. Maybe seven ghouls, I couldn't tell. Where the rest were, I didn't want to contemplate. Other cisterns held humans and orks, some just children, all of them civilians. They looked exhausted, dressed in the hodgepodge of the citizens of the Corridor. Some were crying.

The spirits set us down at the bottom without our guns, but didn't seem to realize the value of what was in our packs. My boots splashed in the slimy rainbow puddles of filth pooled all around, bigger ripples to compete with the small ones from that maddening heartbeat. The queen's eyes bored into me, and I shuddered with the unfamiliar sensation of fear. I knew her power. I knew what it was to face these creatures...or did I? Its veins throbbed under misshapen talons, distorted orbs slowly gestating in its twisted egg sacs. Facing it, my Geiger counter started making crackling sounds, like soymilk hitting Krak-L-Snaps cereal, and I started to have the barest inkling of the horror before me.

The bug shaman approached us, moving like a rich host entertaining in his parlor, despite appearances. He strode confidently up to me, smiling genially. All the while his compatriot moved between us, one after another, examining us like specimens. He pulled Pretty's chin this way and that, following the line of her neck. Slim snarled at him, but he paid it no mind.

"You came," said the bug shaman, "to kill us?"

I locked eyes with him, barely touching his power with mine. It was akin to dipping a toe in lava. He was potent, and on his home turf, with all the power of a queen behind him.

"No," I whispered. "I just wanted our people back. You do what you have to do to survive."

"Indeed!" His smile grew wider, displaying surreally white teeth. "The Invae are alive, like all of us, and like us, they can, and will, do what is necessary to survive. To propagate their species. Not that different from us humans."

"Less and less different every day," rasped the rail-thin man, who had moved on to Slim, examining his datajacks with marked distaste.

"You understand, though, don't you?" The shaman looked to me with something like hope. "You know more than most, being what you are."

"Beautiful," the strange little man said as he got to me, lifting my lip to examine my fangs. I felt like biting his fucking hand off.

"You're more human than the humans. All of you are." He swept his arms to indicate the four of us, and the ghouls in the cisterns. "You all know what it is to live. What it takes to continue living. Life feeds on life, and so on and so on. Nothing lives without doing so at the expense of another. You understand that more than anyone, feeding on your own kind." The shaman put his hand on my shoulder. "You ought to understand what we are doing better than anyone."

"Can't say as I do."

The shaman shook his head, his smile turning sly. "Don't play the fool with me. You know what we're trying to accomplish here. Just as virgin soil is without purpose until it is planted, humans exist to spawn something more wonderful, more complete."

"And you think insects are the right seed to plant?"

The little man spoke up. "Why not? They are adaptive, social, industrious, and far more likely to survive in the world metahumanity is building."

"What are you talking about?"

His eyes bulged even further out of their sockets from behind his greasy gray hair, and I wondered if they might pop out. "My friend, every day hundreds of tons of toxic waste are produced by the corporations, the governments. The people themselves produce this waste. It does not go away, my friend. The earth does not change it. It changes the earth. And with that change, metahumanity, and all life on this planet, is changed as well."

My rad counter was going crazy pointed at him. I wondered if I would glow if and when I got out of here.

"Things seem to change just fine on their own."

The thin wretch before me barked a laugh, sudden and curdled with madness. "Not fast enough for the new world people build of their own free will."

"People don't ask for toxic waste."

"Oh, but they do! They demand it! Every day it's a choice they make, with their plastics and chemicals. By-products they willingly accept for their creature comforts."

"So what? You want to replace humans with bugs?"

His eyes took a sad gleam. "My friend, I want to save them all. Don't you understand? Evolution is a slow, inadequate process, insufficient to keep up with the changes of this brave new world. Even the insects will fall to its ravages in time... without help."

My eyes rolled up to meet his. "Help only you can give?"

He laughed softly. "I'm not unique, or arrogant. I just want to help metahumanity reach its full potential. We are soft beings, my friend. Weak. We're manufacturing our own destruction faster than we can engineer a solution."

"So what's your solution?"

"Progress! Mutation is nothing but fast evolution. Radiation, acid rain, smog, these are the new weather patterns in the world to come. Only the strong will survive that, so I will make everyone strong. But insect spirit investiture is not enough. Other factors must be taken into account. Slow radiation exposure to build resistance, develop positive mutations. Chemical immersions, synthetics ingestion. Magic, as well. Viruses such as yours are an example. Strain III will be something far deadlier in the future if it survives. But perhaps HMHVV can be used to resist it."

"Toxic magic," I hissed.

"Oh, 'toxic' is such a vulgar term. It carries all manner of misnomers. One day, 'toxic' will be the same as 'normal'. I'm not trying to destroy the world. I'm just trying to prepare the people who are destroying it for the consequences of their actions. I'm trying to give them a second chance!"

The insect shaman stepped forward again. "We've seen such marvelous results with the ghoul flesh-forms. I am most eager to see what one of my children will do in the body of a vampire."

"What have you done with my people!?" Needles screamed.

The insect shaman turned to look at Needles as though seeing him for the first time. The queen's head moved in synch.

"I've made them my children. I've accepted them into my fold, and made them my own."

As though on cue, the clack of long claws rattled behind the queen, and pale, twisted forms crawled out. Long black talons, ghastly pale chitin, and bizarrely long teeth with brilliant, multifaceted eyes shining like opals in the wet darkness.

"Oh, no," Pretty moaned.

"They are beautiful, aren't they?" the bug shaman beamed proudly. "Normally there are some difficulties with merging into dual-natured creatures, but, like all problems, it's not impossible, just an obstacle to overcome. With my own abilities and the kind cooperation of the Ant queen, we managed a workaround."

"Ants?"

"Oh, yes, surely you noticed? The changes wrought on the queen pass on to her progeny. I experiment on the drones and warriors, finding beneficial mutations before developing them in the queen. Generation by generation, we build a better hive, a better breed. Before long we'll incorporate other elements into our master race. Other bugs, free spirits, HMHVV strains, toxic magics, blood magic, perhaps even cyberware before long. The possibilities are limitless. Surely you can see that?"

The ghoul-Ants loped over to us, long tongues running over their misshapen teeth, sniffing at us with obvious hunger.

"Of course, there are some unfortunate side effects. The usual hunger for flesh has been amplified far beyond the norm. Perhaps they'll make efficient hunter-killers. I'm really quite curious to see what we'll get from you, though."

My eyes darted to him, and I started struggling. But just as I would have started dissolving into mist, splitting pain, wrenching and burning bright, pierced my chest. I looked down to see a wooden stake in the hands of the toxic shaman, half-buried into my heart.

"I've been waiting a long time for one like you to show up. It hasn't been easy. But I have a long view. It teaches me patience. And now, it is the time for the harvest."

Ah, the stake through the heart. A classic of vampire mythology. Supposedly, it should kill me. It could, with enough force. But the real kicker is that if it's made of wood, my body has that old allergic reaction kick in. My heart stops pumping like it ought to, but I don't die, not for some time. I'm just prevented from taking mist form...or moving at all. No regeneration, no enhanced abilities, nothing. I'm just a wounded man in shock when that kind of wood damage is present in my body.

I went rigid for a moment, hacking and snarling and trying to shape the words for a spell, anything, even here. But I couldn't concentrate enough to string an English phrase together, let alone Latin. Finally, my strength left me, and I slumped in the deformed grasp of my captors. Pain, and the bitter acknowledgement of failure, became my world.

I could hear that toxic bastard talking to the others. "This is an honor. Don't be afraid. Soon, you'll be stronger, safer, a part of something. Devoid of this wretched individuality and loneliness. You will change, and change is the only beauty this world has left to offer."

I could hear screaming, struggling, as Pretty was taken somewhere. Needles spit insults as Slim cried for help. Nothing. I could do nothing. My lolling head saw the destination the flesh-forms carried me to, an open egg sac on one of the highest tiers. The astral came unbidden to my eyes, and within I could almost see the quivering, larval spirit that waited to consume my soul. I couldn't close my eyes. I couldn't look away. The stinking moisture began to enclose me—

An explosion rocked the hive, sending my captors to their knees. I landed halfway over the edge of the tier, the stake holding me from falling down. My unresponsive eyes fell on the depths of the hive. The pale ghoul-flesh forms fell in with the others, swarming from all over to converge on a single passageway, the same we came from. For only a moment, they stood clustered, shoulder to shoulder, clogging the passage, until they were thrown back, a pair of VTOL drones bursting through with heavy machine guns blazing. My eyes slid further down as the first FRT troops emerged.

The weight pulled me down, until it was only the stake holding me aloft. I cringed internally at the sensation of it ripping at my weight, flexing within until...almost...almost...

The wood snapped, the bits falling out of me as I tumbled down floor after floor, humid, wet air billowing past me. I almost smiled at the relief, partially turning to mist, drifting for a full, luxurious second of painless bliss, before I solidified near the floor, gear still on, falling into the muck with a thick splash. I scrambled to my feet, the queen not a meter from me and roaring in fury at the invaders, the bug shaman mirroring her movements.

Her twisted mouth spoke words that made my head spin. I looked up to see a Star officer stop shooting and slowly look down at the queen. She chittered hypnotically as he stared, enthralled, until a ghoul-flesh form tore into him with fangs and mandibles. The soldier didn't scream. Not once, even as he and his killer tumbled over the edge to fall a few feet from me with a sickening crunch.

I reached behind me, pulling a bug bomb from my pack and breaking off the end. The queen looked down at me as I jammed it into a fold of her egg sac, the gray gas spraying out in all directions. She tried to bring her gnarled arms back to pull it free, to block the flood of gasses on its back. It wouldn't kill her, but it would keep her distracted.

I leaped onto a ladder leading up one of the cisterns. I only had a moment before the queen got free of her spray or a drone came down on me. The VTOLs whooshed overhead, their guns never stopping a constant, strobing chatter as they swept over the hordes of flesh forms.

And still more of the abominations come pouring out from the tunnels.

At the top edge of the cistern I looked down. Shaking ghouls... and Needles. I took off my pack and lowered a strap down. He jumped up and grabbed it, and I strained with all my might to give him enough leverage to climb up. He scrambled up quicker than I thought, and dropped to the ground, running for the fallen Star. A full on tackle sent the ghoulish hybrid flying as he scooped up the soldier's assault rifle, rolling to a kneeling position and opening fire on the queen immediately in one smooth motion.

Other ghouls had gotten the same idea, and were climbing up the pack to swarm out. I jerked back. None of them was ready for this kind of fight, safer out of the way. Hanging from the ladder, I pulled my gas mask on and grabbed another bug bomb. I couldn't imagine a better place to use it, so I tossed it down by the queen to keep her busy. At another cistern's lip, I could see Slim, mask down, climbing out, probably on the shoulders of other ghouls. He threw a wave my way and jumped down to hide behind the cistern. I threw him my pack and hit the ground running.

The chatter of gunfire above told me the Lone Star team was still going strong. An explosion rained down bits of drone and another scream let me know they were losing men. I tried to make my way to Needles until I felt white-hot power hit my chest. I was thrown down, clotheslined. My eyes cleared and I looked up into the leering gaze of the toxic shaman.

"I need you to stay here, my friend."

I rolled to dodge another fall of his cudgel, studded with looked like greenish orichalcum. My chest still stung where he had hit me. My regeneration wasn't handling it. Goddamn shaman. It was some kind of weapon focus.

He brought it up in a swing at my chin, missing by centimeters as I jerked a long Cougar fineblade from its sheath at my thigh. It came up, missing his face only barely. He smiled sadly and drew back, adopting a defensive stance.

"I won't kill you, my friend. I have grand plans for you."

"I'd rather you try and kill me," I snarled, swinging at him with my heightened reflexes. The blade seemed to move slowly, arcing through the air as distant gunfire slowed its speed to the languid pace of a relaxed heartbeat. The toxic's eyes followed the path of the blade, whispering words of power that made my flesh crawl. My blade sliced into his arm, drawing blood and striking bone. But his gaze didn't falter. Maddened focus held as he completed his summoning, and the sludge beneath my feet moved to embrace me.

"Shit!"

The shaman smiled again and turned away, apparently confident his toxic water spirit could contain me. Maybe he was right. I tried to move my legs, but it slid up too fast, brackish muck covering my torso and arms. It slid into my mouth as I tried to scream, choking me.

Oh, spirits, no...

My breath stopped, clogged by acrid sludge. A world of difference from water for anyone else, but for someone who has drowned twice, it was a foul homecoming.

Oh god, they've killed me...

...Karl leered at my restrained form as he bent down to take my blood. The girl was dead already. I could hear her screams as they taunted me, chanting blasphemous words to conjure forth dark powers. That was the moment I knew magic was real. They had summoned it here, and the tall one, the one with the blond hair, took Karl and bit into his throat. I could almost see the glow of the girl's soul brightening the room. Mana. Life. It all pulled into Karl right before the blonde... vampire, it had to be a vampire... gently lowered him to the floor.

The beast turned to gaze at me, grinning through Karl's blood. "Take him."

Fangs all over. Piercing moments followed by interminable ecstasy. My terror mingled into it, and I felt myself being drawn in a dozen directions, pulled and sapped, until nothing was left...

"Shall we keep him?"

"We have no use for one so defiant. Give him a proper Salem trial. If he floats, bring him."

"And if he doesn't?"

"He won't."

I struggled vainly, managing to move my arms enough to claw at my mouth. But it was useless. It was in my lungs. I strangled silently, barely able to see the carnage outside.

"Rick, she's dead!" Thrall tried to hold me back, but I slipped from his grasp, leaving him with an empty coat as I dove from the ruined

yacht. The warm Louisiana water pulled me in, but I ignored the panic as I cast about for Gypsi.

The beams from the yacht's spotlights illuminated her in the corona of blood she drifted through. I thought she was floating, but we were both sinking, little trails and clouds of scarlet streaming upward as the light diminished. I swam toward her, cradling her slight body until I passed out...

There wasn't enough sludge to cover all of me, let alone hold me down. I stuck my fingers down my throat to try throwing the vile substance up, but it moved within my lungs and throat, holding down and suppressing my gag.

...The termite queen had chased me through the subway, until we came out by the bridge on Columbus and Wacker. The wall on the other side of the bridge lit up with spotlights, and I knew Knight Errant would be here before long.

Behind me, Needles and my runner team were knee-deep in bugs. My ally was near, smiling demurely at me and seeming calm despite the massive mystical conflagration all around us.

"You don't have to be here," I said.

"There's nowhere else I'd rather be."

I smiled, pulling my sword focus and Redline. The Queen was stuck between me and the bridge. Maybe it was suicide, but if I could push her away from my chummers, drive her back toward those Ares troops, I might just live through it.

The alien intelligence probed at my thoughts. I let her. We might be evenly matched, when all the servants were taken out of the equation. I pulsed a spell of strength and speed into myself and rushed at her. She lowered her troll horns at me, charging across the bridge with a roar to shake the pillars of Heaven.

We met in one brief instant, my blade clashing against her head as she lifted me up with her pincers—

And the world became a firestorm. Falling, screaming, water, and then... Nothing.

I couldn't cast a spell without speaking. My gestures were insufficient. My vision was going hazy...

...the full honey-moon on a calm, black lake...

The impact of purifying cold sent me flying, and my lungs

were suddenly filled with cold, fresh water. I coughed, the crystal fluid gushing from me to join with the rest floating into the air to form into Mene. She stood defiantly across from the toxic spirit, placing herself between me and it, heedless of the horrific astral energies of the toxic hive.

"He's mine, cousin."

The creature burbled in a strange language as I retched on the ground. Mene looked back to me, eyes shining happily.

"I'll discuss this with him. Meanwhile, could you negotiate his release from his Master?"

I nodded, searching about for the toxic shaman. Mene and the toxic water spirit splashed together, mingling and switching compositions like an animate lava lamp. Needles had retreated behind the cistern where Slim was writhing, clutching his face. The corpse of a flesh-form was nearby, and smoke rose from the hacker's face and its body. Needles tossed a spare gun into the cistern, presumably for Pretty, then loaded the Alpha with a green-striped insecticide clip. He was also winding tape around something beside him. Above, the remaining LS drone continued its strafing runs as the Lone Star troops were pushed further and further back down their tunnel. From Slim's eavesdropping, I knew the cavalry would arrive sooner or later, but would we still be alive by then?

The toxic shaman was one level above, holding one hand out to immolate an LS grunt with glowing white radioactive fire as she screamed. I bolted up the gooey ramp, coming up behind him and swinging the sword with all the force I could muster.

Again, the world seemed to slow at the critical moment. Blade met flesh, biting into his neck more deeply than I ever could. It hooked on his vertebrae, but the damage was done. His spell stopped, the burning trooper fell to the ground, still agonizingly alive.

The toxic's neck exploded in magical energies, glowing yellow power erupting forth. I kicked the body into the pit with the queen. The soldier writhed, but there was nothing I could do for her right now.

Above, the fight was going more and more to the bugs. I could hear their screams even from here. I cast my gaze down to the queen, disposing of the second bomb even now. She was covered in the toxic solutions, but seemed less hurt than she should have been. Damn those mutations. Her shaman lay in a heap next to her.

"Red!"

Needles waved for me. I started running to him, but after firing a burst, he waved something with his other hand. An insecticide bottle was taped up to a gray block of plastic explosive. He gestured as though to throw it, like a football. Somehow, the idea of making a pass like that in a war zone with his off-hand made me nervous. I'd have given a lot to be able to cast in this mess right now.

He threw it, and I was surprised just how far it got. Not far enough, of course. It landed on the ramp up to my level, bouncing down toward the first cistern tank. I dropped the sword and dove for it, hitting the ground hard and hearing something *snap* on impact.

The timer on the explosives read five seconds. Ignoring the splitting pain, I sprinted back up the ramp, limping on my injured leg. I came to the spot where I was right above the queen, diving onto her without a second thought.

I landed on the egg sac, eliciting a scream as she twisted to claw at me. Her talons shredded my armor, leaving livid scratches where she grazed me. I jammed the package in the bloated crevasse between the egg sac and her body. She screamed again as she looked down. I flashed her a quick smile and dove—

Only to be snatched in mid-air. The queen held me close, sinking serrated mandibles into my shoulder as I screamed—

Boom.

An entire minute of unconsciousness passed. I came to in time to catch some of the crisping remains rolling down from higher levels. I was being dragged across the grotesque floor, splashing as my head bumped into the puddles within small craters. I looked up at the strong, human hands gripping my ankles. My bleary eyes caught the close-cropped hair of a FRT officer. He turned to look at me.

"You all right, son?"

I nodded. He must have thought I was another Lone Star trooper. I pushed myself up, shaking my head groggily.

"That was a really ballsy move you pulled back there, kid. Stupid as hell, but it worked." He nodded at the burning remains of the queen. A few weaker flesh forms fell from tiers above, snapping as they impacted. LS troops were dispersing through the hive, maybe a dozen of them. Shouted orders, quick, casual.

These were professionals, experienced bug hunters. They were looking for uncorrupted hosts.

"What team are you with?"

He startled me with the question. I was about to make something up when my earbud crackled with Slim's rasping voice.

"Squad Three," I repeated.

The officer, whose tag identified him as Kamer, looked puzzled. "I thought they only sent two squads."

"To this zone. Two-squad groups were sent to other areas. We were closest. I guess we made it in first."

"Looks like," he said, looking upward. "With the queen dead, the rest got disrupted. We're still looking for the victims."

I nodded as though I knew exactly what he was talking about. I looked around. The cisterns were still untouched, but it was only a matter of time before one of them looked inside and decided the best move would be to toss in a grenade.

I looked around, gesturing at the half-decapitated remains of the shaman. "That one wasn't an insect shaman. He was using toxic abilities."

"How do you know?"

"Hell, he told me. They were gloating, supervillain-style. Laid out the whole plot. Evolution of bug spirits and metahumans or something."

He shot me a confused look. "Don't they only come in eco-terrorist and genocide varieties?"

"Sometimes they follow other Twisted paths. This one could be called a mutator."

He smiled. "I thought command said no mages in here."

"I'm not. I've just dealt with toxics before. Believe me, survive one encounter, and you'd want to know everything about them, too."

"Personal fascination?"

"How to kill them, mostly."

He laughed. "Well, looks like you got him."

But what about his bound spirits? Toxics can go berserk, and the rads in here mean a ripe environment for them."

What are you saying?"

"This area isn't secure. Hell, he might not have been the only toxic shaman in here."

He looked at the withered body, shaking his head. "All right, is your squad operational?"

I looked around. Needles and Pretty were trying to look inconspicuous with masks down, searching around the cisterns.

"Yeah, I think we'll be okay. You wanna secure the perimeter, make sure there's evacuation paths? We'll locate any survivors here."

He nodded. "I'll leave two troops here to keep things secure so you can focus on your job."

"Oh, that's not necessary—"

"I insist. You've done enough of the hard work for one night." He smiled and clapped my shoulder. I feigned a smile until he rounded up his squad and made for the tunnels. Needles and Slim came around the side of one of the cisterns, Needles supporting Slim. I noticed a pair of slap-patches on Slim's arm. The two Lone Star troops took up guard positions at the main entrance.

"Shit," Slim hissed over the comm. "What do we do?"

"We'll have to take them out," Needles whispered.

I shook my head. "There's gotta be another way."

He looked at me through his mask. "There isn't."

The pause was a moment only, but long enough for us to convey tensions and arguments. It was fought, won, and lost in total silence.

"Fine." I sighed. "I'll handle it. You get the survivors out. How about you take the ghouls and get them together out of sight? Slim can relax and find us a way out through one of these tunnels. Pretty can get the other potential hosts out of here and to another squad best of any of us."

They nodded, moving to their tasks as I started around the cisterns, picking up one of the fallen Star's snap batons and whipping it ready. I passed the dead shaman. Looking closer, I could smell his own decomposition, already advanced. The queen had just been puppeting his corpse for a mouthpiece. My eyes stopped on the smoking husk of the queen, and the basketball-sized stone orb within...

"I'll be damned..."

I'd only seen it on the news, gray and somewhat rough to the touch, rune-carved in a fashion incomparable to any historical culture. There sat the Bhianchi Orb, pristine despite the gore all around it, amidst the smoking entrails. I peeked just slightly into the astral, resisting the alien compulsions that still polluted the area to focus on the Orb...

Nothing. Magic, certainly, but nothing specific. Nothing identifiable. I picked it up and placed it in my pack. It'd be worth some-thing to the Institute, after all.

I walked carefully, not too quiet, but not loud enough to at-tract their attention. They were both facing outward, into the hall, a blonde woman and a large black man, both human as far as I could tell. I came up behind him, hefting the baton. If I could help it, I wouldn't kill him. Either of them. This didn't have to go down bloody...

They both brought their rifles down and turned to look at me. Even as I hid the baton, an identical series of looks flitted across each of our faces.

Casual. Shock. Recognition.

"*You...*" she whispered.

"Shit," he said, lowering his SPAS-12.

The seconds ticked by as Needles and Slim climbed up the cisterns, helping the ghouls out. Pretty dropped to the ground to run to the ones holding humans, reassuring them that they would be safe soon enough.

"What the frag are *you* doing here?" the male trooper asked.

"Some of our people got snatched. We came to free them."

"What's with the uniforms?" She looked me up and down sus-piciously.

"We didn't feel like getting shot at the moment you spotted us. Why the hell are you here?"

"Massive kidnapping," the black man replied, shouldering his shotgun. "A poorhouse and orphanage. They got away with may-be twenty-eight civilians."

I nodded. "Look, if you're willing, I just want to get my people out of here. We won't go taking anyone with us, just getting our-selves out. Your civilians will be left for you to escort."

She looked pained even as he considered it. "How are we go-ing to explain *that* to the sergeant?" she asked.

He indicated my baton. "You were gonna knock us out?"

I considered the metal in my hand with a shrug. "If I could help it."

He chuckled bitterly. "No dice. I'm not getting left asleep out here while there's hostiles around. No, I think my partner and I need to check out the top of this chamber for the next five min-utes. Then we're going to go down and help all those civilians out of there. How many are there?"

I whispered over my commlink for a head count. Slim responded. "Twenty-three," I told them. "I'll bet you'll find the rest partially transformed in some of the eggs."

They nodded sadly. "Fine," he said. "I expect twenty-three civilians down there."

"You'll have them."

They began walking up the ramp, carefully keeping their eyes away from the bottom of the hive.

"Hey."

They turned back.

"Thanks."

She smiled. "We're even," he said.

"Even it is."

The survivors, eight if the one back at the warren pulled through, trembled and cast darting glances about the gooey walls as we headed out through another tunnel. Barnes sulked among them, shooting reproachful glances at Needles every so often, who was doing his best to ignore him.

His head swathed in bandages, Slim listened closely to his earpiece as a pair of ghouls half-carried him, scanning frequencies to find a way back to the warren without any awkward reunions with friendly Lone Star officers.

I carried the Bhianchi Orb under my arm, idly wondering what powers it really held. Step after step I was worried the background count at the edge of the old Cermak mana warp would start hurting the ghouls, but it never came. Strange.

Mene floated up next to me, hands behind her back and coasting as though she were ice skating beside me. I looked over at her and smiled. She smiled back, pixie-like. "You owe me."

I laughed. "Fine, I owe you."

We emerged from the underground two city blocks away from an entrance to the warren.

The sun would be coming up in a half-hour, and the predawn light made the ghouls nervous. Imagine how I felt.

"What now?"

We all turned to look at the source of the question. Barnes

had stopped, perhaps three meters back, and stood alone, defiant. "What, are we all supposed to come crawling back because you saved us?"

Needles moved to the new front of the crowd, looking more tired than angry. Barnes's eyes narrowed at seeing him. If a man could snarl silently, he did. Needles just stood and waited.

"What do you want, Barnes?" he asked with a voice reminiscent of an exhausted parent.

"You expect I'm going to heel like a good dog just because you came to the rescue? You think I owe you something, now?"

Needles flipped the safety on and slung his rifle over his shoulder. "Barnes, I don't give a fuck any more. You can do whatever you want to do. You wanna come home? You do that. You don't like things, you wanna leave? Then go. No one is forcing you to do anything."

He smirked, sniffing in mocking amusement. "Yeah, but what about the others?" Needles shrugged and turned to address the huddled group of tired ghouls.

"If anybody wants to, they can leave. If you don't like me or the warren, you can go with Barnes, or head out on your own. If you want to come back, though, that's fine, too. Do whatever you want, no one is forcing you to do anything."

The ghouls looked at each other. These were most of the ones whose intellects hadn't quite survived the transformation into being a ghoul, and most were simple-minded at best. One hesitantly loped over to stand by Barnes. Another followed. Barnes's spreading victory smile melted into a sneer as the rest huddled close to Needles.

"Fine!" he shouted. "I only have use for the strong, anyway. Stay out of my way, Needles, or so help me, I'll rend your flesh and bathe in your blood."

Pretty rolled her eyes as Slim snorted in amusement. Needles just shrugged as we turned away to leave.

"Barnes," Needles called over his shoulder. Barnes turned to look.

"Stay the fuck away from my people, or I'll kill you."

Barnes let a glare linger for a moment before running off with his pair of ghouls. The remaining group looked to Needles. He took a deep breath, exhaled.

"Let's go home."

CHAPTER 13

AFTERSHOCKS AND TURNCOATS

We got back to the warren to find a sort of welcoming committee, the women and children swarming to hold us close and mutter their simple words of affection. No sweeping music, no dramatic kisses or fireworks. Just a crowd of twenty-eight people and a free spirit embracing randomly and being close. I recorded it on my contacts, feeling more of a sense of community, love, and pure humanity in that moment than I'd felt in dozens of aboveground towns and families. It was the closest thing to trust and belonging I'd felt since losing my family so many decades ago.

Mene took every opportunity to latch onto me and squeeze me in her approximation of a hug. I cast a glance over her shoulder to see Pretty gazing at me, almost unreadable, before she left the room for the decontamination showers.

I passed the next week relaxing, playing with my new commlink and choosing a few mapsofts, linguasofts, and music chips to go with it. I also pulled out a virtual pet program, a hellhound. I'd wanted a real one since I woke up the first time, but this was just as good. A handful of music chips caught me up to some of what people were listening to these days. Not bad. I'd always loved music, but it was a shattering blow to discover that Shield Wall was long gone. I raised a glass of wasp juice to all the old greats, wistfully aware that I'd never hear something new from the likes of JetBlack or Concrete Dreams again.

On the trid, reports came in of people dropping dead in the street, maybe twenty or so, most from the derelicts and dispossessed of society. It was all carefully glossed over, but from the time of death, I knew it was a bunch of "good merges" who didn't have enough strength to break free of their bond to the queen. I worried about the ones who had managed to break free, becoming free spirits like Mene, but probably far too twisted and alien to find a peaceful place in society. Rumors in the warren spoke of a free roach spirit that had wandered the city for years, making deals with metahumans toward unknown ends. I ruefully wished Lone Star all the luck in the world finding them.

Slim's head was wound with gauzy bandages after a flesh form had spat acid into his face. He had absolutely no free time, and were he not saving his money to go through with the plastic surgery, he might have invested in a sleep regulator to play with all his new toys 24/7. He was almost thankful for the facial wound, as it had finally convinced Needles to give his blessing regarding the surgery.

As soon as things were installed and settled, and someone was taught how to keep an eye on the automated security agents, he'd be off to the same street doc who had worked on Pretty. He'd sat with me for hours, going through skin tones, noses, hair and more, flipping through a catalog of possibilities, but always coming back to the skinny, pale, shaggy-maned boy his icon resembled. To my mind, it was how he had always seen himself, and I couldn't think of anything more perfect for him.

The drones and most of the chips and standard commlinks stayed in their boxes, ready to be taken to Ranes in payment for the job. They filled the greater part of the van, considering the value of the commlinks and sensor equipment we kept. Sleep and eating were things Pretty and I had to remind Slim of as he spent all his waking hours installing cameras and sensors at every entrance to the warren. The specialized bacterial scanners and medical systems went into the two rooms for decontamination. Needles beamed as they were installed. Without them, the Strain III-infested ghoul, Goolah, would surely have died.

Meanwhile, Slim tore apart his old room, setting all of his jury-rigged equipment aside lovingly as he installed the new systems, linking up all the cameras, commlinks, decks, and sensors with as much fiber optic cable as possible to prevent detection. The warren had caught up with the latter half of the twenty-first century at last.

The renegades were welcomed back without a word. They merged seamlessly back into things, apparently cowed by the displays of force Needles had shown in rescuing them and winning a stare-down with Barnes. Combined with the new security system, there was finally a sense of safety in the warren.

Needles called me to his room as he got ready to take Slim out to the cyberdoc. He'd made use of Pretty's makeup skills and took advantage of the cold weather. There would be no need to see anything more than his face until they were safely in the clinic, and a parka, gloves, and broad hood and scarf concealed most of his features. I stood in the doorway as he got ready, but he beckoned me in, closing the door behind me.

"You wanted to see me?"

He slipped on his gloves, focusing on anything but looking me in the eye. "Yeah...I wanted to say...that you were right."

"About what?"

"About here. This place. Me avoiding change. You were right." He finally raised his eyes to look at me. "But I don't think you understood the challenges in keeping a place like this going, or the investment it took to keep it alive all this time."

I nodded. "You're probably right."

"I'm still not sure you do."

"Probably."

He returned to his prepping. "But that doesn't mean you're wrong. That LS patrol was way too quick to arrive, and we've heard too many rumors about corps buying back into the zone. It's only a matter of time before they come down here and flush us out. And there's no damned point in waiting around for it to happen." He finished putting on his gloves and sighed. "I've called the ghouls at Long Pig Farm. Since we're a smaller group, they might be up for merging with us, especially if we bring our contacts and haul."

"That's awesome!"

He nodded. "I'm not entirely comfortable with it, and I'm trying to take my feelings out of the equation. Still, I can't shake the feeling there might be some more to it."

"You're worried they're gonna try to fuck you?"

"Yeah, a bit. There aren't a lot of us, and we have some pretty excellent goods. And the fact that so many of us are feral...it doesn't exactly bode well for integrating into a place that does business with norms." He sighed. "But, if we can pull our weight, we might be able to make it there...." He chuckled. "Heh. Pull our weight? I honestly think it'll be a vacation compared to what we usually deal with."

"That brings up a good point. What about the bug hunting for food?"

"Yeah. I think they live on body bank leavings, which is...not what I wanted, but I can't avoid the reality of what we are forever. But, that's also something on our end of the table. Feeding on clinic scraps makes you lazy. We've been hunting bugs. I'd put any of my ghouls against ten of theirs and call it a fair fight. And we might be able to do some more bug hunting, pull in some bounties for cash, eat the majority, really open up some options for them."

"And you'd be one step closer to bringing your warren into the light."

He smiled softly. "Yeah."

"It's what Sara would have wanted."

He sniffed. "You didn't know her, so that's a little melodramatic. Still...you're probably right. Or, at least it's as close we'll get for now."

He zipped up. "Are you willing to come along after I drop off Slim? You and Pretty can help me out."

"Sure."

Needles was wiping the makeup off as he stopped the van up at the corner of Grove and Washington in what was once Skokie, on the broken gravel of a parking lot behind an old sign for a country club with a newer, raw wood board reading *Long Pig Farms* in spray paint. The suburb had once been shrouded in oak trees before they were taken down for wood, but many stands remained, surrounding the rolling hills of converted golf courses with tall chain-link fences and razor wire. The old clubhouse was an exhibition of passing time, with patched and wooden planks over many windows, yet retaining the mixture of architecture as only a building more than one hundred and fifty years old could. There still remained weathered hints of what must have once been fine architecture.

The three of us got out of the van in the post-dusk light to the wafting stench of livestock.

The reinforced front doors of the compound opened to a pair of ghouls with Uzi IIIs. Between them, dressed in a shabby suit that wasn't too bad for a Corridor ghoul, was a tall man with cybereyes. His talons were trimmed short, his smile conservative and confident. He knew he was in control, and he communicated it without arrogance. I wondered if he was used to this position.

He walked down the front steps, extending his hand to me. "Needles, I presume?"

I smiled. "Afraid not..." I pointed to Needles on my right.

The ghoul adjusted with a chuckle. "My apologies. Matthias Greene, I represent the ghouls of Long Pig Farm. Who are your friends?"

"Pretty." She smiled. Her mask was on. I was grateful for it now.

"Red." I extended my hand, which Greene took. Without letting go, he looked back to Needles.

"A vampire? Does your pack include many other breeds of Infected?" Needles was about to answer when Greene cut him off. "Oh, but where are my manners? Won't you step inside? Winter is coming quickly now." He indicated the door and welcomed us inside.

Pretty leaned close to Needles, whispering, "He's trying to throw you off. Don't let him. Stay cool." He nodded, his face grim. Needles was incredible at rallying the troops, but when it came to negotiations and diplomacy, he was sorely lacking. Still, he was the one who had to conduct the negotiations, or he would lose credit in the pack and at the table.

The interior of the clubhouse was decorated in a classic, luxurious style, though the dust and decay of time had taken its toll. The furniture was done in a style that would have been called modern back in the '50s, and it was worn enough to be that old. We walked past open doors, behind which ghouls were preparing for their day's work, some sharpening tools for the treatment of meats and hides. Greene had an office behind a door labeled "Manager" just off a large sitting room with a stone fireplace stocked generously with wood. Spacious and sparse, with views out to what once had been the golfing greens. The smarter ghouls were leading their brain-damaged cousins, emerging from the bunkhouse and converted bungalows to tend the fields of clover and grains and the lean pigs that happily wandered the hills and wallowed in the muddy pools.

Behind the ancient, wooden desk, Greene sat and steepled his fingers, smiling. "Can I offer you some refreshment? Our pork is specially prepared to be more palatable to a ghoul's tastes."

"Thank you, no."

He shrugged. "Perhaps after, if all goes well."

"Perhaps."

"You seem to be doing quite well for yourselves," Pretty observed.

Greene beamed with pride. "We can't discount luck, but a lot
of effort went into making this place. We've established one of
the few communities outside of Asamando that shelters ghouls
in harmony with its neighbors."

"Well," I said, "Asamando is hardly at peace right now. And
surely you have your complications."

"Certainly. Swine rustlers come around every now and again.
And Humanis sometimes finances attacks, but thus far we've
been able to hold them off with a minimal loss of life."

Pretty looked back toward the door, where the guards had
been. "You don't seem to have much in the way of hardware to
defend yourselves."

Greene's smile deepened. "Not to greet guests, no." He let
that hang in the air for a moment before continuing. "So, to business, then. I'm to understand that you represent a pack around
thirty strong, and you would like to take up residence in our community?"

Needles nodded, relieved to finally get to the point. "Correct."

Pretty interjected. "We have a number of options we're ex-
ploring, but we feel Long Pig Farm has the most to offer our community, and vice-versa."

"How is that?"

"Integration," I said.

Needles picked up immediately where I gave him the starter,
a topic he could focus on. "For almost twenty years I've tried to
keep this pack alive, off the radar of bugs and corps alike. In that
time, I've seen many of them grow up with minimal resources
and learn to make the best of it. Living behind the wall has taught
us the hard way how to stay clean and alive, how to defend our-
selves and how to exhibit restraint. Our diet has primarily been
insect flesh-forms."

Green raised an eyebrow. "Hybrids? Are they still metahuman
enough to provide sustenance?"

Needled grinned. "Absolutely. Nobody minds some missing
bugs, and we manage to pull in enough meat to live very healthily."

"It can't be very appetizing, though."

Needles blinked. "What does that matter?"

"I mean that satisfying hunger is good for basic health, but satisfying taste is good for the mind." Greene chuckled. "Perhaps you've noticed that ghoul problems in the city rarely trace their origin to here?"

"We assumed that was excellent PR," Pretty said.

"No, not at all, though many are willing to give us the benefit of the doubt, considering the products we offer. No, we have found that supplying our population with the meat they crave is often enough to curb their hostility toward other metahumans. After all, a full belly doesn't urge hunting instincts, and feral ghouls are nothing if not instinctual. This way they are much more docile, much more agreeable to mundane tasks."

"You still treat them well?"

"Of course! Everyone has to pull their weight, but their needs are simple, and we provide those simple needs. You really should try our pork. I'll have some brought in." He gestured to someone through the windows flanking the door behind us. "It's quite different from any other you've tasted, I promise," he continued, obviously proud. "We keep them in different groups. One large population is sold to metahumans for profit. Ames of Chicago's Own Pizzeria makes all her sausage from our produce. And the other half is a specially-engineered breed we acquired which, we hope, may prove to be nutritionally viable as a replacement for metahuman flesh within the next ten years."

Our eyes went wide. This wasn't just good for ghouls, but there was a considerable monetary prize from the Draco Foundation for whoever managed to create a viable flesh substitute for ghouls. If they had cracked the mystery, they would be flush with cash and rather famous. From Greene's expression, he obviously knew this.

Needles leaned forward in his chair. "There is nothing I would like more for our people. Being free of human flesh has been one of my main goals with this pack. If you've got a line on a way to make that happen without having to hunt bugs, you've got my support."

"Naturally. But I wonder, isn't it possible that your diet has had some adverse effects on you?"

"What do you mean?"

"I mean, your coloration is a bit grayer than even the rest of us. You're terribly pale. And bug spirits aren't just human, are they? Perhaps whatever changes metahumans into bugs—"

"That's ridiculous," I said. "Ghouls have been eating bugs for a long time. I can guarantee you if there were effects, we'd have seen them by now."

"Guarantee? Are you an expert on bugs?"

"I've been hunting them since the '50s, so, yes, actually."

He considered this as Needles continued. "We all have. And we've got the experience and gear to offer this place a much better sense of security."

"What kind of personnel?"

"Around thirty, several combat-trained, with one technical expert. Very well-equipped, now, which we would bring with us. About half have retained full mental faculties, and all are trained in basic hazmat procedure."

"They've have to be, considering where you were. How did you survive all that time?"

Needles grinned. "We got smart. We got strong. And we stayed together."

Greene pointed his interlaced fingers at him. "Loyalty is important to you?" Needles nodded.

Greene thought for a moment as the door opened and servings of pork were brought in, raw on chipped plastic plates, dented metal silverware. Each was set on the desk for us, the ghouls who served them leaving with smiles. Though the smell wasn't palatable to me, I could detect the odd similarity to human flesh, beyond what one normally associates with pig meat. I could tell Needles and Pretty were tantalized by the scent.

Greene took up his silverware and indicated they should do likewise. When he looked at me, he frowned. "Oh, I'm sorry, I'm afraid we don't have anything to fit your diet." I smiled and pushed my plate away politely.

After Greene tucked in, Needles and Pretty took their first cautious bites. Their self-control was admirable, but I could tell they were engrossed in the flavor.

"Are these the transgenic pigs?" Pretty asked, temporarily too preoccupied with her meal to maintain her usual cool façade.

"Indeed. They don't quite satisfy all our needs yet, but we have a few ways we've managed to enhance the flavor that no one else seems to have figured out."

Needles stopped chewing. "How?"

"Are you familiar with ghoul caps?"

We nodded.

"We are occasionally able to secure small supplies to keep a small cultivation of them for a group of our transgenic pigs. We've found this group is especially appetizing when their diet is supplemented with them. Unfortunately, we've had little luck in maintaining an adequate supply to expand our experiments."

Needles smiled. "Then we do have something more to offer."

"Oh?"

He set down his half-finished plate. "We maintain some small clusters of them in our warren. We can keep them growing, but we never had a need other than to mask the flavor of bug or rat meat, usually just sniffing them. We'd be happy to share our techniques."

Pretty swallowed her last bite, looking up. "And we have a lot of experience behind the wall. It wouldn't be difficult to bring more of them here, and meat to keep them growing in."

"I'm curious," I said, "why the megacorporations aren't more interested in this link. You'd think they would have come to the same conclusions you have."

Greene nodded. "I doubt they have as much perspective on the matter as we do, or as much interest. But every now and again we have curious parties show up to offer payment for medical data on how we are getting along. I suspect the corporation we acquired the pigs from is using us as a testing ground. Which is fine by me, as long as they don't try to take my people. They don't know about the caps, and if they want to offer us a partnership in developing the swine alternative, we'll make quite a bit of money. Maybe enough to become a subsidiary in our own right."

"Which corporation did you get the pigs from?"

Greene smiled. "No offense, but I don't know you quite well enough to go sharing that detail, yet." That was fair. It was worth some nuyen to the right buyer.

"One more reason for us to join forces," Needles said.

Greene nodded. "All right. I admit, we could use the extra security. And getting more ghoul caps is a nice incentive..."

Needles gave him a moment before pushing. "How about this? Come to our warren. Get a look at how we get along. You'll see we're not feral, that we know how to take care of ourselves and work together."

Our host considered it a moment, then smiled. "That's an excellent idea. But first, let me show you around the farm. Make sure you know what you're getting into."

The tour was everything Needles could have hoped for. Long Pig Farm was massive, with grain fields and thousands of swine tended under starlight by ghouls working together in peace. Several times, he observed to Greene where he thought security could be improved, pointing out blind spots and breach points, and indicated that Slim could easily transfer the surveillance equipment for integration.

Greene also gave a tour of the housing facilities, converted tennis courts and bunkhouses made into dormitories. He paid special attention to the care of brain-damaged ghouls, where they slept and played and how they worked under the caring supervision of those still in full possession of their faculties. They were deemed more docile, their feral instincts curbed by honest work and full bellies, and treated as valued if simple members of the community.

Needles was in awe, seeing a glimpse of the world he had always dreamed of building for Sara. He wasn't as happy when a corpse cart came calling, offering the day's scavenging for a supply of fresh pork, but he understood the necessity, and given the promise of the transgenic livestock making such purchases unnecessary in the future, and the logical fact that it would take this much metahuman flesh to keep the farm going until then, he accepted it. It didn't hurt that the ghouls of the farm didn't hunt for live victims, either.

Greene and three armed ghouls returned with us to the warren, making the trip through the sewers without complaint. Needles showed them the housing and Slim's tech lab, explaining that Slim was currently undergoing biosculpting to look more human. Greene hoped more of them might be able to do that in the future, or better, that it would become unnecessary.

Experience had made decontamination look simple for Needles' pack, and Greene watched as a scavenger team returned and was scrubbed inside of ten minutes. Later, he partook of a plate of elfwasp, grimacing at the flavor, but admitting the satisfaction of his appetite. A small pot of ghoul caps on the table turned out to help, after all.

All the while, Needles explained their procedures, told stories of their successes against raiders, bugs, Knight Errant, and Lone Star. Pretty and I smiled to each other. He was a natural leader. In his element, he didn't need our assistance at all.

Finally, Greene looked up from the remains of his meal at Needles. "Be honest, Needles. You need this more than we do?"

"Excuse me?"

"I know very well that Zone lands are being sized up for reclamation by the corps as well as anyone. When they come through here, they'll kick you out. That's why you're looking to join us, isn't it?"

Needles sighed. "Yes. But more than that, even. We are stuck here. We survive and we learn, but this isn't a society. This isn't growing. We've done so much, and we have no way of making it matter, making it change things. It took a long time to realize that. When you spend every day focused on surviving, you forget that there's more to life. If we stay isolated down here, or if we die, we might as well have never been here. And that's not what I want."

"So you want to matter?"

"I want to make a difference, for my pack and for all ghouls. And there are other ghoul communities to join, others that have their acts together, but for the most part they are predators, or they hide like we do. The difference is learning to live in the open. To stop fear from spreading, and remind people that we are part of metahumanity. And as far as Chicago goes, you're the closest I've seen to it."

He smiled before continuing. "And that was before I saw the pigs."

"You're not at all interested in the money if we crack the alternative food source?"

Needles sniffed. "I know very well how to live without money, as you can see. The real payoff is how it will advance Infected interests. It makes us human. Takes away one more thing that makes people fear us. You take cannibalism off the table, and we're just sick. I'm not crazy about pity, but I'll take it over fear."

Greene nodded. "I know what you mean." He sighed. "Well... I have to talk to my people, but as far as I'm concerned, you should join us. Maybe you do need us more than we need you, but it's good for both parties."

He extended his hand, and Needles shook it.

It only took two days of Needles and Greene speaking with the other leaders of Long Pig Farm to ensure a place among them for the pack. Two more weeks went by, with the entire warren in a flurry of activity. Parties had gathered large supplies of the ghoul caps, and electronics and gear were packed up and prepped for transport.

Slim returned, wrapped in sterile bandages and careful to avoid infection as he oversaw the breakdown of equipment through a drone, occasionally complaining that he had just set up a beautiful system only to see it taken down before it could prove its worth. Needles comforted him by telling him there was a much bigger system to be built, which mollified him somewhat.

Even more than that, Slim was eagerly awaiting the removal of his bandages. Pretty would sit by his bed when she was in the warren, listening to him chatter about his hopes and all the things he would do once he could go out among metahumans. She smiled patiently, reminding him not to smile with the bandages, and giving him pointers on what he would have to know and do once he was among the norms. A regular metahuman might have healed by now, but those Infected who could have surgery at all often took longer to heal from it. It would be at least one more week until he was ready to get up. Until then, he maintained only the bare essentials for security and communication with the outside world. Everything else would go.

Pretty spent the rest of her time arranging for transportation of the ghouls. The old panel truck would bring crates and groups over slowly, careful not to attract attention, and taking alternate routes all the time. Moving the gear was the hardest part, but the warren wasted nothing, and the plastic crates from the heist still had their packing foam and fasteners. I drove occasionally to give her a rest, the hours of navigating Chicago's broken roads against a sky heavy with coming snowfall strangely silent, the back of the van with two or three ghouls squeezed between the boxes, nervous and uncertain and hopeful. Often I would look in the mirror and see them watching me.

The rest of the time I remained in the warren, devoting my attention to security. We were all hoping that this sudden increase of activity wouldn't attract attention. LS sweeps had doubled since the hive incident, and that drove bugs, raiders, and gangs to look for new hiding spots. Mene would conceal the van as I led small patrols that dwindled with every night's transportation of ghouls. Before long it was down to just a few of us to move Slim while I stayed behind the sterilize the area and catch up.

The tunnels were clear of the detritus you would find elsewhere in the city's ruins, but that would change with the doors open and a few days' wind to blow trash in. I hoisted an old fire axe and and swung the pick end into patched pipes and old furniture. Everywhere I saw signs of habitation I cracked it apart. The decon stations were already stripped of all useful materiel, the kitchens empty, the tech room nothing but a pair of dead, dangling cables and a clean spot where the Maria Mercurial poster had hung for so long.

My eyes drifted into the astral, and I could see echoes of this place. So many ghouls spending so much time here, the whispers of laughter and tears, fear and perseverance. In the midst of this medley of memory, footsteps sounded behind me, and I turned to see the far clearer form of Needles standing in the doorway.

"Red."

"Hey."

He walked through the door, looking around with vision much like mine.

"It's funny...you stay here so long, you see these residual images and they blend right in with life every day. You forget they're there. And it's only when everyone is gone, and the place is empty, and all you see are the ghosts..."

He hung his head. "Am I doing the right thing?"

"I think you're doing the only thing you can. Which is what you've always done for your people. You can't help being a good man."

He sniffed. "Yeah...well..." He glanced around again. "Think you could wipe all this away?"

I looked around. My skills weren't what they used to be, spells I could only half-remember that might have wiped the astral clean. "Even if I could, would you want me to?"

We walked to the great drain chamber where we had judged the Stars and debated Barnes. Vague visions of the many gathered here, emotional impressions of inspiration and family overcoming those few stains of rebellion and fury. More than anything, this place spoke of what Needles had built, and what it had meant to the lives spent here.

We looked at each other. It was clear. Maybe, even there were a way to wipe it all away, we didn't need to. Maybe the memories of a place deserved to remain, even when everything else was gone. Needles smiled.

We returned to the generator room, cans of kerosene and ammonia from the sterilization chambers the only resources remaining. We spread the chemicals all over the warren, every chamber and every passageway, until the fumes were thick enough to see. I'd be all right, but Needles strapped on a gas mask.

We left by the main door into the Zone, the night still young and the sky clear and cold, not a sign of FAB in the air. Needles pulled off his mask and reached into a pocket to pull out a red-banded incendiary grenade. He turned the timer to four minutes and, after a moment's hesitation, tossed it in. With a final look, we walked in opposite directions. We both needed time alone.

The grenade went off, and the vaporized fuel in the contained space detonated, shaking the ground and echoing across the entirety of the Zone. But the memories remained.

I sat for long hours listening to my music, some new band called Grim Aurora, staring at the Bhianchi Orb. I would hold it in my hands, set it on my lap, assense it, even talk to it. Like most strange puzzles of the mystical world, there were no unreasonable methods in trying to understand it.

Dusk found me in the shadow of a building near Cermak, abandoned by Ares, Lone Star, and bugs alike for now. Assensing from a distance showed the warp was back, practically vibrating through the tunnels leading down to the blast zone. The radiation had tapered off somewhat. I suspected that had to do with the death of the toxic shaman. Without his poisoning influence, the radiation would probably relax back to its usual, regular glow.

I wished I could ask Mene what she had seen when she looked at it, but I had needed to take care of the warren on my own, and had sent her on to help the ghouls settle in. It would be safer for her, away from an unknown artifact and the potential dangers of the Zone. Besides, I needed the time alone with my own thoughts.

I looked at the Orb, tucked under my arm, and took a few experimental steps toward the nearest sign of the warp. Assensing, I saw the warp vanish as I approached. I backed away, and the warp returned.

Interesting.

On a hunch, I set the orb down on the dust and gravel and

moved toward the warp. Stepping right where the warp abruptly began, I assensed—

—BlazingmeltingdeathhotdeathburnsWHYdyingkillingthebomb—

I stumbled back, and it was gone. All the horror of the spirits, the bomb, the ritual, everything. The astral here was clean and pure.

So that's *what it does...* Grinning, I picked it up and tossed it in the air like a beach ball, catching it with an "Oof!" just as my commlink chattered for my attention.

"Hello?"

Slim's icon of a disheveled youth appeared on the screen, smiling. "I just made contact with Ranes."

"Shouldn't you be recovering from surgery or something?"

"I am! I'm almost all healed up, and there's no reason I can't be jacked in while I do. We've set the time and place for the meet. You ready to go with Pretty tonight?"

"Sure." I grinned. "I'll head over now."

Pretty dressed for a casual night out, a thick cable knit sweater and jeans, but I wore my nice suit. I placed a quick call to Halian, offering to buy him a cup of coffee after the meet, and placed the Orb in my bag. Commlink and all its bells and whistles accounted for, we got in the van and made for the meet.

"If this works out, Ranes might become our new fence."

I turned to Pretty with mock surprise. She was initiating conversation, seemingly for its own sake. She smirked at my reaction and flipped me off.

"You think Needles will want us pursuing more jobs like this?"

"Nah," I said. "Despite all its capacity for crime, Needles wants to reintegrate the pack into mainstream society as much as possible, and make a good impression with the Farm. That means living as law-abiding citizens, or at least as close to it as possible."

She nodded, taking a turn on a side road. "He really does have our best interests at heart."

"Yeah, he does."

She looked thoughtful. "You two are good friends."

"Yeah. Well, we used to be. With all that's happened lately, I think I've outstayed my welcome."

She shot me a surprised look, sending her chrome earrings

dancing. "Well, the ghouls in the warren view you as his primary competition for leader of the pack."

"*What?!*"

"Don't sound so surprised. You were the one who defused the situation between Barnes and Needles. Everyone was there to see it. You gave Slim hope that he could live a normal life outside the warren someday. Some of the more sentient ghouls hope for the same thing, and word gets around. Some of us are starting to think Needles will never build anything more substantial than a sanctuary out of the warren. And the ferals may respect Needles now for staring down Barnes last week, but they remember *you* as the one who killed the queen."

I slumped back in my seat, shocked.

"You mean the pack wants me to replace him?"

"I didn't say that...not yet, anyway. But the strongest leads. It's instinctual. And since we're all Infected, you're fair game for the position."

"Pretty, I don't *want* to lead them."

A mask fell into place. "Why not?"

I tried to choose my words carefully. "Well it's...look, I'm...I'm not cut out to lead like he is."

She frowned. "You've done all right so far."

"That wasn't leadership! It was single instances of trouble-shooting. I know how to solve a problem looking at it from the outside. Imagine when Barnes left, how that might have been handled if I had been in Needles's place."

"It might not have happened at all, in that case."

"That's not what I'm saying. I'm saying I'm an outsider. That gives me a unique perspective on things in the warren."

She smiled sadly and slowly shook her head. "You just don't get it."

"What?"

"You still think of yourself as an outsider. But you're the only one in the pack who thinks that, now."

"I've only been here a month!"

"And look how much you've been a part of in that time."

"I don't know the first thing about leading a community."

"You've never tried."

"I'm not cut out for the lifestyle!"

She turned to look at me steadily. "Is there something wrong with it?"

I sighed, knowing there was no way to walk on eggshells any-more. Not with her. I should have learned that lesson a while ago.

"It's me, Marie. *I'm* the one who can't handle it. My life has been a rollercoaster even a born ghoul might be impressed by, and..."

"And you'd rather come home to a sense of normalcy than a pack of flesh eaters?" She sounded hurt.

I fixed her with a frank stare. "Marie, I eat souls to stay alive. I was in hibernation twice, and lost decades of my life, not to men-tion everything else that went with them. I was born seeing whis-pers of magic before the Awakening, and that's before getting turned by a vampire, which spiked dormant genes into elfhood. The only girlfriend I've had in the past sixty years was a shadow-runner that died in my arms. I've won and lost millions of nuyen. Oh, and my ex-ally spirit seems to have taken up obsessing about me as her *raison d'être.* So if anyone has a right to a little normalcy in their life, it's me."

The silence in the van as unbroken but for the rattle of boxes as we passed over bumps, the occasional honk of a distant horn.

"That's my world you're talking about, Rick. My life."

"But it's not mine."

A tear trickled down her cheek. "Why can't it be?"

I hadn't expected that. In my mind, I alternated between ask-ing for an explanation and coming up with an answer when we pulled up. She dabbed her tear away with the sleeve of her sweater, sniffled once, and took a deep breath. A mask fell into place, cold, competent, and confident. She turned to look at me with alien eyes.

"Let's go."

I stepped out of the van into the chill December night, slam-ming the door and looking around. The back alley behind a series of stores was an older part of town, faded red brick barely visible in the muck of built-up pollution. Light fell in that uniquely urban way, reflected in dull carmine against the heavy clouds overhead. Rows of back doors and loading docks lined the alleyway, and in the trash I could hear the scurry of rats fighting for food. Not devil rats; stray wisps of Strain III would consume them. Pretty tapped the horn in sequence, two long, two short, and slammed the door, waiting.

A single silhouette moved from a niche beside one of the loading docks, the glow from his cigarette as he pulled a long drag revealing Ranes's angular, carefully disheveled features.

He grinned. "I take it that's for me?"

"The van isn't," Pretty said with the cold confidence of a seasoned negotiator, "but all the boxes inside labeled 'MCT' are."

Ranes chuckled and gestured, probably beckoning a few goons to come unload the merchandise. I turned to look at Pretty just when my 'link's incoming call beeped urgent. Slim's avatar came up.

"Red, are you at the meet?!"

"Yeah, everything's—"

"Get the hell out of there!"

"Why? What's going on?"

"I cleaned up Pretty's eyecam shots, and got a look at her attackers' faces." A series of mug shots scrolled across my view. "One of 'em could be working for Ranes. If the same thugs see her, they'll blow the meet!"

Through the HUD one of the mug shots passed translucently over one of the goon's faces, matching perfectly for the briefest instant. His eyes turned from me toward Pretty, drifting up her legs to her face and freezing in a moment of horrifying recognition. Pretty's eyes locked on his, and their mirrored expressions let me know all hell was about to break loose.

The goon pulled a revolver from his jacket even as Pretty dove for the back of the van, knocking two others out of the way. The shot rang out loudly in the confined space of the alley, sending everyone dodging for cover. I ran for the back of the van too, finding Pretty with a Streetline Special and a look caught between terror and hatred.

"It's them, Rick, it's them..."

I listened in the silence, the whispers of the goon to Ranes barely audible. "It's her, boss, the one with Edgar when we shot him..."

There was a pause as Pretty and I looked at each other before Ranes' brogue echoed over to us. "Hey, boyo... you listenin'?"

"Yeah," I responded in my Hertfordshire accent.

"I didn't know about your joygirl, there. I thought that was separate business, over and done with. I'm sorry about my boy here pullin' his piece... It won't happen again."

Pretty's eyes bored into mine, demanding vengeance.

"You listening, boyo? It's in the past! Live and let live, right?" I looked to Pretty again. She smoldered.

"How do I know you won't just shoot us now like you tried then?" I called out.

"Boyo!" he called amicably, almost covering the sound of guns being cocked. "If I went and did things like that, how would I ever stay in business?"

I smirked at Pretty, and she handed me one of the Lone Star flash-bangs. "Stay here," I whispered.

I stepped out from cover, the battery-sized flash-bang concealed in my palm. For all his talk of peace, Ranes and his boys were all pointing pistols my way.

"Where's the other one?"

I shrugged. "Staying out of sight until we know you're a man of your word."

He smiled, handling his chromed Ruger with cavalier indifference. "Boyo, you're giving me what's in that van. Why would I ruin my reputation by killing you? 'Sides, bullets cost, and I came here to profit, not to bury."

I walked forward slowly, hands in my pockets, keeping my cool. I could probably survive whatever they threw at me. I just needed to keep them on me, and away from Pretty.

"Could you guys set your guns down? I'm feeling a little antsy with all that iron facing me."

Ranes grinned. "While your girl's back there with shooters of her own?"

"She hasn't got anything."

"Good."

His shot was straight on. In the closed alleyway, it thundered just like it does in the trideos, catching me in the throat and sending me spinning. Pretty's scream echoed strangely as my face pressed against the ground, cold asphalt giving my blood a path to spread. Ranes' worn boot made the mildest splash in the red puddle, the click of the hammer being pulled just before I felt the press of the cold metal barrel against the back of my head.

"You done good, boyo. Shame we didn't get to work together again. Any last words I should pass on to your friends when I find them for the other half of my merchandise?"

I clicked the arming button on the flash-bang and held it up in time to feel my palm burn and hear their yelps of surprise and pain through the explosive *cracks*. A few more gunshots went off, and I rolled away, dizzily jumping up and dashing for the van. Pretty fired a few rounds, clipping one thug and sending him yelping to the ground, clutching his leg.

I crouched next to her. She stared at me with naked relief,

throwing her arms around me and burying her face in my shoulder. "Oh, spirits, I thought they—"

"I'm fine, I'm fine." It was the truth, too. My flesh was already regenerating, nothing but bloodstains on my shirt and neck. Sirens began to wail in the distance.

"Shit."

I reached up to open the back door, pushing Pretty inside just as a security drone flew overhead, spotlight shining right on my face. My commlink beeped as it was scanned. I looked away as gunfire pelted the drone, and it sped forward to start recording the faces of Ranes and his boys. I jumped into the van just as Pretty started the engine and gunned it out of there, almost rolling us as she took a corner hard. I turned to look just as Ranes slammed against the windshield, rolling to the side. I couldn't tell if he survived or not.

We took turn after turn, finally pulling onto the interstate and blending into traffic. One of the advantages of having such a damn old car was its lack of modern transponders. As long as we stayed away from scanning zones, we'd be effectively invisible.

"Pretty...Pretty...Marie, listen to me." She looked up at me, more tears in her eyes. "You've got to get out of here. LS's involved, and they've seen my face. I'm a liability to the warren now."

"It doesn't matter!"

"Yes, it does. I've got to get out of here. Don't you see? It's not just the law. I'm dragging the whole warren down. I'm a threat to Needles staying in charge, right when he's finally got the right idea how to do it. I'm dividing loyalties and second-guessing people, leading them down paths they wouldn't normally take. The way I do things, I'll get everyone in trouble. I'm better off on my own, far away from here."

She didn't respond, only sniffling and pulling off the road near Bucktown.

I knelt in the van next to her, waiting until she could look at me again. She did, her face as naked as I had ever seen it, the features of a heartbroken, scared girl with tears in her eyes.

"What do we do?" she whispered.

"You are going to get out of here. Take this stuff back to the farm. You can still use most of it."

"What about you?"

I looked her in the eye.

"I'll find my own way. Tell the others I didn't make it. Tell Needles you saw me take a few shots to the head before you got out of there."

"But why?"

"Because it's for the best if the warren thinks I'm dead. Then there's no one worrying about me. Let me be dead, at least until things have stabilized there. I swear I'll come back someday."

"You promise?"

"My word."

I grabbed my coat and the bag with the Orb. The windows were down as I slammed the door. I turned to look back and say my goodbyes.

She dashed forward, her lips meeting mine in a shocking moment. Every ounce of passion I had doubted existed in her came rushing to the fore in that instant, blazing through in a single kiss.

She pulled back, fresh tears falling, but not a sob to be seen as she smiled weakly. "I'll kill you if you don't."

The first snowflake of the season drifted onto her cheek, melting to join the tears falling along the curl of her smirk. I smiled with a confidence I didn't feel, and turned to blend into the last of the Christmas shopping crowd.

How ironic. Now she was the honest one with her tears, and I was the one wearing the mask.

CHAPTER 14

ADIEU

The subsprawl streets finally emptied, with all the happy corporate families going home to enjoy a hot cup of Koko choco-sub by the light of the trideo on this first snowfall of the year. Others less fortunate would be huddled in shelters or around steam vents, as Chicago's brutal winters made heat as valuable a resource as clean water.

I walked through it all as casually as I could, constantly checking my HUD to make sure it was in passive/hidden mode. Paranoia was my closest friend right now, and the glow of the coffee house might have been Mecca to my weary gaze. I resisted the urge to burst in and strolled over as casually as I could, finally stopping at the window to gaze inside.

Halian sat at his usual small table, fiddling with his PAN. As he sipped his drink, he caught sight of me through the window and smiled, beckoning me in. Wary of the store's auto-check of my commlink, I gestured for him to come out and join me, instead. His smile faltering, he got up and came outside. It was strange, but in all our meetings, we had been seated, facing each other eye to eye. Looking down on his 1.2-meter-frame, I was reminded just how different we were.

"What's wrong, Rick?"

"I'm in a jam," I began, stopping and darting my gaze about as sirens rang in the distance. That seemed to provide him with ample explanation, and he nodded, beckoning me to follow him. He led me to a midsize sedan parked around the corner, and unlocked it. Getting into his dwarf-sized seat, he activated the heaters and flipped the switch for a white noise generator. My ears popped from the double pressure change and I sighed, sinking into the seat and relaxing for the first time in hours.

"What has happened, my friend?"

I sniffed in derisive laughter. "I trashed my identity."

"That seems like a foolish thing to do."

I nodded, zoning out on the distant street lights and the hypnotic pattern of falling snow in the beam of light.

"Would you care to tell me how it happened?"

"Off the record?"

"Naturally."

I sighed and began my tale of the events of the evening. After wrapping it up where I met with him, the car grew silent. I suddenly became acutely aware of the sanctuary around me, and the danger into which Halian was putting himself by harboring me. For his part, he sat and nodded, taking it all in and thinking before responding.

"You'll need a place to stay while we find another identity for you."

Startled, I looked at him. "You can't put yourself at that kind of risk."

He turned his gaze on me, surprised and amused. "I'm at equal risk every day for the things I do. Sheltering a relatively innocent fugitive hardly seems like a worthy crime to add to the list at this point."

I laughed. "Relatively innocent?"

"You didn't hurt anyone who leads a simple, crime-free life. Those who did get hurt were scum who threw the first punch. If it weren't for your SINless status, I imagine you could have played it off as a mugging and been none the worse for wear."

"You're a complicated cat, Halian."

"Remaining impartial in my information distribution does not preclude my having a moral code."

I conceded the point, and he told me to buckle up. "Where are we going?"

"Someplace they never look for criminals."

The University of Chicago's library boiler room was as warm and welcoming as a log cabin in the woods, sealed up and clean but for a fine layer of dust. A small chair and table sat near the furnace, a couple of hardcopy books and a pitcher and glass sitting fresh and dust-free.

"I keep this handy as a quiet place to think," Halian explained. "For the meager price of a pack of Choco-Bombs and some friendly banter, the janitor never comes in here."

We headed up to his office and grabbed a sleeping bag and some basic toiletries. "Where did you get those?" I asked.

"I'll be going on a camping trip in the NAN when spring rolls around. I keep my gear here. Good thing, eh?"

I smiled and warmed my hands by the fire. He joined me. "You know, you barely know me, Halian."

"I know you well enough, Rick."

"Yeah, but I owe you for this."

"Nonsense. Think nothing of it. And if you must, then consider it a favor for a friend that you can repay however you see fit."

He turned to go to the door, leaving a keycard on the table. "That's to get in and out when you wish. I'm afraid this night's worn on a little longer than I planned, and I'll be needing some sleep. I'll come back tomorrow night after sundown, and we'll decide how to proceed from there."

I smiled as he left, dragging the sleeping bag over by the furnace and setting my suit on the chair. Stretching out and trying to relax, I let my mind wander over the strange events of the day, falling asleep wondering how I got myself into such strange predicaments all the time.

Halian was prompt the next evening, knocking and entering just moments after sundown.

Smiling, he held out his commlink to me. "I've found a friend who may be able to help you. Link your PAN to mine."

Still bleary-eyed, I took out my 'link, merging its PAN with my display and earbuds and watched as a black screen with the print "Audio Only" came up. A warped voice came through.

"I'm told you need a new identity."

That's right."

A pause the length of an eyeblink. *"What specifications are you looking for?"*

I thought about it. "I need to get out of Chicago. Something that will let me carry my gear, not arouse too much suspicion about looking like..."

"An Infected?" the voice finished.

"Yeah. A vampire."

"Heh. Haven't done that bad for yourself, then, have you?"

"Could be worse, I suppose."

"Night travel, or something well-sheltered, then. Where you looking to go?"

Memories of Pretty and her accusations that rang true now in my mind. *You've only ever run away...* It was time to stop running.

"Seattle," I answered.

"I think I can help, Hannibelle. How about you and I handle this later today, while my friend and I work out the details of his to-be identity?"

"Your call, Lens."

The connection cut. I looked at Halian quizzically. "Lens?"

"My decking name in bygone days. I apologize, incidentally. Yes, she knows you are Infected, and can pass for a regular metahuman. It's that very status that gave me the notion to call her first. She tends to sympathize with your kind. I suspect someone close to her was Infected themselves."

"So what did you have in mind? You look like you have a specific idea."

His smile turned devious as he brought up a file on my PAN. Lines of student profiles streamed across the screen. "How do you feel about going back to school?"

"Pardon?"

"My administration-level clearance with the university gives me an in regarding student profiles. Those profiles are connected to shared data dumps with other universities and colleges across the world. I could whip up a student profile for you, establish a level of credibility for the SIN Hannibelle will engineer."

"I didn't know Chicago had campuses worldwide."

"They don't. But a student that does as well as you will have can go almost anywhere there are schools. A transfer, grants from anonymous sources, the works. How would you feel about Oxford?"

I laughed. "You're serious?"

"Absolutely. I can arrange for the files, the uniform, the student history, everything. But you want Seattle, so Seattle University it is. Hannibelle will use her connections to legitimize what we come up with and provide an actual SIN."

"Wow. How much is that gonna cost?"

"Oh, don't worry about it. I'm sure she'd be willing accept an IOU on my part."

"No," I said as I pulled the Bhianchi Orb out of my pack and handed it to him.

His eyes widened. "This is that relic stolen from the Chicago Metaphysical Institute, isn't it?"

I nodded. "There's no way for me to claim the bounty on it, now, but you can. What's more, I'll throw in my observations as to what it does."

"I thought no one knew."

"That's because it was only tested and observed in standard, isolated laboratory conditions, and never in the real world. I'll write it up and you can drop both off for the loot. I think the DIMR would offer some pretty nuyen for the info alone. Keep the payment to cover my costs. Anything above it you can consider a donation to the college or your pet projects."

Halian looked like he was about to object, but he bit back the words, probably sensing I wouldn't relent over this. "Well, Draco Foundation credit is as good as any. Thank you."

Putting the Orb down, he tossed me a passkey. "That's for one of the unused student dorms in the building adjacent to this one. You can rest there until we get this whole mess sorted out. Meantime, your homework assignment is to write up a dossier on your skills and talents. We'll factor those into your profile so you can answer any inquiries naturally, should the question of your identity's veracity arise."

I nodded, smiling and staring at the passkey in my hands. "Thanks, Halian."

"Naturally."

It took a whole three days for Avery J. Dancing, student at UC-Berkeley with an anonymous grant being transferred to U of S, to be born, fleshed out, and legally have lived for the past two decades. I posed for student ID pictures and SIN photos, having gone back to my crazy hair in its hanging scarlet spikes and stubbled goatee. Halian laughed and said I was looking more and more the part every day. While I didn't have the pleasure of speaking with Hannibelle again, Halian explained the process of bribes and information to certain black markets and government officials who slipped in the occasional file, falsifying their histories, and making it look as natural as possible.

In my name, Halian and Hannibelle were able to acquire a student license for possession of an edged weapon (fencing team) and Practice of Thaumaturgy ("A rare Awakened prodigy," my teachers raved.). Plane tickets were purchased and hotel rooms booked. Halian and I even collaborated on letters from my "parents" as physical evidence to corroborate my story, should my luggage, meager as it was, be searched. I loaded a few basic lesson programs onto my 'link, practiced looking like a bored, snobby, rich student, and finally got some new street clothes.

I posed for Halian the day of my flight, in Zoé-knockoff hoodie and jeans and Vashon Island synthleather boots, the perpetual petulant youth. I couldn't keep from smiling. "It actually feels like I'm going off to school."

"If only you could. But they'll have far more checks when you get there. I'm afraid this identity is only going to work as a delinquent student, and even then, it will probably begin falling apart before the year is out."

"As long as it gets me out of the Midwest and into the Seattle shadows, it'll have lasted long enough."

"So, you'll be getting back into the thick of things?" There was a faint note of disappointment.

"I have no money. No identity. I am a no one, with unlicensed skills and a disease that makes me an exile to society. Any job I take is illegal, technically."

He shrugged. "I suppose you have to find your own truth."

"Truth...I suppose that's what's really important here."

"It's my dharma."

I nodded, pulling a chip from my commlink and setting it gently on the table.

Halian picked it up. "What is this?"

"My story. The story of the ghouls of Chicago. Lone Star. The bug spirits. Everything I've seen in the past month."

He cocked an eye at me. "Are you sure you're comfortable giving me this?"

"I am if you keep your word."

"Regarding?"

"That you protect the anonymity of the innocent. Don't tell this story until it's safe to do so. Or release it on the NooseNet. I trust you to do the right thing. Just make sure people know about the plight of those ghouls. Of all the Infected, for that matter. We're people. Not all of us are predisposed to horrifying acts just because of our nature."

He nodded as he pocketed the chip. "I'll see the story is told. Thank you."

I grinned. "Sure. Can I have a ride to the airport?"

O'Hare didn't see as much business now that Chicago was a pariah among UCAS cities, even with the new reclamation and reconstruction effort. Most people simply didn't have the time or inclination to vacation in a place infested with bug spirits or swimming in Strain III. After the breakout, most of the business came from rebuilding, and heavy equipment travels best on the ground. Some parts of the sprawling airport had been closed down entirely, gathering dust and transients. So long as no one was bothered, though, the staff had a don't-ask, don't-tell mentality.

I stood at Terminal 3, handling cross-NAN flights, with my lonely duffel and a long case containing my new sword. I turned to look at Halian, who beamed up at me just like a proud instructor would at his star pupil. What made it so touching was the honesty behind it. How very genuine he was. I think he still thought of me as a child, despite our identical age. And that was fine.

He'd stuck his neck out for me. Spirits knew no one but Needles had done that for me for a long time. It was an unfamiliar feeling to have a friend. I held back the tears that realization inspired as I took his proffered hand and shook it warmly.

"You take care now, Avery. If you ever need anything, you know where to call." I nodded, and he tipped his old houndstooth hat and turned to leave.

"Halian!" I called. He turned back to me.

"Think I can buy you one last cup of coffee?"

"Sorry, Avery, but you know I have class in the morning." He checked the time on his HUD and sighed. "But have a cup for me when you get to Seattle."

"I'll do that," I whispered as he disappeared down an escalator.

The final boarding call went out for my flight, a suborbital straight shot to the Emerald City. I brought up my boarding pass on my PAN and made for the gate when an alarm went off. Ahead of me in line, a uniformed man was shaking his head and waving to the crowd.

"We're very sorry for the inconvenience, lades and gentlemen. There appears to be a technical error. Please take a seat. We'll inform you as soon as the situation is remedied."

The crowd gave a collective groan and turned to find seating, eyes rolling, and grumbles becoming the new ambiance. For my own part, I wished Halian had stuck around.

I flopped down in one of the hundreds of seats for waiting passengers, loaded up a Grim Aurora track (thank goodness they still made *some* good music these days), and fell asleep.

There was no dream, only the briefest whisper of my name in my mind. A voice so familiar I was consumed with it, the warm feeling of water, and a connection as close as twins shared, long-broken for one, and newly-severed for the other. It lasted an eyeblink, long enough to fill a lifetime, dream-wise.

Mene. Still here. She'd follow me anywhere.

The alarm chime broke through into the song, jolting me awake. Second playthrough. 172 minutes. Final boarding call, Seattle Metroplex.

I grabbed my sparse luggage for the sparsely populated flight. Glanced out the window.

Chicago...City of my birth...City of my death.

With one final look, I bid it farewell.

EPILOGUE

FRIENDS OLD AND NEW

Club Penumbra is the one place in Seattle that hasn't changed whatsoever. Matte black on black with faux starlight and laser shows, a callback to the '50s that makes me feel right at home.

The crowds haven't changed much, either. Orks in Sleeping Tiger suits with leopard cuffs and chain link belts, men and women with neon mohawks and platform boots, the familiar hiding spots for hold-outs on nearly everyone. There's even a booth toward the back, just behind some speakers, where four young punks sit with a corper in a fine suit, slick haircut, and an immaculate and very artificial tan. Mr. Johnson, how little you've changed as well.

Even the music is familiar. The voice is a little different, my AR listing an unfamiliar name, but it rings a bell...

"Given dreams now forsaken,
I caught your wandering eye.
You give me life and I take it.
I'd rather bleed you dry."

I grin. Somewhere, behind the holograms, JetBlack is still making music.

Some things, thankfully, never change.

"There," Mene whispers telepathically, and my attention is drawn to a Chinese man in a suit sitting at a table nursing a tonic with lime. I nod and move across the throbbing dance floor. With the earbuds, I can make out the individual sounds of the room even through the music, the clink of glasses, and shouted conversations. I can even hear heartbeats when I focus enough.

But I can't hear the man. As soon as I step to the table, the sound of the club fades. The small box on the table neutralizes the noise. Nothing we say can be heard outside the table.

He looks up, perfect skin, perfect hair, Zeiss cybereyes. His watch is a Fairlight commlink. His cufflinks have sensors. I've caught up with technology, and the more things change, the more they stay the same. Corporate. Wuxing, maybe.

I pull out the chair and sit down, folding my hands. My suit isn't a tenth as good as his, but I keep up with current fashions, and a simple illusion spell has taken me to the tasteful edge. It was an easy spell.

My paradigm works best with my ego. So does talking to a Johnson.

I fold my hands like his. Mimicry is the first step of setting someone at ease. He knows that. And now he knows I know it. I don't win him over on the first level or even the subtext. I am simply communicating my competency. He is impassive, his artificial eyes at ease, but keen. He takes in details without the darting glances to collect it. When he speaks, he retains a Hong Kong accent, but his English is flawless. That is an affectation, a nod to his heritage. Corporate cultural loyalty. Or maybe a ruse. I don't think it is. His aura doesn't show as much, anyway.

"Mr. Johnson? Hannibelle arranged for us to meet?"

"I am afraid I am not a Johnson, Mr. Lang."

My eyes narrow. It's not done this way.

The not-Johnson pulls a secondary commlink, equally expensive as the watch, and hands it to me, a call in progress much like a 20th-century cell phone. The sensors in my own cufflinks don't detect explosives. I put it to my ear.

The voice on the other end is one I have not heard in more than a decade, as calm and cryptic as ever. As always. A single syllable.

"Come."

The not-Johnson drives me to the temple in Chinatown. The rain has been falling since we stepped out of Penumbra, and I'm still getting used to it. The drive is careful over ice and ash, with swinging neoplas lanterns casting their yellow and gold glow through the steam and downpour. The statues and façade are unaffected by the acid. Not-Johnson opens the door, and then an umbrella for me. He walks me to the doors, and I proceed inside alone.

The temple is quiet but for the hammer of rain on the roof. Incense hangs heavy, but my view is clear to the head of the chamber. Su Cheng has not aged a day any more than I have, kneeling before the altar, the three great statues at his back, the sick yellow glow of his eyes casting dirty amber beams in the thin smoke from the braziers.

"Long time, Great Master."

He grins broadly, revealing his crooked yellow teeth, pointed canines unextended. "You are bolder now, young one."

"And older."

"Never as old as I, though."

I shrug. "Product of coincidence."

He nods. "And how was your sleep?"

"I don't remember it. I lost much."

"And gained purpose."

I consider it, hands in my pockets, pensive and irreverent. "I suppose you're right. All it cost was a fortune."

"Fortunes rise and fall, Richard. Time and tide. Other immortals have lost more over the centuries and millennia and Ages, I am sure."

I pause. "Just how old *are* you, Su Cheng?"

He smiles, only a tiny grin this time, and cocks his head slightly to the left. Every movement is calculated, every truth doled out in precise measurements. I wonder what he is trying to lead me to...

"Would you like to rebuild your fortune?" he asks.

"Still fortune-telling these days?"

"Fortune building, when it suits me."

"What do you have in mind?"

"Nothing beyond your means or skill. In fact, what you do best."

"I'm not interested in aligning with any of the syndicates or corps."

He chuckles, a soft grating sound holding a high, keening cackle in its depths. "A man like you does not stay quiet or neutral. But you do stand for yourself. I have always respected that. I do not offer you employment. Simply a contact. A little something to cut your teeth on, and something to put in your back pocket."

I consider. Su Cheng has yet to steer me wrong, and he has no reason to. Syndicate politics aside, the only times I've ever seen his interests are when ours align. It doesn't play to counter my conscience. And besides, my account is just about empty.

"Keep talking."

He spreads his long-taloned fingers over the array of spilled I-Ching tiles and human bones, blackened and cracked open over flame. "What do you see?"

I kneel down, tracing my fingers along the bones. I've made a study of the I-Ching, but it never speaks to me as well as more direct divination. I wish I still had my tarot deck. European styles mixed with Asian philosophies always appealed to me. I have to wait until someone gives me one as a gift, unsolicited. I wonder if Su Cheng knows I'm thinking that.

Probably.

"Tell me, instead."

"You *have* grown bolder."

"Perhaps just more direct."

He inclines his head and traces the end of a nail along the fibrous cracks of the bone, his eyes shining down to dance back and forth along the pattern of golden tiles.

"There is a man at Dante's Inferno. A man who sits among sensuality, comfortable and at ease, seeking those who will do work for him."

The second circle of Hell. Lust. Was the first floor just a lobby, or the first circle, Limbo? I couldn't remember, it had been so long. "Does he work for—"

Su Cheng cuts me off with his free hand without looking up, closing the black nails with a clack that does not echo in the muffling haze of the chamber.

"He does not have work for lone wolves, no matter their skill. He likes a stable of fresh talents."

"I'm not exactly fresh."

"He does not know that. So don't tell him."

"But I do have to build a team?"

"Or at least find a partner."

"That could take a while."

"Tonight it won't." He strokes an errant joss stick where it crosses a foil-stamped stone, eyes on mine.

"You have someone in mind?" Silence. "Maybe a name?" He chuckles.

"Fine. I'll go find my own fate, or whatever you'd like to call this. What about the contact?"

"A man with a name of Inari."

"He's called Inari?"

"I did not say that."

"Inari is a Kitsune fox-god of the harvest."

"Yes."

"A Japanese god."

"I know."

I look around the Taoist temple and its exclusively Chinese trappings. "I didn't know your riddles were multicultural."

"As are my friends."

"Are we friends now?"

He gestures to me. "Isn't this what friends do?"

I stand up. "I'm starting to get some idea just how old you really are." He smiles and bows his head as I begin to depart, but I stop halfway out.

"You know, it's not fortune telling if you make it happen. And it's not friendship if you're using each other."

"Come now, Richard...you're starting to show how young you really are."

He melts into mist and blends into the haze of incense, leaving me to the sound of chimes and rainfall, and to ponder my clue to employment tonight.

Dante's throbs with bass even a block away, where the line ends, even at this late hour. Unlike Penumbra, which seems heedless of the changes of time or the date on the calendar, the Inferno recognizes the season. Sinners and Saints is the theme tonight, non-denominationally holiday-themed in the sense of blasphemy and sin for the sake of entertainment. Men and women alike are dressed as angels, devils, and even stranger in the line, wrapped in AR augmented costumes, Second Skin, latex nuns, leather businesswear and more. Rather pedestrian for the Inferno. The really impressive specimens will already be inside.

I find the end of the line, next to a tall human woman in a top-knot headdress that extends along a leónized body to become a one-piece of cocktail dress and boots, impatiently enduring the whining of her partner, an ork with a collar and leash. I'm considering how long this will take and whether the couple will prove entertaining or exasperating when a flicker in the corner of my eye catches my attention. I abandon the line for the alleyway behind. Devil rats scatter between the dumpsters, which are already auto-compacting their collections of bottles and trash. Business must be booming.

The alleyway stinks of piss, vomit, and spilled, stale synthahol. To my particularly sensitive nose, it is nigh overwhelming, but the footsteps of the man shadowing the girl are too filled with promise. I focus on him. The sound of the man's heartbeat, accelerating with a heady sense of control and lust. He stinks of insecurity, his aura tinged with longing and loneliness and rage. She sways her hips just a little more, subtly curls a finger to hitch her plaid skirt up. I gape. She's playing him.

His pace speeds up and he catches up with her quickly, slapping a hand over her mouth and pressing a knife to her throat. Now that I realize who the hunter is, I can see she knows well enough to play along, squealing and kicking her legs as he lifts her off the ground and presses her to the wall. Maybe it's his first time doing something like this. Maybe he thinks the next time will be easier.

He's already planning next time. I can feel it running off him in the astral like sweat, and so can she. Her blank, unremarkable aura shifts subtly, masking I hadn't noticed drops, and the darkness in her is running tendrils through the connection he's already created with her. Lust. Hate. Fear. She's hunted this way before. And just like the others, he can't look her in the eye as he threatens her, his voice a choked hiss.

"Make one sound and I'll kill you."

Her face is a mask of terror. She nods shakily as his knife slides down to her tank top. He draws close, his body covering hers, the blade slicing one shoulder strap. He shudders as his lips approach her neck. Outwardly, she cringes. Inside, she is assensing him. Finding her own hate. Finding its target in his aura. He feels like a god. She quakes with hunger.

I step from around the corner to approach quietly when she exposes her fangs and clamps her mouth on his neck. His scream stifles almost as quickly as it starts, and he is moaning with the ecstasy he sought tonight and more besides. Her own moans remain, her eyes rolling up in the pleasure of the kill.

I clear my throat, and she comes back to reality, eyes snapping into focus on me through the purple of her hair. They narrow as she glares at me, now supporting the weight of the much larger man, her skin flushing as his grows more and more pale. I wait as she sucks, until she pulls away. Arterial red has sprayed across her chest, lingering crimson in her mouth and the scent of fresh blood fills the alleyway. "What do you want?"

I slide my hand in my pockets, at ease. "Just thought you might need help."

She scowls out a phony smile. "I didn't need help."

"Yeah... I can see that."

She drops the dying rapist to the ground, pulling a small, minty spray out of her jacket and remedying her breath. She looks up and down the alley, then back at me.

"What the hell do you think you're doing?"

"Trying to help you. What were you doing?"

She wipes the blood from her chest, licks it from her fingers as her teeth extend again from the stimulus of feeding. "Hunting."

I smiled with fangs of my own. "Huh. Me, too."

She smirks as she kneels down to the man. He isn't dead yet, moaning and weakly trying to push her away, his tattered soul still flaring with ebbing life. She stares at the wound. "I don't like to share."

I sigh, keeping an eye open at the mouth of the alley. "That's all right. There's plenty of vermin in Seattle for the both of us."

She is too wrapped up in the terror, the blood, even the lingering lust as she drinks her would-be rapist's soul in response. When she raises her head again to look at me, she's not scowling any more. Just suspicious. Good. "Who are you?"

"My name's Rick. My employers know me as Red."

"Employers?"

"Yeah."

"And who are they?"

I keep my eyes at the end of the alley. "It's not my job to know who. That's one of the reasons I get paid so much. But from what I can see, money isn't exactly your problem."

"And what do you see?"

"That you're bored. You're a party girl. Daddy's a lawyer, if I were to guess. You use your looks to get your way. You're a mage. You've got some real talents, and no way to use them, and you feel useless. And—" I focused on her. "—you worry about your father. You worry that he's in danger, and you want to help."

"How the hell do you know that?"

"Your aura shifted with worry and affection when I mentioned him. Not corporate. Mob. Is he thinking of turning state's? Making a run for it?"

She shifted her aura back into a masked form, appearing in the astral to be nothing more than a teenage girl. "Peeking's no fair."

"You use every trick you've got in this business."

"So you're, what, a mercenary?"

"A shadowrunner."

I can't go by her aura anymore, but I can read a face quite well, and she's intrigued. "So, you want me to be a shadowrunner?"

"I suppose yes, I'm offering you the opportunity."

"Why me?"

"I'm kind of charmed at the thought of having a partner who can regenerate. It might be nice not to have to absorb all the bullets for my friends."

"And what makes you think you can trust me?"

"Two reasons. One, if your father is connected, you can't afford to go talking about me without catching Hell in turn."

"And the other reason?"

"My astrologer said I'd meet you tonight."

"Romantic."

"Isn't it?"

"I don't like her," whispers Mene in my mind.

She smirks and snaps her fingers, a spell lifting the gore and grime from her body to fall to the alley floor. She gestures to the body, levitating it into one of the dumpsters as it starts compacting.

"Okay, Rick. I'm game. Let's try this out."

"It's Red, when other folks are around. You'll want some kind of handle, too."

She looks me up and down, considering. "Okay. Call me EB, Red."

"Is that short for something?"

"Yes."

"Your real name?"

"No."

"Are you going to tell me?"

She smirks and starts walking to the mouth of the alleyway. "All good things, Mr. Shadowrunner." With a grin, I follow.

With EB at my side, getting into the club is easy. *A pair of amazing biosculpt jobs,* thinks the bouncer as we subtly influence his mind to let us by. The cursing at the head of the line vanishes in the wash of pulsing bass as the door opens into the First Circle. I guess there's no lobby after all.

Limbo, though Cacophony would suit it better, given the screams and bustle of the crowd writhing to the waz-step or whatever they're calling it these days. The lights strobe too quickly to make out details of the crowd. EB seems even more blasé about it than I am. I'm happy enough to lead the way to a roped off ramp leading down to Lust. EB whispers something in the augmented bouncer's ear, who grins as she opens the rope for us.

Lust is low-lit, subtle scents I can recognize as phero-stims pumped into the air, warm colors and soundproofed against upstairs, even as we look up to see the boots and strobes. In here there are lounges and booths, reclining chairs in alien baroque fashion while we get a better look at the people in their fetishistic finest. EB is tame, and I'm utterly bland against a crowd of body-mod enthusiasts, symbiote-clothed celebrities, even one man wearing illusory magical flame and very little else. Beside them, the present AR patrons can't hold a candle. A club dancer is on stage, moving to vintage trip-hop. Body mods, magic, or astounding makeup make her appear to be a sexualized hybrid of human and reindeer among falling snowflakes and rose petals.

I head to the bar, EB in tow, and tell the bartender I'm meeting a new acquaintance here, someone with a name that has to do with foxes. She grins and takes the fifty nuyen I offer, gesturing toward the round corner booth by the stage. In the low light, clad all in violet to offset an auburn ponytail, is the fixer. He lets his IR glasses fall down his nose and looks us up and down, eyes lingering on EB, before speaking.

"Help you?" A hint of UK drawl. Educated upper-crust, but still sleazy.

"I understand you're looking for talent."

"Depends on the talent, huh? What are you good at?"

"Getting into clubs, for one. Coming here. Finding you."

He grins with his eyes, and gestures for us to join him. His mouth never approaches the emotion.

"Reynard," he offers, by way of introduction. Ah. Reynard the Fox. Su Cheng's prophecies have a sense of humor.

"I'm Red. This is EB. And this—" I indicate the swirl of materializing water forming into feminine dimensions. "—is Mene."

"Charmed," he says as he takes EB's hand and raises it to kiss. She smoothly slides hers out of his, twisting lightly to caress in the departure. He likes that she's playful. He likes the initiative. If EB can handle a fight, can keep her edge then as she's doing now, then this is a good start.

Mene, meanwhile, remembers the professionalism of when we did this before, and whether its become inherent to her nature or she just wants to impress me, she's cool as can be.

Reynard orders a round of Blind Reapers he'll end up finishing on his own, and leans back expansively in the booth as he takes us in. "So. Runners. Wiz. I've got a need, but I'm not going to hire people sight unseen."

"You want us to prove ourselves?" EB seems eager at the prospect. I can sense Mene rolling her eyes internally.

"Heh. Everything has a price in the shadows, love. Su Cheng says you check, so you check. But I want to see results."

I blink. Smile. Every step leads me back to this. The club. The table. The Johnson.

"Let's hear what you have in mind."

ABOUT THE AUTHOR

Kevin R. Czarnecki has been playing *Shadowrun* since he was 12, and aspired to be an author, actor, and Ghostbuster since he was a kid. Now that this novel is done, he has accomplished all three and can die a happy man. You can also find some of his work in *Run Faster*. He has a Bachelors Degree in Voice Over and a minor in Fiction Writing from Columbia College Chicago.

Kevin lives in a pre-Bug Chicago, where he works as a freelance writer and voice-over performer.

NO JOB TOO SMALL

BY RUSSELL ZIMMERMAN • COMING SOON!

DOWN THESE DARK STREETS...

Most folks see Puyallup as the worst Seattle's got to offer; a tangled mess of metahumanity and greed, poverty and ghettoes, vice and corruption, where the crime is more organized than the government. They call it a Barrens, an armpit, a cesspool.

Jimmy Kincaid, though, calls it home. Walking the line between the shadows and the desperate light, semi-legit like only a Puyallup brat and former cop can be, he insists Puyallup has a heart and a soul, that it's a place of life, magic, and starving hope. A former combat mage, now as burnt out as his neighborhood, he does what he can to police the worst excesses of the crime-riddled city he loves.

In the darkness of the Seattle Sprawl, what's one more murder?

To Kincaid, it's everything. He's got a dead mentor, a hermetic group in need, and a mysterious file that might have been worth killing for. To unlock the data and get a little justice, he'll face the worst the Sprawl has to offer, wading through blood, darkness, and a murderous web of lies.

It's a good thing he's got friends—in high and low places...

CHAPTER 1

It wasn't raining, but that couldn't last. For once I didn't have my collar flipped up against the slush and cold water drizzling down my back, didn't have my hat jammed tight on my head against a Pacific wind that carried shivers.

It was a nice day. Nice days never last long in Puyallup, and the fair weather just made my mood even fouler; I had work to do, naturally. Lots of it. The shining sun didn't help the street any, it was still empty. Folks were scared.

The Better-Than-Life den, a tenement building taken over by dealers and burners, waited for me just down the street. BTL chips, intricate computer programs carrying fake memories and false experiences, tailor-written entertainment that overrode safety protocols, made for a bad hobby, but a good business. This particular chip-head hole, a place run by a two-bit razorguy who called himself Tinman on account of a chromed-up arm and leg, was a real dive. The place had been operating for about six weeks. Tinman had muscled out most of the decent folks in the building, taken sledgehammers to the walls and the citizens that stood in his way, and turned a handful of apartments into his own little wasteland. It was one part recording studio, a programming center for chip creation and reproduction, and one part safe place where his clients themselves, the burnouts who used these chips to escape reality and walk a mile in someone else's shoes, could squat and fry.

Slotting BTL chips was dangerous work. I knew that better than most. A beetle-head had the rest of his brain turned off, just sat there, eyes wide shut, tasting fake food, feeling fake women, slinging fake spells, living a fake life. You lived a movie instead of watching it, and that just wasn't safe—an addict soon left reality behind for the 24/7 fantasy. You couldn't chip out just anywhere. Tinman was tough enough and scary enough that no one messed with his customers while they were sprawled out in his joint.

Well, almost no one.

An ork punk stood out front, all synth-leather and broad shoulders, no neck to speak of, and not much in his head but plugs and meanness. A shotgun was within arm's reach, and Tinman made sure the whole neighborhood knew the double-barrel was packing explosive ammo; nothing in half-measures, no expense spared. The street muscle was big and dumb, even for an ork. A doorman's number one job was always to look scarier than the door he stood next to.

"Hoi, chummer," I said around an unlit Target dangling at the edge of my mouth. "Got a light?"

He didn't reach into his coat to help a brother out, naturally. This wasn't that kind of neighborhood, and he wasn't that kind of guy. He did roll his eyes, though, and that was opening enough for me.

My left fist came up fast, hit him just under his warty chin, then my right swung around in a big overhand that smashed square into a yellowed tusk. One wingtip flew up between his thighs to keep the pain coming and mess with his balance, and as I stepped back down I put all my weight and forward momentum into another big right and he dropped. Even an ork-thick skull didn't help much against a decent punch and the added oomph of the densiplast plates sewn into the knuckles of my lucky gloves. That's why they were lucky.

I stooped to grab the old shotgun propped against the wall, and pointedly looked up, square at their small security camera, as I straightened.

"Yo, Tinny." I broke the shotgun open, made sure it was loaded, then snapped it shut with a flick of my wrist. "What did I tell you?"

I knew that a few rooms away, Tinman and his chiphead buddies would be getting hollered at by their security man right now. I knew they'd start scrambling around, going for guns, shouting, cursing a lot. I knew they'd recognize me. I knew Tinman and his boys thought they were safe behind their door, that it would buy them time.

I also knew they were rocking a Gatehouse Nine series security door, with an up-gunned Draco-Hoard Maglock sporting a thumbprint scanner and RFID chip sensors. I knew they could buzz the door open from inside, or the ork doorman could open it, but only when the biomonitor—a solid model, not too shabby, even compared to my top of the line headware Corpsman—read steady vitals. I knew Tinman thought he'd been really smart when he installed it, invested heavily in it, told the whole neighborhood about it, showed it off to every chiphead junky screw-up that walked past it.

I knew Tinman was an idiot, though, who hadn't worried about properly reinforcing the doorframe itself in this crumbling, half-dead, piece of crap apartment. I'd talked to those junkies, seen the door myself, done a little homework, and put the schematics and installation instructions into the supercomputer I kept hidden in my skull.

I leaned into it as I wedged the shotgun's muzzle snug against the door, opposite the fancy-pants Maglock, right where my headware computer told me it was 285 mm away from the top of the door. I dipped my head and tugged the brim of my hat down low, then pulled the trigger and waited for the bits of hinge and doorframe to stop flying.

"Knock, knock," I rolled with the recoil, then took a knee before slamming the old Stoeger shotgun's muzzle exactly 320 mm away from the bottom of the door. One hinge down, one to go.

After the second shot, it just took a few kicks to send several thousands of nuyen worth of security door and top-of-the-line electronics thumping to the ground. I dropped the shotgun, drew my Colt from its holster, and let the muzzle lead me in.

One of Tinman's muscleheads greeted me in the entrance hallway. His Ares Predator barked, and I took two to the chest—giving him a wolfish grin over the iron sights of my Model 2061—

before I blasted him to the floor with a trio of shots.

It wasn't his fault, really. He'd lined up his shots better'n most, but how was he supposed to know what a cheater I was? My ally spirit, Ariana, floated just overhead, watching over me from the other side of reality. Bobbing and idling on the astral plane, she was tethered to me by a handful of protective spells, wards of armor and vitality, sustained enchantments that increased my strength and speed. She longed to join me, but I'd made her promise to stay put and help out from the other side. As magical friends go, she's pretty great. I was making a statement here, settling the books with blood and bullets instead of magical flash; but that didn't mean I wasn't above using a little mojo to tip the balance of things in my favor.

I put two more into the downed razorboy's chest just for punctuation, adding to the noise, making sure everyone had been jerked out of their chip-ride by real life.

"Hands up and move fast if you want to live, beetle-heads!" I hollered in my best Lone Star command voice. "I see a gun, I'm putting down the man holding it!"

I let them flood past me, then, Colt at the ready but sliding the smartlink targeting pip over skinny form after skinny form, all of them in rags and cheap vending-machine clothes, most with the red eyes of deep-dream BTL junkies.

I was glad for my usual cyberoptics' color filters, making them all look just a step removed from real life, just a shade less close to me, greyscale images as they shambled by, sparing me the most specific details of their many ailments. Here and there they were polka-dotted with open sores, more than a few had cracked lips and bitten-ragged fingernails, raw infections around hastily-implanted chipjacks. My cyberoptics took it all in, my headware categorized it all, the Sideways gene-treatment that made me live my life in slow-motion ensured I noticed every little detail. Six, then eight, then a dozen, all dark-toothed and grimy, rail-thin from malnourishment, bundles of knees and elbows scrambling in fear, they pushed and jostled past me, scrambling over the corpse of Tinman's bouncer. Even my headware couldn't tell me who, but some enterprising soul in their mad rush had still had enough smarts to grab the man's gun, another his belt, and someone darted away with his left boot.

I figured the doorman out front would get a more thorough Puyallup rolling, if he hadn't already.

My Colt up and ready, I knifed around the corner and into the main hallway. It had been a long time since Fast Response Team training on room clearance, but the basics stuck with you, and it's not like my life ever let me get real rusty at this sort of thing. My smartlink pip and iron sights led the way, rounding corners and sweeping into rooms.

Sweeping the first room, I saw nothing but an assortment of filthy pillows and sweat-stained mattresses scattered on the floor, empty chip cases and broken glass bottles, protein bar wrappers, stains in the corners, something green-grey growing up the far wall. Rough edges scarred the room, where flimsy interior walls had once separated this into two apartments, and less-than-great care had been taken with the demolition and clean-up process. No one that used this place cared—about anything except slotting in. It was the playroom, where chipheads could squat and zone out for hours or days, so long as the nuyen kept coming. You could probably burn this place to the ground and it'd never smell clean.

My gene-tweaked neuroproteins and Transys headware supercomputer desperately sought patterns in the chaos, counted every piece of detritus in the place, tried to feed me clues about behavioral patterns based on forensic evidence, but eventually gave up. There wasn't a pattern to be found there. There was no logic to it. The rooms where chipheads killed themselves didn't have to make sense. My gut already knew that, it just took my head a while to agree.

My cyberaudio suite picked up the sound of a hammer being cocked as I turned to step back into the hall, and Ari's mojo and my Sideways helped me lurch backwards as a pistol round slapped into the doorframe where my head had been. There were limits to Ari's magical protection. I had a tac-vest on under my Kevlar-laced long coat, which had helped with the shot to the chest, but nothing but her mojo was protecting my face. A head shot would've done a number on me.

I emptied the rest of my magazine out into the hallway, in the general direction of the shooter, but it was enough to my ear upgrades to tell me more of a story. As I grabbed a fresh mag from my belt and slapped it home, one guy grunted, the other cursed. I had good ears. I made out scuffs of shoes on the floor, separate footfalls as someone ground loose plaster into the floorboards, the rustle of cheap synthleather against an interior wall, the just-audible whine of a cheap external smartlink's battery pack. Sounded like two guys.

"Listen boys, this is between me an' your boss. No one else has to die here. Now drop those pop guns and lay down, or I'm gonna lay you down."

I didn't expect them to surrender, don't get me wrong. Anyone working as this sort of low-rent muscle was bottom of the barrel, even where Puyallup was concerned. I knew Tinman's guys, and I knew what caliber of punk he kept on the payroll. I knew what they did. They were the used-ups and the burn-outs, the guys running secondhand implants a generation or two behind, the guys who'd do anything to anyone for a job and a taste of making folks afraid, the sort of skull-fried thugs who took their payment in goods instead of nuyen. Tinman didn't hire 'em 'cause they were the introspective sort, given to pondering philosophical questions of life and death, the morality of their place of employment, or the odds of getting out of the business in one piece. No, he hired them 'cause they worked cheap.

The streams of profanity and bravado they sent down the hallway did what I needed, though; confirmed numbers and location. Say what you want about Lone Star—hell, I'll cuss 'em out right with you—but before they let me go, they gave me some pretty handy headware.

I came around the corner while they were still cussing at me and shouting threats. I watched the ammo marker on my smartlink display dip as I poured round after round into, or rather through, the wall one of them was using for cover. Plaster flew, then blood, then I heard him tumble to the ground. A split-second later, so did my second empty magazine. As I pulled a fresh one off my belt, a round whizzed past my head so close it sounded like a clap in my ear.

The thug crowed insults at my family in a gutter-lingo bastard child of Spanish and Japanese—my vocabulary of curses and profanities was terribly global—and fired at me again, his troll-sized Ruger wheelgun looking absurdly oversized; partially because he was just a human struggling to hold it in two hands, partially because every gun looks a bit bigger when you're staring down the barrel. He fired again, but the recoil from the first shot still had him unsteady and aiming high.

My slide slammed forward, mental commands chambered a fresh round, and I lined up the targeting reticule as he staggered and tried to line up his stupid-big Ruger again. My shot smacked into his forehead and left a mess on the wall behind him as he dropped to the stained carpet.

I angled my Colt as I rounded the corner, shifting the plane of the sights and smartlink, leaning around with my smartgun's muzzle leading the way. I snapped off a quick shot as one more of Tinman's boys lunged back into a side room halfway down the hallway, reticule hovering over a jacket so ugly even my color filters didn't fully spare me, and was rewarded by a grunt of pain. I ducked back around the corner as his gun-arm stuck out into the hallway and a long burst of autofire rang out.

He laid on his trigger, and I waited it out. Plaster and paint flew as his blocky little submachinegun chattered, and I stayed out of sight while my headware and Sideways-infused compulsion counted the rounds. Thirty-two. Even Tinman's second-rate muscle weren't stupid enough to spray and pray with their only ammo, so as soon as I heard his empty magazine hit the floor, I made a big show of waving my arm around the corner like I was about to come out—sure enough, I snatched it back just in time, and he leaned on the trigger again.

My Transys Avalon and TacWhisper, headware computer and cyberears, worked their magic again. As soon as thirty-two distinct firing sounds were registered, I went around the corner again, this time catching him in the middle of fumbling for his next magazine. My reticule danced square in his center-of-mass as I advanced down the hallway. I slid my point of aim higher, past the faintly glowing plaid pattern of the world's ugliest armored jacket, and right at the bridge of his nose, I squeezed the trigger just so.

I didn't get a satisfying bang and the buck of recoil. My smartlink pip dissolved in a burst of static, I got four different pop-up displays warning me about malfunctions, and my magazine fell right out of the bottom of my Colt.

Well, crap.

A mental command shoved the warning messages out of my field of vision even as my audio suite picked up a giggle from the side room Ugly Jacket had been ducking into.

It only took us an eyeblink, both standing there with empty guns. I could've tugged the knife from my pocket and tried my luck. I could've gone for my wand and seen what combat mojo I could whip up, keeping my distance and using old instincts and the flickers of power I still clung to. I could've reached to the offside of my belt for my last reload, betting I'd be quicker than Ugly Jacket. Instead, I just rushed him while he fumbled at the pocket of his ridiculously baggy cargo shorts, trying to free another magazine.

Empty or not, a gun's still a weapon, or at least a tool. The Colt Model 2061, the commemorative 150th anniversary edition of that seminal semi-automatic handgun, is a well-crafted machine of violence. My particular model, an academy graduation gift from my father, is gun-blued and traditional, even for 1911 clones, with tasteful—and real—rosewood grips, simple ergonomics, an unobtrusive internal smartlink, and a traditionalist's wary view of modern lightweight polymers. In other words, even unloaded, the thing's a handy 1.12 kilograms of metal and wood, and not something any rational human being wants to get cracked in the face with.

My shoulder slammed into Ugly Jacket's ugly jacket, and both of us hit the ground, him with his neck wedged against the doorframe and my weight blasting the air from his lungs. A single, long cyberspur burst from the back of his left hand—he had a second port, but must've sold off that other blade—and swiped wildly at me.

I reared back as he slashed, then grabbed him by the forearm. Leaning forward, I pinned his blade-hand against his side and, holding him beneath me, lifted my blocky pistol and smashed him in the head with it. Then again. And again. And again. It only took those few swings, gun butt sharp and hard against human flesh and bone, before he stopped struggling.

Snarling, I lurched to my feet and saw a pair of scuffed combat boots poking out amid a tangle of wires and cables beneath a workbench. Three strides carried me across the room, and thanks to Ari's loaned mojo, one good kick sent the bench and the punk beneath it flying. My optics snapped a quick look while he was in midair, and for an instant the light flashed against a glossy touchscreen tablet strapped to his wrist. His fingertips danced over it even as he half-slumped against a wall, and I knew what had happened to my smartlink.

Moving smoothly and calmly, I reached for my last magazine and fed it into the empty well of my Colt. A thumb-swipe against the slide release snapped it forward, chambering a fresh round. I lifted it, fingers certain and grip comfortable, and lined up my front and rear sights, smartlink targeting pip nowhere to be seen. He typed faster, licking cracked lips.

"I turned off my wireless after you tried that the first time." I didn't quite smile as I said it.

He stopped tapping at the softly glowing screen of his cyberdeck, and raised a hand to block the sight of me, like not seeing it coming meant it wasn't. The Colt bucked in my hand, and his arm fell. The Sprawl had one less hacker in it.

I looked around, and immediately regretted it. My lawman's gut didn't obsess over details needlessly, but implants did; I didn't have time to play Count The Cord in a room like this. I was in their workshop, where the chips were burnt and mass-produced. The workbench I'd splintered against the wall was covered in now-broken electronics, tangled masses of wires—most of them patched and re-patched time and again, even now a few sparking—leading from device to device, banks of processors, chip burners, replicators, and simrig terminals. This was where the memories and experiences were synthesized and programmed, which meant...

A glance showed me where the thickest bundle of wires headed, and the rough-hewn hole in the wall, leading next door, betrayed the scuff of steel on steel to my ears. Tinman. Finally.

I waited, letting my cyberears do their work while rebooting my smartlink and running antivirus protocols with quick mental commands. The next room was well-lit, and the soft whir of recording equipment could be heard. The whisper of static told me audio gear was live, as well.

"We had an agreement, Tinman."

I took a step along the braid of wires, Colt up.

"Fuck you, Kincaid!"

"Three little rules, Tinman. Three little rules, and you couldn't even follow them."

A boxy little Cobra submachinegun snaked around the corner at me, held in a tinned-chrome hand. I didn't duck out of the way and wait it out like I had with his gun-thug's Cobra down the hall. Instead I put a double-tap into the wall even as his muzzle rounded the corner, earning a grunt of pain from the other side of the drywall and his gun withdrawing.

"I said no selling to kids."

I fired into the plaster again, a little further from the hole, blasting right where my thermoptics showed his heat leaking into the wall.

I remembered the mother who'd come to me three days ago, asking me to do something about Tinman and his little nest. She told me her son was a good boy—they always do—but that he'd fallen in with a bad crowd—they always do. She had told me he was too young for this sort of thing, but that Tinman's crew had lent him the money for a 'jack, then charged him ridiculous interest to put him in a deep hole. She told me they'd pushed him into peddling chips at school to pay them back, and when Knight Errant had taken her son away, they hadn't cared about the rest. She told me how the ork manning the door had beaten her when she'd confronted them. She came to my office, begging, bruised, offering enchiladas and prayers if I could help her. I'd almost stormed the place and killed them right then.

"I said no snuff."

I fired again, methodically, blasting clean through the thin interior wall, putting round after round into him. He had dermal plating, I knew, and who-knows-what other combat augs.

There was nothing wrong with him enough bullets couldn't fix, though.

I remembered the chips my investigation had turned up, the chips I'd had a friend scan—not wanting to slot them, and wanting Skip and Trace to know I wasn't wanting to slot them—and the way they'd almost turned even her bounty hunter's stomach. Trace didn't get green around the gills very easily, and just bouncing through thirty-second intervals of a forty-minute BTL chip, even with all the safety filters churning on her hand-crafted cyberdeck, it had been enough to knock her speechless and grim. She'd just nodded at me instead of going into detail, and her girlfriend, Skip, had wanted to punch me for asking the favor in the first place.

Tinman and his boys were selling murder-porn, the experience of killing someone, the high of ending an innocent life in tortuous detail. Snuff chips were bad juju. The worst kind of karma out there. They were killing people just for kicks, and then selling the thrill to anyone who wanted to slot the chip. I'd almost stormed the place and killed them right then.

"And I said *no Turbo Bunny*."

I emptied the rest of the magazine through the wall into him, still slowly walking forward, still cycling through vision modes, smartlink pip dancing over his heat signature as the air filled with plaster dust.

I remembered my friend, my ex; the girl who'd gotten me into BTL chips all those years ago, and the girl who'd helped me get off them. I remembered seeing her during my three days of stakeout, wanting to shout at her or shoot at her, but instead forcing myself to just watch her come and go on her own. You couldn't help someone else when they were craving—they had to help themselves. Her sleek racing bike had slowed to a crawl once, come to a full stop a second time, and the third and fourth she'd pulled up to the curb, taken her helmet off, let her hair flow gorgeous and long and elf-perfect, my cybereyes zooming in and leaving no doubt about who she was. She'd stopped, but she'd never gotten off her bike. I'd heard them cat-calling her, seen Tinman out front waving at her, offering her discounts, and then cursing as she'd pulled away. She'd been tempted, but she hadn't bought anything. It stung that she hadn't called me. It stung that she'd known to come here, and they'd tried their damnedest to get the claws back in her, despite my warning. I'd almost stormed the place and killed them right then.

"Three little rules, Tinman. Just three. And you had to fuck up every single one of them."

He crawled away from me on his belly, scratching chromed-up arms through a pool of blood, trying to reach the gun he'd dropped. I stepped up and into this last room, their recording studio, and stooped down to pick up his dropped Cobra.

"No kids. No killing. No Tee-Bee. That was it. All you had to do was follow those three rules, and it was live and let live. I know you paid off Knight Errant. I know you keep the peace in this neighborhood. I know you say you mostly leave folks alone. I know you keep your beetle-heads safe. I know you say you're just offering folks a distraction, and that even SINless folks've got a right to get away every once in a while. I know all that."

Tinman rolled over onto his back, groaning, looking up at me from a tiled floor with a drain in the middle. Half his head was shining from a sweat-sheen of fear, the other half gleaming chrome in the hard lights of the room. His metal side—the arm, the leg, half of his face—scraped and skittered on the tiles as he tried to drag himself away, leaking almost as much hydraulic and battery fluid as blood. He'd chromed himself up to look tough, inhuman, intimidating. Now he was just a broken piece of machinery.

There were lights and cameras all over the room, some of them pulled down by his crawling and tumbling, others still on, still rolling, still recording. This was where they made the movies, this two-bit studio, right here. This is where they killed for fun and profit, where they spent hours and hours making the recordings they pushed on kids and burnouts, making a new generation of psychos and junky chipheads.

"Three rules, and you couldn't do it past, what, a month?"

I leveled the boxy Cobra.

"Puyallup's tired of your shit, Tinman. The neighborhood doesn't want you here. And that means I don't either."

He whimpered something, but I was way beyond listening. I emptied the magazine into him, making sure.

Sending a message.

I left all the equipment running as I left, fishing my pack of Targets from inside my coat, letting a smoke hang from my mouth as I stepped over corpses and cables, making my way back outside into the Puyallup ash. A soft rain was falling, and I held onto my smoke, leaned my head back, and peered up into the ash-grey clouds overhead. My cyberoptics flicked from side to side, glancing around at windows, curtains opening, the neighborhood coming back to life, just a little.

I listened to the rain as I walked down the street to my Ford a few doors down. Ari's spells slipped away from me, the mild tingle of being cocooned in upkept enhancements ended, and soon she was hovering in the air next to me, moving her legs, even though she wasn't walking. She was a creature of aether and will, imagination and power, summoned from the metaplane of elemental earth—giving her coppery skin, silver-shining hair, eyes like jewels—but with powers that transcended those of a normal spirit or elemental.

She was also probably my best friend.

Ariana spun like a schoolgirl and made a point of physically manifesting enough to stomp on a small puddle, giggling, whirling.

The street came alive, bit by bit, just minutes after the last gunshots echoed away. It hadn't taken me long to recover my empty magazines, make sure the down were down, and saunter outside, but the neighborhood responded quickly, nevertheless. Everyone knew what had been happening in that BTL den, and everyone knew it wouldn't happen there any more.

An old ork with wisps of white hair clinging in a semicircle over his ears gave me a one-tusked nod from a stoop. A tow-headed little girl gaped and waved at Ariana with her secondhand dolly's little plastic arm, then ducked shyly back from her window. Someone turned their radio back on, filling the street with music instead of gunfire. Mrs. Ramirez appeared on the sidewalk after a few moments, hurrying against the rain as she left a warm tray on the hood of my car.

I allowed myself a smile, willed some of the street's life energy into my control, and squinted down at the end of my cigarette. The cherry smoldered to life, and for once no wave of exhaustion followed even this minor spell. Ari beamed at me. The streets were life. Life was power. Power was magic.

I waved at Mrs. Ramirez before picking up the tray of enchiladas and sliding a few days' worth of supper onto the passenger seat of my big Ford. Ari drifted soundlessly through the side of the car and into the back seat, and then we drove off.

Simple as that. No one would call Knight Errant for Tinman and his crew. The footage might show up on the Matrix somewhere, though, posted in dark corners that the cops didn't care about, and all the right people would learn all the right things from it.

Puyallup is bad enough already. The locals don't want any more of your trouble here. And if you're too naughty, Jimmy Kincaid will pay you a visit.

NO JOB TOO SMALL

BY RUSSELL ZIMMERMAN

COMING SOON!

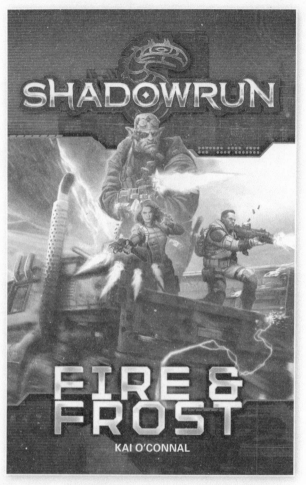

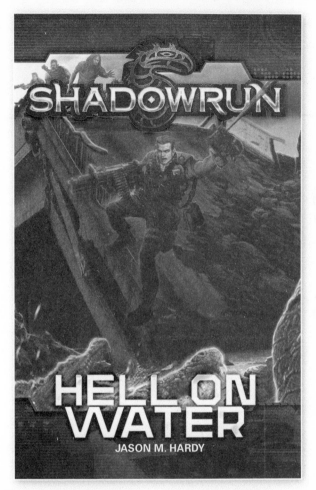